3/26/2015

S0-AWP-849

HUDSON'S MERCHANTS AND WHALERS

HUDSON!

I LOVE YOUR NAME
AND I HOPE YOU LOVE
LEARNING ABOUT WHALERS!

LOVE

TESS AMATO

HUDSON'S MERCHANTS AND WHALERS

The Rise and Fall of a River Port
1783–1850

Margaret B. Schram

BLACK·DOME

Published by

Black Dome Press Corp.
1011 Route 296
Hensonville, New York 12439
www.blackdomepress.com
Tel: (518) 734-6357

First Edition Paperback 2004
Copyright © 2004 Black Dome Press Corp.

All rights reserved. No part of this publication may be reproduced in any form, stored in a retrieval system, or transmitted in any form by any means, electronic, mechanical, photocopying, recording or otherwise, except by a newspaper or other reviewer who wishes to quote brief passages in connection with a review, without prior written permission from the publisher.

Library of Congress Cataloging-in-Publication Data

Schram, Margaret B.
    Hudson's merchants and whalers : the rise and fall of a river port, 1783-1850 / by Margaret B. Schram.-- 1st pbk. ed.
        p. cm.
    Includes bibliographical references and index.
    ISBN 1-883789-39-7 (pbk.)
    1. Hudson (N.Y.)--History--18th century. 2. Hudson (N.Y.)--History--19th century. 3. Harbors--New York (State)--Hudson--History. 4. Hudson (N.Y.)--Commerce--History. 5. Whaling--New York (State)--Hudson--History. I. Title.

F129.H8S37 2004
974.7'303--dc22
                                2004000711

Front cover:
Becalmed in the Hudson Highlands, oil painting by Len Tantillo. The vessel represented is the Hudson whale ship *Huron*.

Designed by Carol Clement, Artemisia, Inc.

Printed in the USA

10   9   8   7   6   5   4   3   2   1

This book is dedicated to my husband, the late
Earl Schram, Jr. His encouragement made it possible.
I wish he had lived to see it in print.

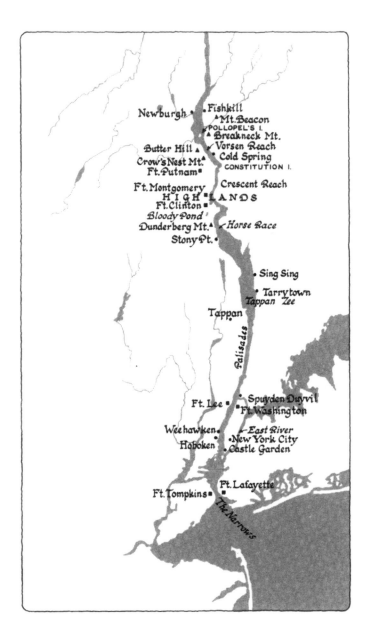
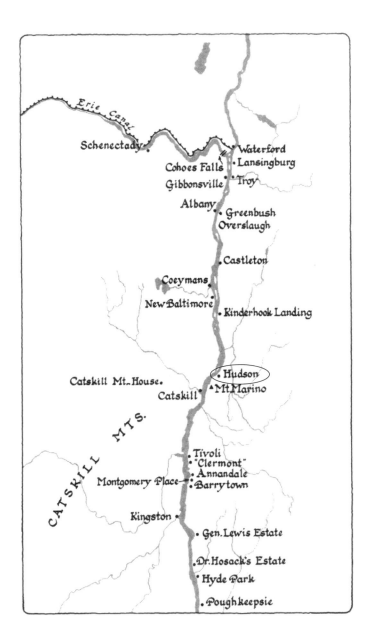

Maps of the Hudson Valley, reprinted from Roland Van Zandt, *Chronicles of the Hudson*, 1971. © Black Dome Press Corp.

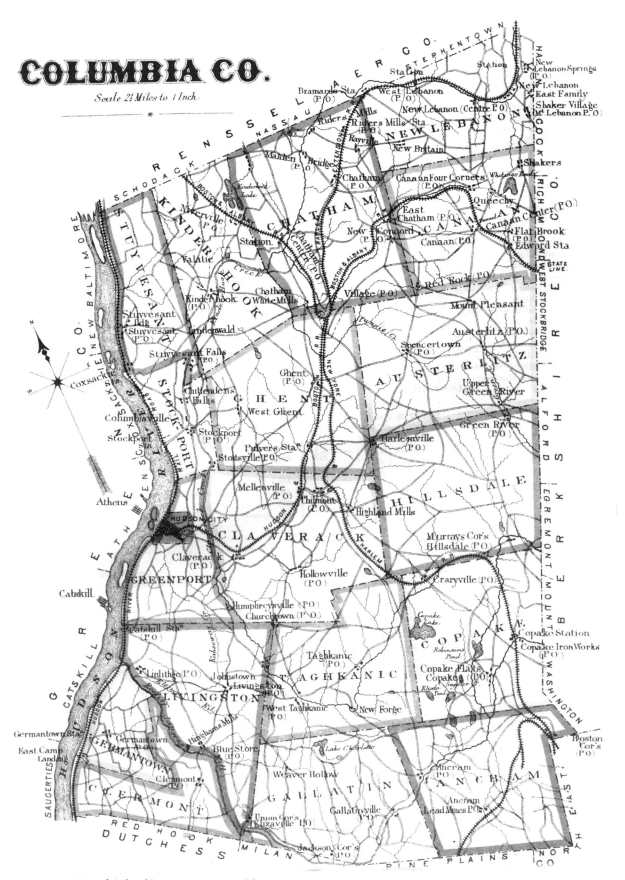

Map of Columbia County, reprinted from Captain Franklin Ellis, *History of Columbia County*, 1878.

FOREWORD

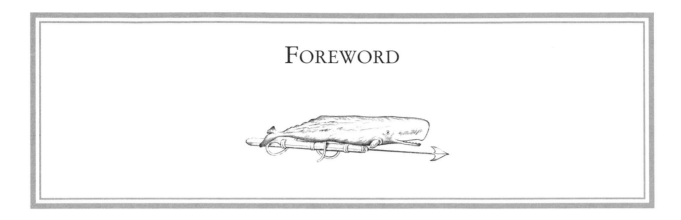

American maritime history, particularly whaling history, has seen a strong resurgence in recent years. Popular press publishing houses have recognized the compelling, perhaps perennial, certainly intrinsic fascination of seafaring stories. Some are wild tales involving the seeming retribution of nature in the form of great whales attacking and destroying sailing ships like the whale ship *Essex* of Nantucket. Others describe atrocious mutinies, or illuminate the life and times of individuals. Ethnic and racial stories, like Native American whaling culture on the northwestern coast of North America, became important after the Makah tribe re-instituted their traditional hunt of migrating gray whales, and the Native Alaskan whaling story has generated several important books. Still others document the history of black sailors and the broad social history of maritime trades, including the roles of women at sea and in coastal communities ashore. All vivify and clarify an important piece of our history.

Whaling history, of course, is an endlessly stimulating subject. Not only are the whalemen's stories fascinating, but the ramifications of the industry are yet to be fully plumbed. American whalers and their polyglot crews, for better or for worse, visited locations on the globe that rarely, if ever, had contact with Western civilization. They hunted animals about which they knew little and observed geography, flora and fauna about which they knew even less. The value of their observations about these features, as well as other natural phenomena of all sorts including comets, earthquakes, volcanoes and ice, weather, winds and currents, cultural conditions, interactions and accidents, are coming under increasing scrutiny. Their presence in far-flung ports demanded the installation of American governmental representatives in the form of consuls to look after the interests of American citizens and American commerce, thus stabilizing U.S. sovereignty in international relations. Whaling inspired superb, mediocre and poor contemporaneous 19th-century literature, even the worst of which is useful, and the best of which is iconographic.

Current writings on maritime and whaling history inform popular and scholarly opinion and open the gates to further study. The *sources* from which popular authors draw, however, are perhaps the most important books of all. As a professional librarian of whaling history I most rely upon books of reference. Those books with good indices, useful lists, extensive bibliographies and ironclad citations, and with appendices full of extracts or entire primary sources, are of greatest value.

The reasons for the importance of these types of books are several. For one thing, they provide quick answers to often-labyrinthine questions. More importantly, though, a complete history of the American whale fishery in one volume is an impossible undertaking. There are too many facets of the story strung out over too long a period of time to give due justice to them all. In 1838, for example, over 400 vessels from 34 separate ports between Wiscasset, Maine, and Wilmington, Delaware, and from up the Hudson River ventured out into the aqueous globe to obtain a cargo of oil and baleen. Every port, indeed every voyage, is worthy of examination. The surviving documentation for these voyages, including outfitting records, crew and other personal biographies, owners' accounts, logbooks and journals showing the whaling grounds visited, contacts made, species hunted, not to mention the shipbuilding histories of the vessels themselves, would collectively make an interesting read for almost every voyage. By 1844, while the number of ports had lessened slightly, the number of vessels had increased to over 600, making it far and away the largest such fleet in the world. This was an industry with a gross value approaching 30 million dollars that fetched cargoes worth between 6 and 9 million dollars annually, placing the whale fishery among the top ten mercantile endeavors in the U.S.A.

Every one of these thirty-odd ports has an important story that needs telling. Thus far, only about half of them have been systematically examined in any meaningful way. Margaret Schram's *Hudson's Merchants and Whalers* allows for exactly the type of systematic documentation of people and vessels that the history of the port demands. The origins of Hudson, New York, as a whaling and sealing port are steeped in the primary facts of American whaling history. The port was settled by Nantucket emigrants seeking a safe, deep-water port from which to pursue their trade while avoiding the ravages of war in post-Revolutionary America. That Hudson enjoyed the success in these fisheries that it did is dependent upon the expertise of the people who settled there. This is the exact reason that so many of the 34 whaling ports in 1838 did not survive in the fishery. They lacked the infrastructure that was present in the ports of Nantucket, Provincetown, New Bedford, Fairhaven, New London and Sag Harbor. It is no coincidence that several of these ports, among the earliest recorded whaling centers in North America, survived right up to the turn of the 19th century, while those seeking easy money in the boom years failed.

In this book Margaret Schram has uncovered documentation of Hudson voyages in the late 18th century and in the early years of the 19th. These are often the most elusive voyages, even for the largest ports, simply because the documentation has not survived or never existed in the first place; time and fire have taken their toll on many collections of historical records. This information about these voyages has never before been published in any other whaling history, making *Hudson's Merchants and Whalers* a valuable reference tool and important addition to any whaling history library.

Michael P. Dyer
Librarian
New Bedford Whaling Museum
February, 2004

Acknowledgments

This book had a long gestation because of circumstances beyond my control. I am thankful to the friends and relatives who encouraged me to continue. Debbie Allen, the tireless owner, publisher and editor of Black Dome Press Corp. assured me that the book was worth finishing, and gently but emphatically steered me toward what came to be excellent therapy.

Once started, I managed to bother an amazing number of people, but all were kind, patient and eager to help. The greatest victim was the librarian of the Claverack Free Library, Sally Alderdice. My demand for obscure books from remote libraries was endless. The final insult came when I requested Thomas Jefferson's letters, expecting about six books. Over thirty arrived, neatly packed in boxes.

I am in debt to Steve Hoare, whose editing of this book turned a rambling manuscript into a smooth, literate creation. Special thanks to Len Tantillo, premier maritime artist, who kindly consented to the use of his work for the book's cover, and also furnished extra copies for reviewers. Carol Clement of Artemisia designed a beautiful book. Michael Dyer, librarian of the New Bedford Whaling Museum, readily agreed to write the foreword; I thank him for his kind words and for lending his erudition in the subject of whaling to place my book in perspective. Special gratitude to my son Charles, who read the manuscript and offered advice.

The following is an alphabetical list of others whose knowledge and expertise made this book possible. Each of their contributions was essential: artist John Alderdice, whose drawings illustrate many pages; Raymond Beecher and the staff at the Vedder Memorial Research Library; proofreader Matina Billias; Roderic Blackburn, expert on the Hudson Valley Dutch—and on many other topics; Helen Brownell, director of the Easton Library; Kathleen Bucholsky, town clerk of Greenport; the Columbia County Clerk's Office staff; Susan Daley, who typed the first, large manuscript; Karen Del Principe, museum manager of the FASNY Museum of Firefighting; Christopher Densmore, curator of the Friends Historical Library, Swarthmore College; William Droege, expert on local breweries; Patricia Fenoff, historian of the City of Hudson; Stuart Frank, director of the Kendall Institute, New Bedford Whaling Museum; Charles and Mary Hallenbeck, who gave early encouragement; Mary Howell, historian of Columbia County; the staff of the Hudson City Clerk's Office, City Hall, Hudson; Michael Lapides, Kendall Institute, New Bedford Whaling Museum; Helen M. McLallen, curator of the Columbia County Historical Society; proofreader Erin Mulligan; Elizabeth Oldham, research associate of the Nantucket Historical Association; Randall Park of the Franklin D. Roosevelt Presidential Library; author Ruth Piwonka—a wealth of historical information; proofreader Eric Raetz; Robert Ragaini, whose photographs grace these pages; Newfoundland artist Jane Sasonow-White; Mrs. Paul Szasz, local Quaker authority; and Ron Toelke Associates.

The images in this book are from the author's collection unless otherwise noted.

CONTENTS

PROLOGUE

A Miracle City

In May of 1985, I was involved in a public controversy regarding Hudson's status as a whaling port. I had committed the ultimate sin of correcting a beloved public figure's assertion that Hudson was the premier whaling port in the United States. (Actually, Hudson rated eighteenth in number of vessels and twenty-fourth in number of voyages.)[1] A war of words, which I entitled "A Tempest in a Trypot," ensued in the local newspaper.

To reinforce my conviction that Hudson was in fact a minor whaling port, I wrote to the leading whaling museums in America to solicit their assessments. They all substantiated my opinion. The following excerpt is from just one of the many responses I received.

> I can readily understand your difficulty in attempting to dissuade those who put forth the extravagant claims on Hudson as a premier whaling port. Whaling was a part of Hudson's early history, but never to the extent of importance as it was in New England ports such as Nantucket, New Bedford and New London.
>
> I believe Hudson, from its beginnings, recognized that their shipping activities depended on the amount of trade it could accomplish by bringing farming and other products to other coastal ports. A number of Hudson's ships made excellent whaling and sealing voyages, but Hudson did not enjoy the prosperity from these ventures as did other whaling ports.
>
> The enterprising spirit of Hudson's founders had much to do with the subsequent success of its citizens in the shipping business. While whaling had a role in its activities it was not in any sense a major role, and this was a factor which indicates the careful planning of the townspeople.
>
> Director Edouard A. Stackpole
> The Peter Foulger Museum
> Nantucket, Massachusetts
> (April 30, 1985)[2]

I had long admired the late Edouard A. Stackpole's (1903–1993) scholarly works on American whaling, and I treasure his letter and its clear explanation of Hudson's early history.

The truth is always more interesting than fiction. Hudson may not have been the premier whaling port in the United States, but whaling and related industries were of great importance to Hudson in its early days, and the story of how the city grew under the guiding hands of a group of merchants and seamen into a thriving maritime port and a city of unparalleled growth and prosperity is fascinating. In the first few decades following Hudson's founding in 1783 the Proprietors, as the founders were known—predominantly Quakers from the Revolutionary War-torn east coast—and their credo of hard work produced a

View of Hudson from Athens. Hudson River Portfolio (1820-1826), No. 13. Engraved by Hill, after a watercolor by Wall.
(Courtesy of Rami's Frame Shop, Hudson, New York.)

city that rivaled Albany and New York in maritime activity.

As rapid as its rise was its decline. By 1850 Hudson was no longer a busy river port, and its citizens were concerned about the future. This story will explain the events in those first sixty-seven years that brought about the rise and fall in Hudson's status as a major river port, as well as depict what provided early Hudsonians with their excitements and misfortunes. There will be little mention of churches, cemeteries, and the illustrious residents so beloved by Victorian writers. These subjects fill other, readily available history books. Rather, this book will take a new look into the early history of the city and explain why certain events occurred.

The transformation from a small, sleepy, post-Revolutionary War settlement with a scattering of dwellings, into a bustling river port city and regional commercial center with whale ships and merchant vessels loading and unloading, took but a few short years. John Lambert, an English traveler, arrived in Hudson from Albany in November 1807 and wrote the following:

In the evening we arrived at Hudson. This town is of modern construction, and, like Troy [New York], consists of one very long street. The houses are of wood or brick, many of them built with taste, and all spacious and commodious. Shops and warehouses are numerous, and there are several large inns, from which I conceived that a considerable trade was carried on between this town and the interior.

It has the appearance of a thriving settlement, and its situation is elevated and advantageous for commerce. There are several large brick warehouses near the wharves for the reception of goods, and a great many small vessels sail continually between this town and New York. Ship-building is carried on here, and a vessel of three or four hundred tons was just ready for launching. Several other vessels of that size were also in the harbor.[3]

One early writer described Hudson's phenomenal growth as resembling "a mushroom springing from the earth."[4] Under the remarkable leadership of the men from New England, a quiet Dutch landing became a thriving city. Visitors recorded in most laudatory terms the new city's bustling streets filled with stores and elegant houses. (The city at that time, of course, had different dimensions than the Hudson of today. Deacon H.P. Skinner, who came to Hudson in 1798, reminisced in 1854 that "all business was down below Third Street and but a few buildings of any kind above that street.")[5]

Schooner. The schooner differs from the brig chiefly in the rig of the mainmast.

Brig. A two-masted, square-rigged vessel.

Travelers arriving by boat marveled at the array of vessels at the wharves and the frames of ships in stocks being constructed along the shore. Laban Paddock, a ship master, wrote in his memoirs of 1853 that "the Proprietors brought a fleet of vessels; ships, schooners, brigs and sloops, and went largely into the foreign trade, particularly with [the] West Indies. The writer has seen 15 sails of vessels loaded and ready to sail at one time. Ship building was carried on for many years. The writer for many years annually packed 4000 lbs. of shad for home consumption and 1000 lbs. of herring for the West India trade."[6]

In 1790 the population of Hudson was 2,584 persons. By 1800 it had swelled to 4,048 individuals. In 1814 it reached 4,725 people; in 1820 it was 5,310; and in 1830 it had reached 5,672.[7] By 1850 the population was 6,286 people. These population increases stemmed from the fame of this successful city spreading afar. New families moved to the town, the men seeking employment in the many industries that were starting up. Most of these immigrants were from the New England coast, particularly Rhode Island and Nantucket. They were hoping for the same advantages and Quaker ties that had brought the original Proprietors to the town.

The maritime industry required a vast supply of skilled workers aside from the sailors and whalers. Shipbuilding required carpenters, rope makers, sailmakers, blacksmiths, caulkers, and a host of other specialized mechanics. The oil works that refined the whale oil gave occupation to many. Men were needed to keep ledgers in the warehouses. Chandlers were required to supply the ships with equipment and all of the supplies needed for a voyage. Bakers had to make the special "ship biscuits" (hardtack) that would keep for a long voyage.

Sloop. A vessel with one mast.

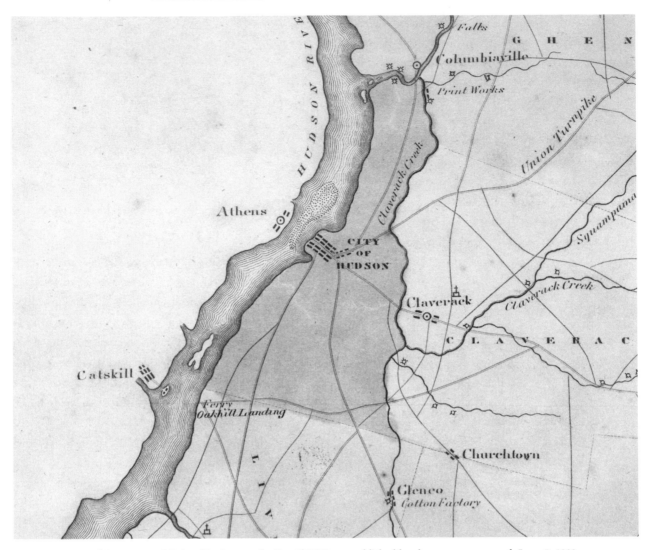

Detail from map of Columbia County, by David W. Burr, published by the surveyor general, June 5, 1829.

Coopers were in high demand to make the barrels that carried water and an assortment of salted meats, plus the barrels (usually in "knock-down" shape) to bring home the whale oil. Carters in great numbers were required to haul all of these items to the ships, and then carry away the oil and other goods after the ships returned.

Tanneries were in operation from the days of the founding of the city, and remained an important industry. Seal hides, as well as the hides from the slaughterhouses along the bays and some imported Spanish hides, provided the material necessary for tanning. Asheries used the ashes brought in by farmers to make potash. Candles and soap also were produced.

As more and more families settled in Hudson, more services and supplies were needed, requiring a still-greater workforce. From the simplest farmer selling foodstuffs and meats at the markets, to the housewrights that built the houses, barns, and out-buildings, each occupation created the need for yet more workers. The prosperity of the city grew with the population, setting in motion a vibrant, successful Hudson.

Most of the turn-of-the-nineteenth-century residents in the countryside around Hudson had never seen anything like it. Imagine the assault on their senses as a farm family traveled into Hudson. Along with the prosperity and surging population came something not so pleasant—the stench.

Visitors from other cities and those living in Hudson were accustomed to the smells and considered it a way of life; however, for a family from a remote farm on the Massachusetts border wagoning in for the first time, the stench of the booming port city must have been surprising and overwhelming. First they were greeted by a pall of smoke hanging over the city from hundreds of smoking chimneys. Closer in, the smell from a city full of privies and manure piles filled the air. (In those times every household had a small barn in which were kept the family horse, perhaps a cow, some pigs to eat refuse, and lots of chickens.) Add to that the slaughterhouses with the offal floating in the bay, the tanneries, the soap factory, and the many other businesses that contributed to the questionable scents in the air. The only thing that did not smell was the whale oil; the odor had been boiled out of it aboard ship.

The country folk also must have been surprised by the noise. Carts and wagons rumbled by on the street, and hammers pounded everywhere from houses and ships being built. There were herds of cattle complaining as they were led to the slaughterhouses, men shouting orders along the waterfront, and the occasional blast as a new street was being hewn from rock. All in all, the first trip to the new city must have been quite an eye and ear-opener for the visiting country folk.

The City of Hudson was a miracle. Only the right combination of men with the right vision and business sense could have accomplished so much in such a short time. Hudson's shipping was second in the State of New York only to New York City's, an amazing accomplishment considering Hudson is 120 miles from the sea. The time was right for such an endeavor, but the times were soon to change.

The River that Flows Two Ways

Among all the rivers of the world the Hudson is acknowledged queen, decked with romance, jewelled with poetry, clad with history, and crowned with beauty.

Wallace Bruce, *The Hudson,* 1913[1]

Most stories have heroes or heroines, and if this account must conform to that formula, our heroine will be the river. Without the river, there would be no story. She brought fame and prosperity to the city, and when the city turned its back on her—in the form of iron rails across her shores—the prosperity ceased.

She was born of glaciers, glaciers so high and heavy that the land beneath subsided.[2] As the climate warmed, the glaciers melted, and the water from that immense quantity of ice created a part of the Hudson Valley. The river was created below sea level, surging far out to sea in a bed that was formed when the glaciers absorbed the waters and lowered the sea level. When the seas rose again, the water flowed into this deep bed, beginning the tidal action that remains today.

This river has had many names. In 1524, thirty-five years after the discovery of America (if one discounts the Vikings), Giovanni da Verrazano sailed into the "narrows" and described her as "the River of the Mountains." The next year a Portuguese named Gomez, employed by Spain, named her the "Rio San Antonio." The Dutch gave her many names: the Mauritius, after Prince Maurice of Nassau, the Manhattan River, the Nassau River, and the North River (the Delaware was the South River, and the Connecticut the Fresh River). It was the English who named her the

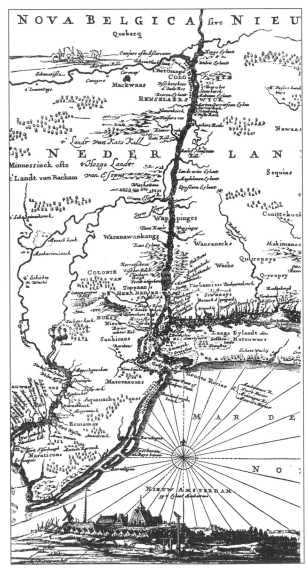

Detail from Montanus's map, 1671, showing Dutch territory along the Hudson, Mohawk and Connecticut rivers. (Courtesy of the New York State Library.)

The Hudson River north from Promenade Hill. Photo by Robert Ragaini.

Hudson.[3] In her 315-mile journey, she is a mountain stream, a canal, a fiord, and an estuary.

Viewed from the shore, the river appears as a beautiful, placid, wide ribbon of slow-moving water. That appearance is, however, a deception. The twice-daily tides push upstream where they collide with the fresh water entering the river from its hundreds of feeder rivers, streams, and creeks pushing downriver. One of the Native American names for her was "The River that Flows Two Ways." This constant flow of fresh water prevents the brackish, salty water from moving far upstream.

The river is broad and shallow between Troy and Kingston, filled with mud flats, sandbars, snags, and islands of silt and mud. Many of these are covered with just enough water at high tide to trap the unsuspecting boater. Silt from the tributaries feeding the Hudson flow in with each freshet, adding more obstacles. The river narrows and deepens

below Hyde Park, deepening to over one hundred feet as the cliffs range closer to the shore. These Highlands presented another problem for sailing ships. As the river makes its first deep curves in the long journey south, the currents become rapid and the wind has a tendency to blow strongly through the canyons. The "Horse Race," as it was called,[4] was so difficult to navigate that sometimes fleets of sloops would have to wait near Peekskill until the wind changed.

Because of the shallow water, as well as the silt and sandbars, the river above the City of Hudson was considered too treacherous for deep-draft vessels, and the city was proclaimed "the head of navigation" on the river (a boast it used until the 1930s).[5] Henry Hudson experienced the problem when his ship ran aground in 1609 on a bank of "Oze" (ooze—mud or slime). It took a high tide to free the ship.[6] Complaints from steamboat companies finally forced the state and federal governments to deepen the channel and remove snags, beginning in 1831. Each spring flood would create new obstacles and rearrange old ones, and the efforts continued. The Overslaugh Bar, near Castleton, where Henry Hudson went aground, was dredged in the 1860s. Serious dredging began in 1932 when a twenty-seven-foot channel was dug from Hudson to Albany.[7] In 1960 the river channel was deepened to thirty-four feet and widened to four hundred feet. The dredged silt was deposited haphazardly on the islands and bays of the river, changing the topography forever.

The river—at least her upper, slow, shallow, salt-free half—would freeze solid during the winter months. From December through March, navigation was at a halt. The advent of the icebreaker relieved this situation. The spring breakup of the ice was (and still is) an event to be celebrated and dreaded, depending on the amount of snow accumulation during the winter. Heavy snow melting in the mountains would send torrents of water and ice down the tributaries to join with blocks of ice in the river, inundating the low shoreline and grinding away any structures (and livestock) in its path. The Dutch at Fort Orange (Albany) suffered several devastating losses in the seventeenth century from the rampaging ice.

Hendrick Hudson's *The Half Moon*,
from *Ter-Centenary of the Hudson*, Wallkill Valley Publishing Ass'n., 1909.

A Little Different: Claverack Landing, 1661–1783

Meanwhile, the defendant and his wife and their daughter together attacked the said Bensingh and beat him, and took the bits and bridles off the horses so that they ran away without control.

Court Minutes of Albany, Rensselaerwyck and Schenectady,
Volume II, October 1, 1678[1]

This incident took place in 1678 on the road from the community of Claverack to the Hudson River. The defendant, Gerrit Visbeek, claimed he had owned the land for over twenty years and had made the road to the river. The future City of Hudson would be built on Claverack Landing.

The name Claverack comes from the Dutch words *klaver rack*. A "rack," or "reach," was used by the early Dutch mariners to define a certain distance on the river. Each rack was assigned a name, sometimes reflecting some obvious, fixed landmark easily identified from mid-river. There were fourteen in all, and some of the other names were Seylmaker's (sailmaker's) Reach, Crescent Reach, and Lange (long) Reach.[2] In this case, the *clavers* (or *klavers*) were extensive, tall, bare, clay cliffs just north of the present-day City of Hudson. The original Van Hoesen deed of 1662 mentions land containing "three of the Clavers," forever proving that the name had nothing to do with fields of clover.[3] "The Klaverrack" referred to in early documents

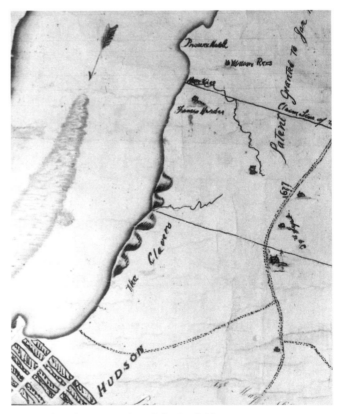

The Clavers. Section of the Penfield Map, 1799.[4]
(Courtesy of the Columbia County Historical Society, Kinderhook, New York.) Photo by Michael Fredericks, Jr.

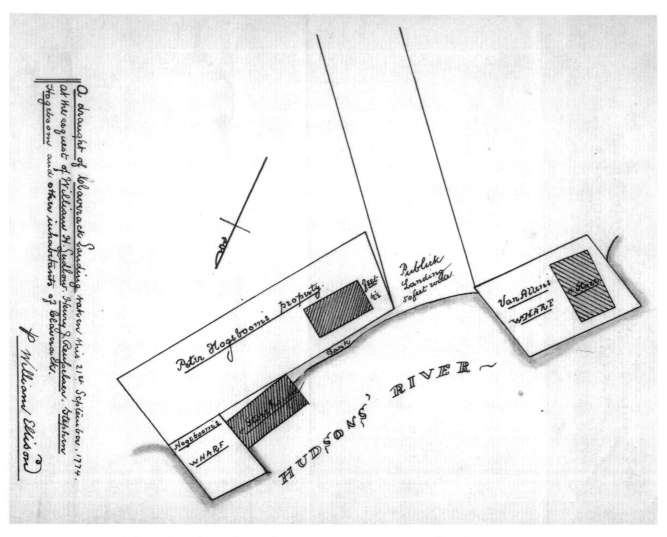

A map of Claverack Landing "taken in the year 1774." (Courtesy of the Office of the Columbia County Clerk.)

meant the land on the east bank of the Hudson River from the Stottville (Major Abram's) Creek on the north, to the northern boundary of the Livingston Manor on the south.

Albany County, formed in 1683, originally included all of the land in what is now Columbia County. In 1772, Claverack was one of four districts that divided the future county, but it was still part of Albany County. It wasn't until 1786 that the present Columbia County was formed, with the inland hamlet of Claverack as its county seat.

Claverack Landing was the riverside access for farm produce to be shipped by sloop, canoe, or scow to other communities on the river. A "waggon road" ran eastward to the prosperous community of Claverack, located four miles inland on the Post Road from Albany to New York. There were two wharves and some storehouses at the landing. A rural settlement developed nearby, growing not so much from an influx of newcomers, but by wills that divided existing farms among offspring.

The area had been purchased by Jan Frans Van Hoesen from American Indians in 1661. Though this land was originally included in the Van Rensselaer purchase in 1649, Van Hoesen managed to defy the Van Rensselaer interests and maintain his ownership.[5] As late as 1773 John Van Rensselaer, proprietor of what was then called "the Lower Manor," was trying to reclaim the land. It was Van Hoesen's family descendants, multiplying through the years, as well as a few family friends, that lived in the Claverack Landing area in the late seven-

A QUAINT OLD DOCUMENT.

AN "INDIAN" DEED.

Original Deed of the Lands now Occupied as the Site of the City of Hudson—A Literal Translation of the Genuine Old Deed—Curious Phraseology and odd Metes and Bounds—A Peculiar Consideration as the Purchase Price.

Translation.

Appeared before me Johannes Provoost, etc., two Indians, one named Panitepiet, or in Dutch Kesjen Wey, and the other Hans Vos, or in Indian Tatınkenat, both owners, and commissioned by the other owners of the land, lying in the Klaverrack, on the East bank [of the river], who declare in the presence of the after named witneffes, that they have sold, granted and conveyed as by these presents they do, to and for the behoof of Jan Franfe Van Hoesem, a parcel of land, lying in the aforesaid Klaverrack, extending from the little Kill (*Killetie*) of Jan Henderickse, *alias root-haer*, to the land of Slichtenhorst, in which parcel of land are comprehended three of the *Klavers*, on the south side of said *root-haer*, and extending towards the wood about an *uyrgaens*, * until beyond the great Kil, and further, of such magnitude as the grantors have bounded it by the woods and Kils; for a certain sum in goods to these grantees paid, amounting to about five hundred guilders in beavers, for which they promise the aforesaid land, to free from further actions or pretensions of the other Indians, who may sinisterly lay claim thereto.

Thus done in the presence of Gerret Fjsbeek and Carsten Claebsen [Timmerman] as witneffes hereto invited, on this 5th of June, A. D. 1662, in Fort Orange.

    This is the mark ⋈ . — of Panietepiet, with his own hand set.

    This is the mark of U–U–U–of TATANKENAT, WITH HIS OWN HAND SET.

GERRET VISBEECK.

THIS IS THE MARK, ⊲ [——of CARSTEN CLAESSEN, with his own hand set.

Acknowledged before me,

    LA MONTÁGNE, *Clerk at Fort Orange.*

On this 11th day of June, A. D. 1664, appeared before me as above an Indian, named Sickaneeck, or by the Dutch named Teunis, one of the proprietors of the above written land, who acknowledges and declares that, on the 5th of June, 1662, with Panietepiet and Keesie Wey, he sold the above mentioned land to Jan Francen Van Hoesen, and was fully paid and satisfied therefor, and frees him from all claims of the other Indians.

Done *ut supra*.

    This is the mark * * * of SICKANEECK, alias TEUNIS, with his own hand set.

(*) As far as one can go in an hour's time.

*** The original manuscript has designated upon it as the mark a picture or character of an animal similar to that of a horse.

Copy of the Van Hoesen deed, June 11, 1664, reprinted from Robert M. Terry, *The Hudsonian: Old Times and New*, 1895.

teenth and early eighteenth centuries. A school, a gristmill and a canoe ferry served the inhabitants. Though the Claverack Landing families shared Dutch roots with their eastern neighbors, in another respect they were entirely different. Van Hoesen's patent was free of the Van Rensselaer manorial obligations. Landing residents owned their land free of any rent or other accountability to the "manor lord." While those inland chafed under the tenant system, those living on the Van Hoesen lands had the advantage of ignoring the deference due to the Van Rensselaers. They could sell their land freely, without permission or having to pay the hated quarter of the sale price to the landlord.[6]

In 1679, Volkie, the widow of Jan Frans Van Hoesen, and her new husband, Gerrit Visbeek, were living near the river and close to the road leading inland from the river. Mayhem resulted when they attacked a local farmer for using the road on his way to the river. Visbeek's claim to ownership of the road was denied in court.[7]

In that same year Marie Van Rensselaer petitioned the court to have a house built near the river "for those who live inland—for their accommodation near the strand" near Gerrit Visbeek's. Visbeek was to give a valid deed after payment was made.[8] This indicates that Claverack Landing was used for shipping purposes at an early date, and that the title of the land was free of manorial claims.

In 1745 Francis Hardick (or Herdyk), the heir and the son-in-law of Jan Frans Van Hoesen, sold to Jeremiah Hogeboom a large and important parcel of land on the North Bay and the slope above it. The land contained the only viable stream in the area, where the Hogebooms built a gristmill.[9] They also built and maintained a wharf and storehouse on the river at the edge of the bay. In 1760, Peter Fonda had docks on the southern shore of the South Bay, and a farm on the hill nearby, owned by Van Rensselaer.

Another factor that set the Claverack Landing residents apart was their religion. New Netherland was founded by the Dutch, who established the Calvinist doctrines of the Dutch Reformed Church as their national religion. They tried to exclude other religions in their settlements, but the diverse beliefs of the immigrants required tolerance. Generations of traditions spawned suspicion, however, and even a difference in Protestant beliefs loomed large in the small world of these Dutch set-

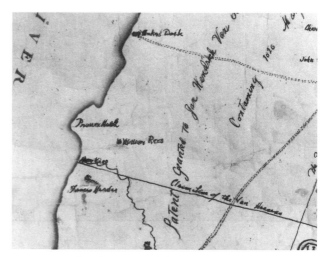

Praewenhoeck. Section of the Penfield Map, 1799.[10]
(Courtesy of the Columbia County Historical Society, Kinderhook, New York.) Photo by Michael Fredericks, Jr.

tlements. Most of the Claverack Landing folk were Lutherans, at least those descended from the Van Hoesen line, but their neighbors were Dutch Reformed. Denied the right to build a Lutheran church at the landing by the Reformed Dutch elders, the Van Hoesen heirs and their friends canoed across the river to Loonenbergh, named for the Van Loon family, which is now upper Athens.[11] There, they and the Loonenbergh congregation founded a church in 1704 and worshiped their Lutheran religion in the Dutch language.

William Herdyk married a daughter of one of the earliest Lutheran ministers in America, Daniel Falckner. William's sister, Gerritje, married Pastor Justus Falckner (1672–1723). They lived on Herdyk land two miles north of Hudson at a site then called Praewenhoeck,[12] later changed to Praven Hook, and now known as Priming Hook.

Today's Partition Street partially follows the route of the old "Waggon Road" that led from the river to Claverack and to the inland communities. The street's name is derived from the partition of lands between the Van Hoesen heirs. Son-in-law William Herdyk (or Hardick; not necessarily the same William Herdyk who married the daughter of Daniel Falkner—each generation of Herdyks had a William) received the section of the holdings from today's Ferry Street northward to the patent

boundaries. Johannes Van Hoesen came into possession of the land to the south of the "Waggon Road."

In terms of agriculture, the subsistence of colonial life, the lands near the river were poor. Histories mention orchards on the slopes near the South Bay, and forests on the north. The land in between was hilly, rocky, and mostly clay. Those Van Hoesens that settled on the rich bottom lands of the Claverack Creek had the advantage in farming. But the river offered seasonal runs of herring, shad, and sturgeon that could be netted in great quantities, then dried or pickled and shipped off to other markets.

Colonel John Van Alen, who had married Catherine, one of the later Van Hoesen heirs, purchased the land south of the present-day Ferry and Partition streets, which included a landing site on the South Bay. Four years later, in 1768, he sought "500 yards of land under water, to the north of Rocky Point, now Promenade Hill, near his dwelling house at Claverack and to the same distance to the south of said point, along the Hudson River, for the breadth of 100 yards into said river." This was the beginning of the demand for "water lots." Col. Van Alen constructed a wharf and warehouse in that vicinity, and his large brick house on the street opposite was a focal point until destroyed by the fire of 1838.[13]

Various types of vessels plied the Hudson in these early times. The Dutch yachts were cumbersome and, in the formative years of the colony, equipped with small cannons. Agents for the patroons and well-to-do citizens used the yachts for carrying people and merchandise. Barks (barkentines) and skiffs also were used on the river. Canoes, either dugouts or bark-covered, are mentioned frequently in the early records for both travel and freight. They were the vessel for the average colonist because they were simple to acquire and easy for one person to manage. The ferry from Claverack Landing to Loonenbergh was a canoe. When a wagon and team needed to cross, two canoes were lashed together and covered with

View of Partition Street. The western section follows the route of the old "waggon road." Photo by Robert Ragaini.

Sloops, from a painting of Clinton Point near Poughkeepsie, reprinted from Thomas Hunt, *The History of Clermont*.
Photo by Robert Ragaini.

planks to support the wagon. The horses were lashed to the side and compelled to swim across. When the river froze solid, a horse-pulled sleigh provided transportation and recreation.

Because the river was shallow, sloops—originating in the Netherlands as canal boats—became the carrying vessel of choice for Hudson River skippers. Over one hundred sloops plied the river by 1800, stopping at Claverack Landing to pick up or deliver cargo. Flour, grain, lumber, and hay were just a few of the products shipped from the landing.

The Hogebooms and Van Alen may have had their own sloops, but that fact is never mentioned. What is known is that they had warehouses to store goods until a vessel arrived, and a store where scarce items, brought in by sloops, could be purchased.

Claverack Landing was a unique community, its inhabitants differing from those of the surrounding countryside by their freedoms and their religion. The stage was set for a meeting of two groups of people, both of which held beliefs divergent from their countrymen.

Between the Devil and the Deep Blue Sea: The Quaker Whalers of Nantucket

[The whalers of Nantucket] carried the most perilous mode of hardy industry to the extent to which it is pushed by this recent people.

Edmund Burke, "On Conciliation with America,"
speech in the House of Commons, March 22, 1775

On the little island of Nantucket, whaling and the industries allied with it had been the only business of the inhabitants. Before the Revolutionary War, the island sent out over one hundred ships sailing as far as the Falkland Islands to kill whales and bring home the oil. The market for this oil was Britain, and the ships returning to the island were filled with the necessary supplies for island use and trade. The island population was predominantly Quaker, or as they preferred to be known, "the Society of Friends." Nonviolence was their creed; war was contrary to their beliefs. Their dependency on Britain as a market for their oil, and their insistence on neutrality, caused the island Quakers to be caught between two warring countries at the outbreak of hostilities. To the British, they were Americans. To the Americans, they were loyalists, allied to the British cause.[1] In some ways the latter was true, for the older oil merchants of the island were tied economically to the British firms and, though no British troops invaded the island, bands of loyalists from the American mainland came in droves seeking sanctuary.

Blockades were preventing vessels from entering or leaving the island, and the New England ports were forbidden to send goods unless it could be determined that they were to be used by the Nantucketers, and not to "aid the enemy."[2] A ship from the American side came to the island and took away fifty whaleboats, escalating tensions. Nantucket ships at sea were seized and their crews captured and imprisoned. A time of hunger and cold fell on the island as it ran short of food and fuel. By the end of the Revolutionary War, 1,200 Nantucket men had been captured, killed, or lost at sea.[3] Nantucket managed to have a few ships licensed by both British and American authorities, but by the end of the war few remained of the original one hundred or more ships that sailed before the conflict.

When the hostilities ceased, the final blow arrived. Britain imposed a tariff on incoming oil that made any profit impossible.[4] There was no market for whale oil in the new United States; Americans had become used to using tallow (animal fat) for their lighting. To make matters worse, new whaling ports sprang up all over the Atlantic coast when a bounty was declared on whale oil. With no market left, the Nantucket whalers were without the only industry they knew. To further aggravate matters, a generational schism had developed during the war. The young men of Nantucket resented the loyalist leanings of the elders who felt the survival of Nantucket rested with Britain.[5] The younger generation felt the future lay with the new country. These differences were to play a part in the future City of Hudson.

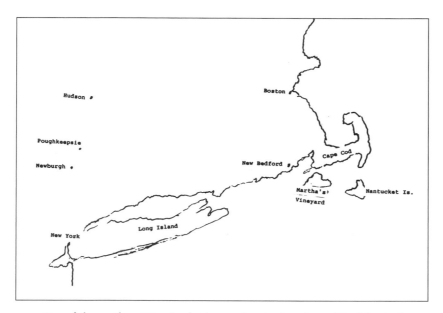

Map of the southern New England coast showing locations of the islands of Nantucket and Martha's Vineyard.

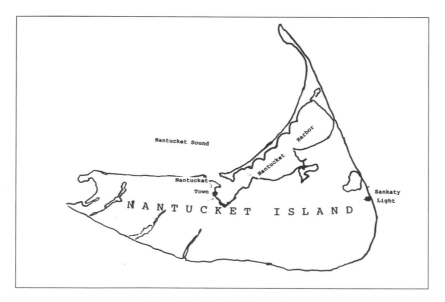

Map of the island of Nantucket.

Five Quakers, Six Opinions: Migrations from Nantucket

[The Nantucket whalers are] *a race apart from the mainstream of American or European life.*

Thomas Jefferson,
"Report of the Secretary of State on the Subject
of the Cod and Whale Fisheries," Philadelphia, 1791[1]

The close of the Revolutionary War found Nantucket Island ready to restart its whaling industry, but without a market for the oil. The Nantucket leaders failed to win approval by the Massachusetts Legislature to have the island declared a neutral state and, therefore, not subject to the British duty. Many whalemen accepted offers from British whaling firms and served on British ships for the growing British whaling fleet. The Southern Whale Fishery, the name for the new grounds found in the southern Atlantic off the coast of Brazil, was the stimulus for the British whaling companies to control sperm whale imports.[2] Sperm whale oil and the valuable "head matter," called spermaceti and used for candles, had a lucrative market for the British firms.

Migration by groups of Quakers from the 14.5-x-3.5-mile island of Nantucket was a common occurrence. Burgeoning families led to a shortage of space and opportunities. The problem of consanguinity, with bloodlines limited to such a small area and a religious prohibition against marrying non-Quakers, plus the constant fear of war, contributed to the movement of families away from Nantucket. They would move "off-island" to the mainland where there were other settlements of Friends.

It seemed reasonable to assign all the Quaker migrations to the reasons stated above, but while researching the fate of the present Quaker meeting in Hudson, I learned of another catalyst for the movement of Quaker families from one location to another. Quakers have long been considered peaceful, quiet, and amenable so it came as a surprise to learn that many of the migrations occurred because of disagreements within the meeting. Even before the serious split between Hicksite and Orthodox Quakers that occurred in 1828 (see Appendix A, "Quakers and the Hudson Meeting"), vehement squabbles took place resulting in families packing up and moving to new communities to join another meeting or begin a new one. Perhaps the Quaker emphasis on independent decisions, plus the lack of a defining authoritative body, allowed these internal disputes to reach such a level. An expression told to me by an active member of the Quaker meeting illustrates Quaker fractiousness: "five Quakers, six opinions."[3]

Many of the settlements to which Nantucket families relocated were far inland, indicating that Nantucket whalers could make the transition to farmers. One will find the same Nantucket family names, such as Folger, Macy, Starbuck, Coffin, and Bunker, in areas throughout the eastern states. One such early settlement was in Easton, Washington

ilies packed up their households and moved to these inland areas.

After the war, as more and more whaling captains and crew left the island to sail for Britain, plans for a larger exodus were being made. Negotiations were brewing with the governor of Nova Scotia for a contingent of Nantucket families to set up a whaling town in Dartmouth, across the harbor from Halifax. Residency on this British soil would free whale oil from the tariff. The move occurred in 1786. Forty families (over 170 people), some house frames, and 150 whalemen moved to this new settlement.[5]

All in a Day's Work, by Charles Raleigh, 1878-1880. (Courtesy of The New Bedford Whaling Museum.)

County, near Saratoga. Nantucket Quakers began moving there during the 1760s, and the families with Nantucket names flourished and built a meetinghouse.[4] Others settled in the Nine Partners Patent and the Oblong in Dutchess County. In the 1770s there was an active settlement near Greensboro, South Carolina. In 1776, fearing the worst in the accelerating war, many Nantucket fam-

Another group of New England Quakers had strong ties to the new country. Several had served the American cause during the war in ways other than actual combat. Now they chose to risk their fortunes in a financial venture that would move them far from their homes and the sea. With the high duty imposed on oil by Britain, and little demand for oil in the States, these men were deter-

The Captain Daniel Folger House, once located in Easton, New York. Photo donated to the Easton Library by Theresa & Gilbert Pratt. (Courtesy of the Easton Library, Greenwich, New York.)

mined to find a safe port for commercial shipping. Eighteen highly successful men of various occupations banded together to find a site for their future port. They hoped to select an area that would furnish an unlimited supply of marketable goods and be free of the threat of foreign invasion.

During the British occupation of New York City, the lower Hudson River had been closed to navigation. A treaty of peace was finally signed after a two-year conference in Paris and was ratified by Congress in January of 1784. As soon as hostilities ceased, a Nantucket schooner sailed up to Newburgh with fish, whale oil, and rum.[6] New England Quakers knew the river well. Before the war, they had traded with the river communities and visited relations in Dutchess and Saratoga Counties. They probably knew of the deep water

that extended almost to the shoreline at Claverack Landing, and the presence of great forests of hardwoods suitable for shipbuilding—something that Nantucket and the other highly populated New England towns lacked. A growing supply of vessels was, of course, a necessity for the growth of a port. A vast area of farms also was there to provide products suitable for trade. It has been written that the Nantucket Quakers who founded the City of Hudson searched many places before "discovering" Claverack Landing, but they already knew of it, and they knew that it was reputed to be "the head of Navigation" on the river.[7] This meant that vessels of deep draft would have difficulty beyond that point.

Two New England Quaker men came up the Hudson River to negotiate with the owners of Claverack Landing.

North Quaker Meeting House, located on State Route 40, Town of Easton. Drawing by Rebecca Butler MacKenzie. (Courtesy of the Easton Library, Greenwich, New York.)

Those Yankee Heathen: Clash of Cultures, 1783–1785

From an old-time English history we read that Hudson grew more rapidly than any other town in America except Baltimore. Standing at the head of ship navigation it would naturally become a great port.

Wallace Bruce, *The Hudson*, 1913

No mention or document exists to describe the meeting and negotiations in the summer of 1783 between Thomas Jenkins, who represented the Proprietors, and the affected residents of Claverack Landing, but agreements were made and money passed hands. The first purchase, in July of 1783, was the store and wharf belonging to Peter Hogeboom. That wharf was to become the city dock.[1] Two more parcels were purchased from the widow of Francis Hardick, and the leaders returned to their home ports and packed up their families for the move to the landing.

"When the whalers came to Hudson" captures the popular misconception regarding the founders, but they were not all whalers. The City of Hudson could not have been so adequately planned and plotted had the organizers been off to sea for several years at a time. Some were seamen, but more were artisans and businessmen. Many had their fingers in an array of commercial and civic activities, and those pursuits were directed to making the city a successful port. The men who founded Hudson are usually called "the Proprietors," but "the Nantucket Navigators" is the name they gave themselves.[2] "Entrepreneurs" would be the best word to describe them. Their hometowns were divided between Nantucket, Providence, and Martha's Vineyard. It is known that the Proprietors brought with them a good sum of money to invest in the enterprise. Estimates have ranged from $100,000 to $500,000.

Seth Jenkins, John Alsop, and their families were first to arrive.[3] They lived aboard their ships while their houses were being built on the north side of Franklin Square. More Proprietors arrived the following year with their families and their vessels, some carrying the frames of their future homes. Over a period of a few years, the lands of the descendants of the first Van Hoesen were sold to the Proprietors. The rest of the countryside looked on with horror while these sales were being made. The histories name some families that welcomed the New Englanders, but the silence was deafening from the hundreds of others who considered the newcomers the hated Yankees and, far worse, practically heathen with their weird Quaker notions. ("Yankees," from the Dutch *Jan Kees*—literally "John Cheese"—was a disparaging nickname that the Dutch colonists in New York applied to the British colonists in New England.)

Stephen Paddock was one Proprietor who brought the frame of his house, which was constructed on North Front Street. This seems to be contrary to the Proprietors' Association's rules that stipulated that no structures could be built until the roadways were set out. The rules also state that "no person shall fix his house without such direction from a majority of the committee as they think proper."[4] Another provision declared that "no person shall extend his steps more than four feet from his door or 'seller' way." It was a very planned development.

In May of 1784, the Proprietors held their first meeting, at which a committee was formed to "reg-ulate streets." This was no easy task, considering the obstacles facing them. Building lots were divided among the members in each block, known in Quaker terms as a "Square." In November of 1784, they agreed unanimously to name the city "Hudson."[5]

The Proprietors hired Samuel Edmonds, formerly a clerk for Col. Van Alen, in the double capacity of bookkeeper and spy. He spoke both Dutch and English and was able to inform the Proprietors of any machinations the Dutch countryfolk might plan to their disadvantage.[6]

Building the road that became South Front Street began in June of 1784. Blasting and digging were required, and a bridge was needed over a ravine containing a running stream that entered into the South Bay. This was at the base of the present Union Street.[7]

A walk through Hudson in 1783 would have shown a site much different from today. A rock cliff

View of Hudson & the Catskill Mountains, "drawn from nature" by Jacques Gerard Milbert, *Amerique Septentrionale*, c.1820, Plate 3, No. 11. The view is from Mt. Merino looking across the South Bay.

rose from the river, narrowing into a ridge eastward. The top of this ridge was broken by deep ravines in several places where Main (later Warren) Street was constructed. In the area of Fourth Street, another ravine cut through from north to south and was known as "the great Hollow." It required a bridge with stone abutments. (Remains of this hollow can be seen just west of the Hudson Library's parking lot.) Another ravine, between Fifth and Sixth streets, slowed progress, but was considered "out in the country." In 1798, Fourth Street was considered to be the eastern end of the city, with most of the dwellings and stores concentrated below Second Street and along Front Street. Main Street, which became Warren in 1799, was a ridge extending from the river eastward.[8] The land sloped down on each side, and it took years and a great deal of fill to create the flat city of today.

The drying puddle of wetlands of today's South Bay was once an enormous bay of water fed by streams from inland (Krishna's Kill was one) and washed fresh by the river's tides. The North Bay extended over a much greater area than today. The two bays that bound the city on each side were known in colonial Dutch days as the Souder Bought (South Bay) and the Norder Bought (North Bay). William Strickland, a visitor in 1799, commented that the bays are "in part dry at low water, the tide rising here five feet, which is as much as the usual height of it at the coast."[9] This should dispel the statement appearing in early histories that the South Bay was covered with ships "enough to walk across the Bay over the decks of the vessels." A shipyard was located at the point of the South Bay near the river, but only scows and barges could navigate the rest. The North Bay was never deep enough to carry widespread maritime activity.

The completion in 1851 of the Hudson River Railroad, which ran along the front of the city and across the river access to the two bays, spelled the beginning of the end of these two bodies of water. Earlier, the South Bay's northern shore extended nearly to Cross Street, and an inlet's water lapped near the present railroad station. The eastern shore

View over the South Bay toward the New York State Training School for Girls, now a New York State correctional facility. Postcard, 1908.

was well beyond the Third Street Bay Road, the water reaching the base of the hill of the Hudson Correctional Facility. Most water rights along the northern shore of the South Bay were wiped out by the construction of the Hudson and Berkshire Railroad in 1838. In 1848 the Hudson Iron Works set up furnaces on piles in the South Bay. The intention was to fill with debris and cinders the ninety acres of the bay that was part of the purchase. The firm went out of business, however, after "reclaiming" twelve acres.[10] The North Bay also suffered from being filled and deprived of river waters by the railroad.

The impetus that led to the building of Hudson's shipping port was not the South Bay, as is frequently suggested, but the extraordinary depth of the water in front of the city between the two bays. The water level drops off to a great depth just beyond the shoreline, allowing deep-draft ships to dock safely.

The major disadvantage restricting the maritime success of the city was the fact that the river was frozen over for nearly one-third of the year. Above the salt tide, the river froze solid from December to March. A survey made from 1825 to 1844, inclusively, showed the river closed by ice for an average of 135 days annually.[11] Before the days of the modern icebreakers, no sailing ships—in fact, no ships at all—could reach the port of Hudson while the river was frozen. This made schedules on sailing ships unpredictable. To arrive in New York City with a full cargo and not be able to sail upriver to unload in Hudson until spring was a great hardship for all concerned.

Despite this disadvantage, the Proprietors realized they had the perfect site. Memories of the threat of foreign invasion of their New England homelands created the desire for a port far from the possibility of marauding enemies. The Hudson shipping interests solved the ice problem by sending off their last cargos for the winter just before the river froze. The vessels would sail to a southern port, such as Charleston, where they would harbor for the winter, trading from that port to Europe and back. The ships would return to Hudson with another cargo in the spring when the ice had broken.

From the Jaws of a Whale: The Founding Fathers, 1783–1784

All of them were men of influence, intelligence and activity, and are described physically as stout, well formed, noble looking men.

Stephen Miller, *Sketches of Hudson*, 1862

It would be helpful to know more about the character of the men who contributed to the astonishing success of Hudson, but unfortunately Victorian histories have a tendency to overrate virtues and ignore shortcomings. The following is a list of those who signed the articles of agreement stating that they were joint proprietors in the tract of land purchased by Thomas Jenkins, and that their purpose was to establish a commercial settlement. A few disappeared into the countryside to become farmers.

Stephen Paddock, from Nantucket
Thomas Jenkins, from Providence
Joseph Barnard, from Nantucket
Reuben Macy, from Nantucket
Benjamin Folger, from Nantucket
John Alsop, from Providence
Seth Jenkins, from Providence
Charles Jenkins, from Nantucket
William Wall, from Providence
Ezra Reed, origin unknown
Hezekiah Dayton, from Providence
Gideaon Gardner, from Nantucket
David Lawrence, from Providence

John Thurston, from Providence
Reuben Folger, from Nantucket
Nathaniel Greene, from Providence
Titus Morgan, from Newport

Added in 1785 were:
Alexander Coffin, from Nantucket
Lemuel Jenkins, from Edgartown
William Minturn, from Nantucket
*Benjamin Starbuck, from Nantucket
Shubael Worth, from Nantucket
*John Cartwright, from Nantucket
Paul Hussey, from Nantucket
John Allen, from Edgartown
Marshall Jenkins, from Edgartown
Deborah Jenkins, from Nantucket
*These two did not settle in Hudson.

Others added in later years were:
Benjamin Hussey, Samuel Mansfield,
Walter Folger, Daniel Paddock, Peleg Clark[1]

Proprietary ownership was common in Quaker communities. The rules for the proprietorship of Hudson, written before the search for the future port began, read in part: "That the subscribers, with a group of other American colonists, appeared before a hearing at the British House of Commons to protest the Restraining Act. Jenkins explained the importance of whaling to Nantucket, and also vowed that they "would not live under the military Government of Halifax," a prophecy that held true for Seth Jenkins and his brother, Thomas.[5]

Thomas Jenkins is described as having the "uniting and dignified, princely air of an old school gentleman, with the address and energy of a man of business." "Standing on his wharf with his gold-headed cane in his hand, watching and directing the preparations for the sailing of his ships, his bearing and manner was authoritive, but his nature was kind and genial." His Hudson residence, across the street from what was the Worth Hotel, was considered too palatial by Quaker standards of plainness, however, and he was accused of being "somewhat aristocratic."[6]

David Lawrence "was a man of keen observation and ready wit; of strong sense and stronger prejudice.

Portrait of Thomas Jenkins, c. 1780-1795.
(Courtesy of the City of Hudson.) Photo by Robert Ragaini.

being joint partners of a certain tract of land, for the purpose of establishing a commercial settlement, on the principles of equity, each to subscribe for each part of the tract, shall settle therein in person, and carry his stock on or before 1785."[2] The Proprietors' Association's articles stated that the association should consist of not more than thirty members, and all of them should be merchants or "concerned in navigating the deep."[3]

The two leaders of the enterprise were Thomas and Seth Jenkins, whose businesses had been disrupted by the war. Originally Seth Jenkins was a London trade skipper, and Thomas Jenkins was a whale oil merchant. Of Seth it is said "that he gave most unstintedly of his time and personal service, besides employing his wealth and influence for the prosperity of all concerned."[4] Just before the American Revolution erupted, Parliament enacted the Restraining Act of 1775, which curtailed trade and fishing—including whaling—in an effort to subdue the colonists. On May 2, 1775, Seth Jenkins,

Portrait of Alexander Coffin, c. 1825-1830.
(Courtesy of the City of Hudson.) Photo by Robert Ragaini.

In the Whale's Jaws, from "Huntsmen of the Sea," *Harper's New Monthly Magazine,* c. 1870.

In his old age, gouty, irritable and sarcastic."[7] "A man of strict integrity and good sense but excessively odd" described Squire Worth.[8] Hezekiah Dayton was "a good citizen and an upright man, fond of argument, reasoning in all things, but in all things unreasonable, never convinced and never convincing."[9]

Joining the Proprietors in 1775, Alexander Coffin, a former shipmaster, was a strong advocate of the American cause during the Revolutionary War. Among other things, he was a dispatch carrier from John Adams in Amsterdam, Holland, to the Continental Congress in Philadelphia. He was described as a man who was "frank, generous, warmhearted and brave as Caesar, but withall, hot as a pepper pot, fierce as a northeaster, yet neither rude, aggressive or implacable."[10]

The description (probably modified) of Cotton Gelston, written in times when praise was preferred, portrays a troubled personality. He "was a man of violent passions, and was frequently involved in brawls, verbally and physically, with his cohorts and friends."[11]

Though not a Proprietor, Ezekial Gilbert was active in the affairs of the city. He had moved from Claverack to Claverack Landing in 1785, becoming its first lawyer. It was said of him "that he was not a man of great talents," leading one to wonder at the extent of his lack of "talents"—he did go on to become a representative of Congress in 1790.[12]

When Marshall Jenkins joined the Proprietors in 1785, he brought with him a horrible memory. Fourteen years earlier, his name had been featured in the following news item: "We learn from Edgartown that a vessel lately arrived there from a whaling voyage. ... one Marshall Jenkins, with others, being in a boat that struck a whale. She turned and bit the boat in two ... took Jenkins in her mouth ... and went down with him, but on rising, threw him into one part of the boat whence he was taken on board the vessel by the crew ... being much bruised. In a fortnight after ... he perfectly recovered. This account we have from undoubted authority." (*Post Boy,* October 12, 1771)[13]

Seals, Whales, and Too Many Sleighs: The Port of Hudson, 1784–1800

Their lives have ever been one continual round of hair-breadth escapes ... Many a tale of danger and toil and suffering, startling, severe, and horrible, has illuminated the pages of the history of this pursuit, and scarce any, even the humblest of these hardy mariners, but can, from his own experience, narrate truths stranger than fiction.

Alexander Starbuck, *History of the American Whale Fishery*, 1877

One piece of valuable waterfront still belonged to Col. John Van Alen. He had already donated land to the Proprietors for their burial ground "forever, and for no other use."[1] (This portion of the cemetery is in the old northwestern section. The inscriptions on the old stones face west, while all the other, later stones have inscriptions facing east. This would indicate that the earliest access to the "burying ground" was from the most northwest corner. The immense cemetery today is the result of later land donations and purchases.) The colonel died before negotiations for his waterfront property were completed, but his wife was able to conclude the sale. This included the wharf, store, his house, and all the land lying between Ferry Street and the South Bay running easterly to Front Street, as well as water rights. (Mrs. Van Alen also received a "house lot" on the first square and Main Street.) The sale was finalized in November of 1784.[2]

A market house was constructed on Front Street near Main Street, to be paid for by the Proprietors. (In 1799 a second marketplace was erected "on the jail square," the northwest corner of Fourth and Warren streets. It took the name of the "Upper Market.")[3] Lots were set aside for a schoolhouse and for a meetinghouse for the Society of Friends.

The division of the water rights was essential for a port city. Eighteen men signed the articles and divided the waterfront amicably among themselves.

The former Hogeboom dock was enlarged to be used as the city dock, and was named the Hudson Wharf. This was at the bottom of what is now, appropriately, Dock Street.

Quaker burying ground, northwest section of the Cedar Park Cemetery. Photo by Robert Ragaini.

In 1784 Titus Morgan applied to build a ship-yard "adjoining the Northernmost street," at the base of State Street. His lease was extended to four years because he agreed to make a road "from Market Street to the river, passable for wagons, etc., at his expense." This was the beginning of North Front Street, and the Morgan shipyard was at the foot of State Street. In 1785, because of the "extra cost and expenses of blowing open said road," his lease was extended from four to ten years.[4] Apparently the expense was more than Morgan could handle, because the following advertisement appeared in the *Hudson Weekly Gazette*: "... escaped from the subscriber a man of the name of Titus Morgan, ship carpenter, etc., etc. November 27, 1786, Henry Lyon, Constable."[5]

In March of the following year, all of Titus Morgan's property was offered for sale by Henry Gano and Thomas Frothingham.[6] John Hathaway, ship owner and merchant, received Titus Morgan's share. In 1788 a James Morgan advertised as a ship and boat builder at Hudson. Titus is not known to have had children, so James may have been his brother.

Capt. Abiel Cheney took over the Morgan ship-yard, while other yards were opened immediately afterward by Obed Sears, Marshall Jenkins, John T. Lacy, and others. The histories state that the first ship launched in Hudson was the *Hudson*, of 300 tons and commanded by Capt. Robert Folger. This may be true, but the first *Hudson* listed in the Shipping News was the sailing to Rhode Island of the sloop *Hudson*, with Hathaway as master. A ship, also named the *Hudson*, of 266 tons, was registered in 1803.[7]

Shipbuilding was one of the most important industries in Hudson. The yards employed a great number of artisans: ship carpenters, caulkers, riggers, blacksmiths and sailmakers. Between 1785 and 1800, thirty-two vessels were constructed in city yards: twelve ships, ten brigs, three schooners, and seven sloops. Deacon Skinner wrote the following in 1854: "Robert Jenkins and sons made much money by ship building. Each shipyard turned out at least one ship a year. R.J. & sons annually sent one [ship] to New York [to be] freighted to England and sold there."[8] Launching days were great celebrations, proclaimed as holidays. Cannons were fired, the militia fired muskets, and people cheered as the boat slid into the river. Thomas and Marshall Jenkins opened shipyards in Athens, perhaps because of lack of room at the waterfront in

built a hemp and ducking ("duck" being a linen canvas) factory on Third Street where material for sails was made, which was then sent to the sail lofts to be fitted to the ships.[10]

The newly discovered copy of the Shipping News from the *Hudson Weekly Gazette* covering portions of the year 1785 to 1797 presents a new and exciting view of shipping from the port of Hudson. Specific dates list the type of vessel, its name, and the port or destination to which it sailed or from which it arrived. By reading the destinations, the international problems that beset Hudson's shipping industry in the final years of the eighteenth century are clearly illustrated. The constant stream of ships, brigs, schooners, and sloops

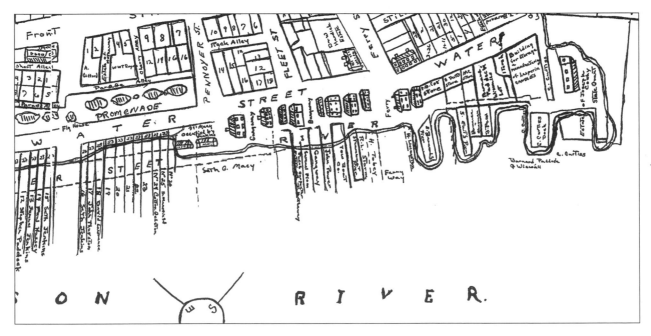

Section of map of Hudson, 1839, showing a portion of the waterfront with the division of water rights among the Proprietors. (Courtesy of the Office of the Columbia County Clerk.)

Hudson or a desire to be closer to a good supply of ship timbers. It is not known if their Athens launchings had the same degree of festivity.

Of the industries allied with shipbuilding, one was the ropewalk of Thomas Jenkins, Josiah Olcott, and others, which was 600 feet long and supplied the ropes necessary for sailing vessels. This ropewalk was north of State Street and had the name "Rope Alley."[9] Seth Jenkins and Stephen Paddock

leaving Hudson to trade in the West Indies in the earlier records, to just a few leaving monthly by 1797, clearly shows the effects of the Quasi-War with France (see below) and the insurrections on the island of Hispaniola.[11]

The British had forbade American vessels from trading with any of their West Indian ports (as well as Canadian ports), but Hudson had been able to trade with the French West Indies. The port most

Sketch of wooden shipbuilding, reprinted from Paul C. Morris, *Maritime Sketches*, Orleans, Mass., The Lower Cape Publishing Co., 1985. (Courtesy of Signy A. Morris.)

mentioned in the Shipping News was Cape Francois in Santo Domingo, now the Dominican Republic. (It took the assistance of Michael Dyer, Librarian of the Kendall Institute, New Bedford Whaling Museum to locate this port.) Santo Domingo was the richest of the French possessions, with extensive exports of sugar, coffee, and cotton. Port au Prince in Haiti was another popular port for Hudson vessels.

The southern ports of the United States rated low in destination, contrary to local histories that emphasized Charleston as a primary trading partner. At the end of each day's listings in the Shipping News is the comment, "three [or four, or more] sloops and coasters." The coasters were small vessels involved in trade with nearby coastal cities.

By 1785, twenty-five vessels were owned by Hudson. The city, just two years after its founding, ranked second in shipping in the state, with New York City being first. Shipping was the primary industry of Hudson, which was exactly what the Proprietors had planned. The inland inhabitants

who had been so prejudiced against the wily Yankees found that the new port city of Hudson was to their advantage. Products from the countryside poured into the wharves and warehouses. The *New York Journal* of February 3, 1786, reported that 1,200 sleighs entered the city over a period of several days carrying produce of all sorts to be shipped out when the river opened.[12] *The Balance* in a March 1802 article mentions 2,800 sleighs entering the city *in one day*.[13] For over a century, every local history has repeated these extraordinary figures, but did any writer consider what total chaos would have occurred if these figures were accurate? It is true that farmers preferred to haul their farm products by sleigh during the winter when the roads were snowpacked or icy. Goods brought to the harbor in March and February would be the first shipped when the river opened. But the heavily laden sleighs, the hooves of all the horses and oxen, plus the attendant steaming droppings, would have turned the streets into a fetid soup and brought sleigh runners to a grinding halt.

A traffic jam of momentous proportions would have ensued in the still-small city. Each sleigh would have needed to stop on Water Street where the warehouses and docks were located. There, sleighs had to be unloaded, the goods tallied, and papers signed, which would have caused an incredible bottleneck if such a large number of sleighs had to be processed. Could the hometown newspapers have exaggerated, as they were prone to do, or did an extra zero accidentally find its way to the end of each figure?

The products carried from inland to the port were in great quantities and varieties. Grains, onions, potatoes, cheese, lard, butter, beeswax, and apples were a few of the items. Slaughterhouses near the river packed beef, pork, smoked hams, and horse meat. Forest products included boards, hoops and staves for barrels, shingles, and firewood. Also exported were fish—herring, shad, and sturgeon—which were either smoked or pickled.[14]

Advertisements in the *Hudson Weekly Gazette* frequently proclaim that the advertiser will take an assortment of goods in lieu of cash. This shows the importance of the shipping trade among the residents. Goods could be consigned on an outgoing vessel in the expectation of a profit. An example is the advertisement the printer of the *Gazette* placed in February 1790: "The printer advertises that he will receive as payment, wood boards, planks, staves, wheat, rye, Indian corn, flour, buckwheat, butter, cream, hogs lard, tallow, beef and pork, beeswax, wool and flax, worsted and cotton, linen and tow cloth, shoes, cotton and linen, and all kinds of country produce.[15]

The remnants of a section of Rope Alley. Photo by Robert Ragaini.

Oxen pulling a laden cart, drawn by John Alderdice.

On May 21, 1795, Henry Malcolm advertised that the last session of Congress had made Hudson a port of entry, covering all the waters of the Hudson River above Hudson and as far south as Catskill, and that he was appointed collector of the district.[16] A customhouse was constructed near the river, and two government officers kept records of the arrival of vessels and collected fees. (Hudson would cease to be a port of entry in 1815.)

Much of Hudson's merchant marine trade was with the Caribbean ports and U.S. coastal ports from New York southward. Products listed shipped by Hudson vessels were beef, pork, shad, herring, staves, leather, grain and hay, lumber, and other assorted country products. Products returning to Hudson were cotton, sugar, tobacco, indigo, and rice. Other foreign ports with which Hudson traded were Cork and Dublin in Ireland, Amsterdam, Hamburg, the Canary Islands, Lisbon, Dieppe (France), and, occasionally, St. Petersburg (Russia) and Copenhagen. Gibraltar, and Madeira imported lumber via Hudson ships, while Hudson River herring found a ready market in all the above ports, as well as in Bordeaux and Sardinia.[17]

One destination presents a problem. In June and July of 1785, there were two voyages to Halifax, Nova Scotia—one by the brig *Hero*, and one by the brig *Industry*.[18] American ships were not welcome

there, and were specifically forbidden to fish or whale off the Canadian coast. (It wasn't until 1910 that fishing rights to the area around Nova Scotia were finally granted to American vessels.) Negotiations were then in progress for a contingent of Nantucketers to move from their island to Dartmouth, Nova Scotia, across the bay from Halifax. Two Nantucket British loyalists, Samuel Starbuck and Timothy Folger, began the talks in July of 1785. As a result of these talks, some Nantucketers moved to Nova Scotia in November 1785, and many more in 1786. Were some of Hudson's "Nantucket Navigators" providing assistance to their fellow Nantucketers?

Not mentioned in local histories is the steady stream of sloops running to and from the island of Nantucket. Latham Bunker advertised in May 1786 that the sloop *Ann*, lying at Thurston's wharf, would be accommodating passengers bound for Boston via Nantucket. Soon the sloop *Sally*, with Barker as master, also was sailing for Nantucket. The *Ann* sailed to Nantucket under Bunker through 1787; then, in 1788, Bunker advertised a Hudson packet to Nantucket. (A packet was a small vessel carrying passengers, mail, and some cargo, that was supposed to follow a specific time schedule.) By

Whaling schooner *Amelia* of New Bedford, Massachusetts, drawn by C.S. Raleigh, reprinted from *The Fisheries and Fishing Industries of the United States*, G.B. Goode, ed., Government Printing Office, Washington, D.C., 1884-1887.

1792, Barker was sailing the sloop *Nancy* to and from Nantucket.[19]

The Quasi-War with France

Although they achieved astounding success in a few short years, the beginning of the end of the ambitious plans and labors of the Hudson "Nantucket Navigators" followed fast on the heels of success—in 1797. France had sent money, troops, and ships to help defeat Britain in the American Revolution. Suddenly, but not surprisingly, given the international politics of the times, France became the enemy. Earlier, in 1778, the future United States and France formed an alliance that promised the United States would come to the aid of France in any future war in return for French aid during the Revolution.[1]

In 1789 the revolution in France began. At first the basic theory of liberty, equality, and fraternity espoused by the insurgents appealed to Americans, who had fought and won their own war against monarchial despotism. The Jeffersonian "Republicans," opposed to monarchy, aristocracy, and privilege, celebrated with public displays of support.[2]

In Hudson, the anniversary of the storming of the Bastille brought forth a discharge of cannons and a parade by the men of Captain Frothingham's artillery. The "caps of liberty," as well as the "national cockade of the Republic of France"—both symbols of the French Revolution—were displayed by many of the participants. At a special dinner the members were addressed as "citizen"—another earmark of the revolution. Toasts were

Painting of the American frigate *Constellation* capturing the French national frigate *L'Insurgente*, February 9, 1799. (Courtesy of the Franklin D. Roosevelt Presidential Library.)

given to all things relating to this overthrow of monarchy, including the representative of France, Citizen Genet, who had been sent by France to incite Americans to war against England.[3] (Genet overstepped his bounds and his public career was ended.)

The French Revolution soon became bloody, and the original victors became victims when counterrevolutions brought on more bloodshed. The monarch, Louis XVI, was guillotined in January of 1793, and his queen the following year. The dynastic rulers of Europe viewed this extreme *lese-majeste* with horror as their realms were being overrun by *émigrés*, mostly monarchists, fleeing France. In 1792 France declared war on Austria, Prussia, and Sardinia, and added Britain, the United Netherlands, and Spain in 1793. The United States, instead of honoring its 1778 alliance, issued a Proclamation of Neutrality. Then, in 1794, a commercial treaty was signed between the United States and Britain. This treaty, known as the Jay Treaty, was ratified in 1795. It still curtailed American shipping to the British West Indies and Canada, but Britain was allowed to trade with the United States on a "most favored nation" basis.[4]

France was furious! It considered the Jay Treaty an abrogation of the earlier American agreement with France. American interests were split— the Federalists favored England, and the Jeffersonian Republicans backed France. While the politicians argued, France fumed. Finally, in 1797, France's privateers began to prey on American commercial shipping, including whalers. By 1798 all commerce between France and America was suspended. This was the beginning of what is known as the Quasi-War with France. The name comes from the fact that though the hostilities were real (and entirely at sea), war was never declared. Americans were angry enough at the depredations on their marine interests to declare war on France, but cooler heads, particularly President John Adams, knew that the fledgling nation was in no position to go to war. So Adams called it a "half-war" and proceeded to have Congress reorganize a

navy and the Marine Corps. American vessels were captured in the English Channel and, especially, in the West Indies. The French used their island of Guadeloupe to set up prize courts to validate their claims to American ships. The situation worsened by 1798, with over 200 captured American vessels and countless seamen wounded or imprisoned in the French West Indies.[5] Congress declared that the United States was free from any earlier treaty with France and encouraged the nation's warships to capture any French vessels in American waters. American port cities began building warships to aid in the conflict.[6]

The ports and the ocean routes used by the Hudson trading vessels were precisely in the range of the French privateers. They had the choice between risking the chance of capture or a sinking, or giving up the sea entirely. Lumbering whale ships sailing home through Caribbean waters had no chance against the swift privateers. The Hudson whale ship *American Hero* was one of the vessels documented as captured by the French. Its owners' attempts to collect reimbursement under the French Spoilation Claims continued until 1885. The U.S. government assumed the $3,750,000 in claims by American merchants after the Louisiana Purchase, but the government procrastinated until 1885, with the descendants receiving a share of $4,800,000 allotted.[7]

Illustrating the effects on Hudson shipping, the following notice appeared in the *Hudson Weekly Gazette* on July 9, 1795: "Adv. That the price of carrying goods to and from New York will be raised from this time and given a list of prices. The rise in the price of provision occasioned by the recent disturbance in Europe. [signed] Robert Folger, Jonathan Hathaway, Samuel Edmonds."[8]

Napoleon, appointed Commander of the French Army of the Interior, managed to defeat most of the European coalition arrayed against him except Britain. In 1789 a *coup d'état* overthrew the French Directory, and a consulate form of government was created with Napoleon as First Consul. In 1799 he negotiated the Treaty of Morfontaine with the

American commissioners, thus ending the Quasi-War between France and America.[9] France declared, in reference to American shipping, that "free ships make free goods."[10] French commerce in the West Indies, however, had been destroyed by the war.

At the same time, Napoleon forced Spain to cede the Louisiana Territory to France. There were many more years of troubles to come.

The First Whaling Voyages

Gathering information on Hudson's early whaling ships is like putting together a puzzle. There are many sources; unfortunately, they do not agree. The list became clearer when Mr. Raymond Beecher directed me to a book in the Greene County Historical Society's Vedder Memorial Library in Coxsackie. The *Annals of Hudson* con-tains a handwritten copy of portions of the *Hudson Weekly Gazette* for the years 1785 through 1797. Included are sections of the Hudson Shipping News, which listed the arrival and departure of most vessels during those years. Many of the whaling and sealing voyages listed do not appear in any other standard source. To an enthusiast of Hudson's whaling industry, this was like finding a gold mine.

Some entries state "whaling voyage," while others may be identified as whaling voyages because the destinations given are obviously whaling grounds. When Brazil or Guiana (later Suriname) is listed as the destination, students of whaling know that this refers to the whaling ground off the coast of the country. Entries for trading voyages give a port city as destination. Beginning in 1791 and continuing until the Shipping News ends in 1797, the decrease in foreign and Caribbean trade is obvious. Months pass with lists of sloops traveling between Hudson and New York, or upriver to Albany or Troy, with few desti-

THE ATTACK

The Attack, drawn by Francis Allyn Olmstead, reprinted from *Incidents of a Whaling Voyage*, 1839-1840, Tuttle Publishing, Boston, Massachusetts.

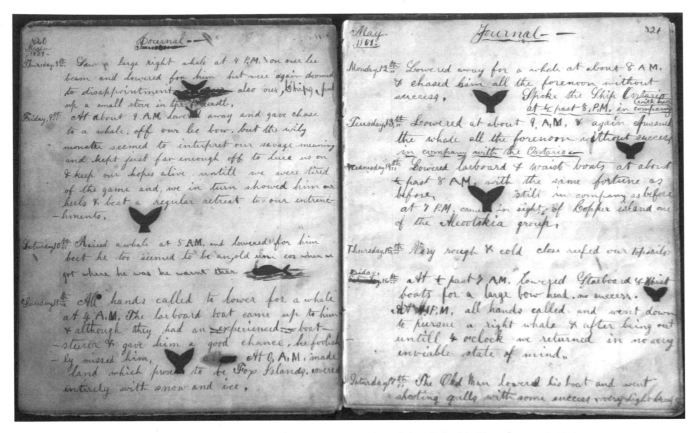

Two pages from the journal of James L. Harris aboard the whale ship *Tamerlane*, 1850-1851.
(The New Bedford Whaling Museum.) Photo by Robert Ragaini.
A drawing of a whale's tail indicates the whale was lost. A drawing of the full whale signifies a kill.

A Tough Old Bull, painting by W.H. Overend, c.1850.
(Courtesy of The New Bedford Whaling Museum.)

nations elsewhere. It is obvious that the adventurous voyages are being curtailed.

Other sources are Starbuck's *History of the American Whale Fishery* and the newly released *Whaling Masters and Whaling Voyages Sailing from American Ports* by Judith Navas Lund. The books by Edouard A. Stackpole, Ivan T. Sanderson, and Granville Allen Mawer, to name just a few, give tantalizing glimpses of Hudson whalers and sealers. Reconcile all these sources with the local histories and contemporary newspapers, and add to that mix some personal narratives from the period, and some form of a list can be presented. The following is what is known of the first fifteen years of Hudson's whaling:

DATE	VESSEL	TYPE	CAPTAIN	VOYAGE DETAILS
June 1785 (arrived)	*Claverack*	Brig	Casel	Brazil; 350 Bbls. Oil
Sept. 1785 (sailed)	*Claverack*	Brig	Worth	Brazil
July 1786 (arrived)	*Claverack*	Brig	Worth	Brazil
1785–1786	*Hudson*	Sloop	Robert Folger	(built in Hudson)[1]
July 1785 (arrived)	*Dolphin*	Brig	Bunker	Brazil
Sept. 1785 (sailed)	*Dolphin*	Brig	Coffin	Brazil
July 1786 (arrived)	*Dolphin*	Brig	Coffin	Brazil
Aug. 1786 (sailed)	*Dolphin*	Brig	Coffin	Guiana
Oct. 5, 1786 (arrived)	*Dolphin*(?)	Brig	Barnard	Iceland
June 1787 (arrived)	*Dolphin*	Brig	Coffin	Whaling voyage
June 1787 (sailed)	*Dolphin*	Brig	Coffin	Whaling voyage
July 1787 (arrived)	*Dolphin*	Brig	Folger (?)	Whaling voyage
Oct. 1787 (sailed)	*Dolphin*	Brig	Coffin	Whaling voyage
July 1788 (arrived)	*Dolphin*	Brig	Coffin	Whaling voyage
Sept. 1785 (arrived)	*Nancy*	Sloop	Merchant	Whaling voyage
June 1786 (sailed)	*Nancy*	Sloop	Coffin	Suriname
Sept. 1786 (sailed)	*Nancy*	Sloop	Coffin	Suriname
1793	*Nancy*	Brig	John Barnard	Falkland Islands; sealing[2]
May 1794 (arrived)	*Nancy*	Brig	Barnard	Falkland Islands; fur & hair seal skins
Oct. 1794 (sailed)	*Nancy*	Brig	Barnard	Falkland Islands; whaling & sealing
May 11, 1786 (sailed)	*Desire*	Brig	Barnard	Iceland
May 1786 (sailed)	*Columbia*	Brig	Bunker	Cape of Good Hope
Aug. 1794 (sailed)	*Columbia*	Ship	Bunker	So. Georgia: whaling & sealing
May 1796 (arrived)	*Columbia*	Bark	Bunker	So. Georgia
June 1796 (cleared)	*Columbia*	Bark	Bunker	South Seas
Nov. 1797 (arrived)	*Columbia*	Bark	Bunker	Falkland Islands
Oct. 1787 (sailed)	*Prudence*	Brig	Clark	Whaling voyage
Sept. 1788 (sailed)	*Prudence*	Brig	Swain	Whaling voyage
July 1789 (arrived)	*Prudence*	Brig	Swain	Whaling voyage
Oct. 1789 (sailed)	*Prudence*	Brig	Swain	Whaling voyage
April 1791 (arrived)	*Prudence*	Brig	Solomon Bunker	Whaling voyage
July 1792 (arrived)	*Prudence*	Brig	Bunker	Whaling voyage
Sept. 1792	*Prudence*	Brig	Bunker; Valentine Barnard, mate[3]	
July 1793 (arrived)	*Prudence*	Brig	Bunker	Brazil
Nov. 1786 (sailed)	*Liberty*	Brig	Hussey	Suriname
July 1787 (arrived)	*Liberty*	Brig	Hussey	Suriname
Aug. 1787 (sailed)	*Liberty*	Brig	Folger	Whaling voyage
1788 (arrived)	*Liberty*	Brig	Bunker	Whaling voyage
1788–1789	*Liberty*	Brig	Bunker	Brazil; 355 Bbls. Whale[4]
1789–1790	Liberty	Brig	Paul Bunker	Whaling voyage[5]
Aug. 1786 (sailed)	*Juno*	Ship	Barnard	Brazil
June 1787 (arrived)	*Juno*	Ship	Barnard	Whaling voyage
Nov. 1788 (sailed)	*Juno*	Ship	Clark	Whaling voyage
Oct. 1789 (arrived)	*Juno*	Ship	Clark	Whaling voyage
Aug. 1796 (cleared)	*Juno*	Ship	Paul Bunker	Falkland Islands; sealing

(The sloop *Betsy* sailed with the *Juno* for sealing in the Falklands. Bunker returned with 2000 seal skins.)

c.1795	*Oswego*	Ship		(built in Hudson, 1795)[6]
1797–1799	*Oswego*	Ship	George Clark	Delogoa Bay (southeast coast of Africa); 1,100 Bbls. Sperm, 100 Bbls. Whale
July 1799 (sailed)	*Thomas*	Brig	Jenkins	So. Georgia; sealing
Sept. 1792 (arrived)	*Recovery*	Brig	Paddock	Falkland Islands; whaling & sealing
July 1797	*Maria*	Brig	Barnard	So. Georgia; sealing[7]
1795–1797	*American Hero*	Ship	Solomon Bunker	Pacific (built in Hudson, 1793)[8]

Reports at the time boasted that this vessel brought back the largest cargo of sperm oil in that year.

1797–?	*American Hero*	Ship		Pacific[9]

This voyage is problematical. This is the vessel captured by the French in the Quasi-War. The ship disappears from all records after 1797. Starbuck places William Pitts as master.[10] Stackpole lists Levi Joy, of Hudson, as master. (Joy was still living in retirement in Hudson in 1839, at age 76.)[11]

Sept. 1793 (sailed)	*Hero*	Brig	Barnard	Falkland Islands
May 1794 (arrived)	*Hero*	Brig	Barnard	Falkland Islands
Aug. 1794 (arrived)	*Hero*	Brig	Clark	So. Georgia
1799	*Ajax*		Pinkham	Sealing[12]

In October 1792 the schooner *Jenny*, with Fisher as master, and the sloop *Polly*, with Dimmick as master, arrived back in Hudson from a "fishing voyage."[13]

Whaling voyages, like those above, were usually listed using the following format: the date of the sailing, the name of the vessel, the class of vessel (ship, bark, etc.), and the tonnage. Next is the name of the captain (master) and the managing owner or agent. This is followed by "Whaling Ground." The use of the word "ground" in whaling means deep

waxy spermaceti and the high wax content in the blubber of this whale, it was more valuable than others. "Whale" was the oil made from the blubber of the baleen whales and the blackfish (pilot whale). "Whalebone," another category, is not bone, but the fringed plates of baleen that fill the upper jaws of the baleen whales, serving as strainers of their food. These plates, several hundred of them reaching to different lengths depending on the whale, are actually made of keratin, like human fingernails. The value of this baleen, or "whalebone," came from its

Attacking a [right] *Whale with the Hand Harpoon*, c. 1835-1840.

ocean, not land. It is the name given to those specific spots in the world's oceans where migrating whales were known to congregate at certain times of the year. Some grounds are easily identified, such as "Brazil," "Canary Island," and the "Charleston." The "Twelve-Forty" was located east of Trinidad in the area of latitude 12°, longitude 40°. The whaling masters would head for these grounds, moving on to the next if no whales appeared.[14] The dates of sailing and return are listed next. The "result of the voyage" is divided into three categories. The first is "Sperm," referring to the oil made from the blubber and head matter (or spermaceti) from the sperm whale (see Appendix B, "Whales"). Because of the

flexibility in an age before thin steel and plastics. The abbreviation "Bbls." stands for barrels. A barrel contains 31.5 gallons, and the whalemen referred to barrels of all sizes as "casks." Starbuck, in his *History of the American Whale Fishery*, adds a space for comments after each voyage. These comments are a gold mine of information.

The comments often use the phrase, "last reported to have ___ Bbls sperm oil, etc." "Last reported" indicates it is from information picked up by another ship, usually homeward bound, and relayed to the shipping news when that ship reached home port. Many whaling ships congregated at foreign ports for "refreshments" (in the true meaning of the word—"taking on fresh food"), or on the whaling grounds. There the captains exchanged news and cargo information. Entered into the ship log, for example, would be: "'Spoke' the Beaver, 250 Bbls. Sperm." These informal get-togethers between the crews and the ships' officers were called "gams." The most picturesque gam was that of two ships meeting in the vast expanse of ocean. Excitement would reign as the crews anticipated seeing new faces after months of enduring the same crewmates. There was a possibility of news from

deep bay known as Post Office Bay. Half of an open cask nailed to a post sunk in the ground was the most famous mailbox in the whaling world.[16] There, letters were left in the hopes a homeward-bound ship would pick them up. Whalers anchoring there to stock up on the giant Galapagos tortoises (their meat was treasured) and pumpkins searched the barrel hoping for letters. Captains left information on their cargoes, other ships they had "spoken," and what grounds they planned to whale.

On the Galapagos Islands, whalemen capture turtles for fresh meat. *Harper's Weekly*, August, 1858.
(Courtesy of General Research Division, New York Public Library, Astor, Lenox & Tilden Foundations.)

home or a chance to send a letter. (The fact that the *Liberty*, a Hudson ship, was in the Pacific between 1790 and 1793 had to come from such an encounter, because there is no official record of the *Liberty* rounding Cape Horn.)[15]

Another source of information was located on a bleak island in the Pacific Ocean. Charles Island (Floreana Island) in the Galapagos Islands held a

The curious voyages to Iceland, which may or may not have been for whaling, were the only North Atlantic destinations for Hudson's whalers and sealers. The North Atlantic was where to find the right whale (a baleen whale that has lots of blubber, is easily killed, and does not sink when killed—thus, "right"). The right was once the whale of choice, but they had all but disappeared from fear

Whale oil lamps. The center lamp is a watchman's lantern. It has a small oil burner inside,
and the convex lens concentrates the light much like a flashlight. Photo by Robert Ragaini.

of man and overkilling. The sperm whale was what made money. Its head was full of future candles, and its blubber made lamps glow brighter and cleaner.[17] Sperm whales like the tropical waters, so the whalers followed that route, which became known as the Southern Fishery. They sailed off to the Azores, picking up fresh water, supplies, and some Portuguese Azorean whalers who made excellent additions to the crew. The voyage continued on to the grounds off the coast of Africa, using currents from there to travel on to the Brazil Grounds or down to the Falkland Islands for seal. The route home might include the Twelve-Forty Grounds. These short, safe trips were known as "Plum Pudding Whaling."

In 1789 the British whaler *Emelia*, captained and crewed by Nantucket men, made the first trip by a whaling vessel around South America's Cape Horn and into the Pacific. Ships had been rounding Africa's Cape of Good Hope for years, particularly the Dutch and British pursuing their spice interests in the East Indies and India. The southern tip of South America, however, was at a lower latitude, and its rocky, icy, storm-swept shores appeared impossible for a sailing ship to navigate around. Ferdinand Magellan had discovered and sailed through a narrow strait near the southern tip of South America in 1520, but this strait was rejected by the whalers. During the summer months south of the equator, whalers considered the Cape

Horn route the safer passage. The crews called Cape Horn "Cape Stiff," and not every vessel made it through successfully. Once the word spread that the Pacific was filled with sperm whales, the Pacific Grounds became the destination for most whalers.[18] By 1793 a Hudson ship was whaling in the Pacific.

As explained in detail in the "Blubber to Oil" section of Appendix B, the blubber was removed from the whale alongside the ship, a process called "cutting-in." The strips of blubber were then cut into smaller pieces and boiled ("tried out") in "try-pots" located on the deck. After being reduced to a liquid oil at a high enough temperature to keep it from becoming rancid, the oil was cooled and stored in casks in the hold. A whaling voyage required experienced officers and a crew of at least twenty men. Whaleboats, with their harpoons, lances, and other whaling gear, were essential, as well as provisions for a year or more.

Sealing required a large supply of salt and pegs. The salt was picked up in the Cape Verde islands, and thousands of pegs (used to hold down the hides) were made by the crew during the trip. Crews were left on the islands where seals were known to congregate. There, they slaughtered the seals, and skinned and prepared the hides.[19] The ship would return after a few months to pick up the men and the hides (see "Sealing" in Appendix B).

When the whale ships returned to port with their cargoes, the oil was graded and taken to the oil and candle works. Thomas Jenkins ran such a factory on Diamond (Columbia) Street, between First and Second streets. Histories state that Tallyrand, on his visit through the United States, visited the Jenkins factory. He was especially interested in the

Painting of a U.S. frigate struck by a squall off Cape Horn, June 25, 1847.
(Courtesy of the Franklin D. Roosevelt Presidential Library.)

Heard Island, oil on canvas. © Mystic Seaport, Mystic CT.
A crew from the whale ship *Corinthian* slaughters and trys out elephant seals, c. 1855.

mysteries regarding making spermaceti candles. The manufacturing of these candles had been a closely kept secret for years. (The reader can learn how in the "Spermaceti Candles" section of Appendix B.) Spermaceti candles gave a pure, bright, smokeless light, and had no odor when burned, as opposed to tallow (animal fat) candles. Another oil and candle factory was run by Cotton Gelston on the southeast corner of Second and State streets. (The Barnard-Curtiss factory did not operate until the later period of Hudson whaling.)

Tanneries were established early in the city's history. Hides from the sealing ships, as well as a constant supply from cattle slaughtered in the slaughterhouses nearby, poured into the city. Hides also were imported from some foreign ports. Shoe leather was the primary product. David Bunker and Redwood Easton opened a tannery near the mill site on the northwest corner of the city. Robert Taylor,

Nathan Sears, Marshall Jenkins, Giles Frary, and David Bunker all operated tanneries on the North and South Bays.[20] Later, most of the tanneries were located along the South Bay. There is today a short road called Tanners Lane (south on Front, east on Cross Street), a remnant of this industry. Whale and seal oils were used in the tanning process. The oil from the elephant seal (it may be disconcerting to see "elephant oil" listed!) rendered the leather waterproof. Hemlock bark, a source of tannin, was brought by barges from the Catskills and the Helderbergs. Oak bark from the Taghkanic Hills also was used.[21]

There are remarkable adventure tales from the sealers. Paul Bunker left Hudson for sealing in 1797 in the ship *Juno*, together with the sloop *Betsy*, sailing to Patagonia for seals with another sealing captain from New Haven. In Patagonia they were captured by Spaniards who insisted they were

Englishmen, the current enemy of Spain. The two captains made a miraculous escape and saved their ships from being seized.[22]

In 1797, Proprietor Alexander Coffin, writing from Hudson, sent a letter to Chancellor Robert R. Livingston in Clermont advocating the destruction of the British whaling fleet in the Southern Fishery. In his letter he mentions the numbers of ships in the American whaling fleet: "Thirty-seven from Nantucket, twelve to fifteen from New Bedford, four from Hudson, and about twenty additional from New York, Connecticut and Massachusetts. Their voyages lasted up to twelve to twenty-four months."[23]

Whale gaugers test the quality and quantity of oil, reprinted from *Harper's Weekly*, June, 1860. (Courtesy of General Research Division, New York Public Library, Astor, Lenox & Tilden Foundations.)

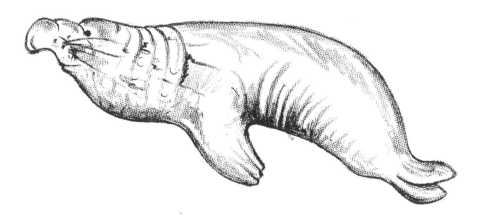

An elephant seal, drawn by John Alderdice.

Rum, Arsenic, and Plumes: The City Of Hudson, 1784–1800

[Hudson] was entirely settled by people from the New England states, the most active and enterprising people ... in the world.

William Strickland, a visitor to Hudson in 1797

$\mathcal{I}$n February 1785 the Proprietors' Association voted to petition the state for the purpose of "getting ourselves incorporated with city privileges." A committee was named to travel to New York City to meet with the General Assembly and use their influence to get it passed "at this session."[1]

Why a city, and why such a rush? This was an indication of a problem looming for the Proprietors, as evidenced by the following entry from April 1785: "Laboring under many inconveniences by laying out their money's for the good of the settlement, [we] do agree to sell a certain gore [a small, triangular piece] of land lying between the warehouse and house lots, which sum so raised shall be appropriated for the use of the Proprietors." The Proprietors had spent a great amount of their own combined funds to open roads, build bridges, and provide water and all the other improvements necessary to make a successful community. It is obvious that the sale or rental of house lots was not sufficient to cover expenses. But as a chartered city, money could be raised by taxes and "assessments" on all the residents of the city.

The boundaries of the city were described as follows: "Beginning in a channel in the Hudson River, directly opposite Major Abraham's (Stottville) Creek; up the middle of the creek to the place where The Claverack Creek empties into Major Abraham's Creek, thence up the middle of said Claverack Creek until the said creek strikes the line of the Manor of Livingston; thence along the line of said Manor of Livingston to the east side of Hudson's River; thence into the said River 180 feet below high water mark to the place of beginning, keeping the same distance of 180 feet all along from

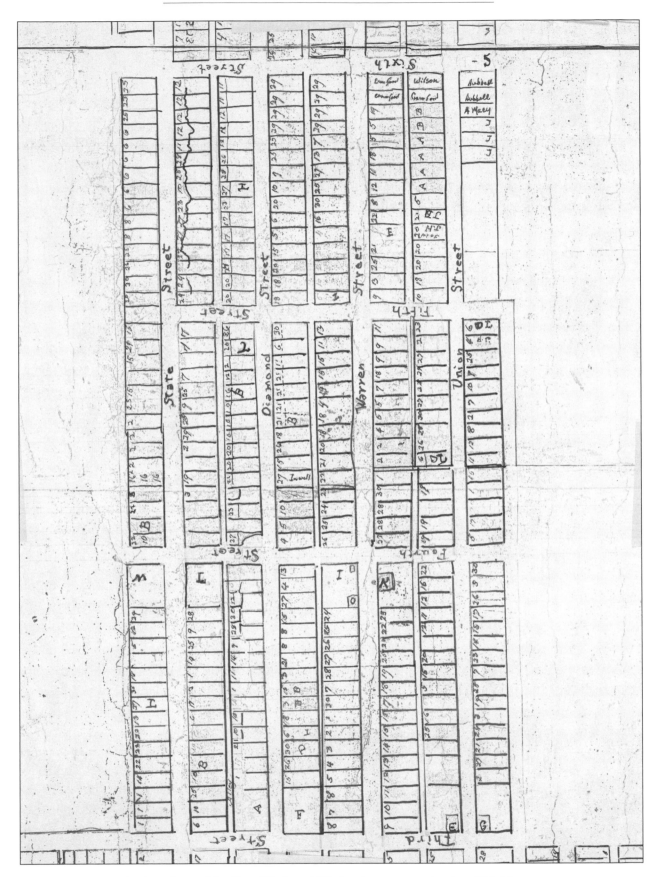

Section of map of the City of Hudson, 1801, showing a narrow city above Third Street.
(Courtesy of the Office of the Columbia County Clerk.)

high water mark aforesaid."[2] (The 180 feet below high water is the water rights privileges, explained later.) This covered a large tract of land, and in the tax list of 1797, 126 men within the city limits were wealthy enough to be taxed on an assessment of over £200 ($500) and upwards.[3]

There was some fairness in the taxing. Inhabitants in what was known as the "compact part" of the city had property taxes levied in support of those services within the city itself. The "compact part" ran from the South Bay to what is now Seventh Street, along Seventh to Clinton Street, and west to the river below Mill Street.[4]

On May 3, 1785, Seth Jenkins, now mayor, having been appointed by the governor and the Council of Appointments, announced the incorpo-

ration of the City of Hudson, the third chartered city in the state. It was still a part of the District of Claverack within the County of Albany. It is said that a great celebration occurred, with firing of cannons, flags flying, and many cheers.[5] Officers had been appointed, but a Common Council had to be elected "by all freemen within the city and the liberties of Hudson."[6]

Laws required a full set of officers and committees to govern the city. The men of the Proprietors' Association were elected or appointed to positions within the city government. It was fortunate that the same officers controlled both city bodies. In April of 1787, the Proprietors surrendered all the roads and public squares to the new city. The Common Council was left with the duty of providing all the services, such as water, policing, fire protection, street repairs, etc., and acquiring the funds for these services. At the same time, the Proprietors continued their own meetings, having control of most of the land in the city. They also had their own businesses to run, as well as to supervise their vast holdings.

The Common Council had a stocks and whipping post set up near the lower market. An example of a typical punishment was reported in the *Hudson Weekly Gazette* in August 1787: "On Thursday last, one John Bennett alias Wm. Smith was convicted in this city for stealing a canoe and received thirty-nine stripes at the public post."[7] The stocks and whipping post were later moved near the new jail on Fourth Street.

Another form of punishment was to have the offender tied to the tail of a cart, and at each street corner receive a certain number of lashes. When the limits of the city were reached, he was set loose and banned from the city forever. In the summer of 1785, the council ordered that a "gaol" (jail) thirty feet long, fifteen feet wide, and one story high be built. It was constructed of logs on the corner of Fourth Street and Prison Alley, and was in use until 1805.[8] In 1786 construction began on a city hall, located where the present Presbyterian church now stands, but it was not finished for many years.[9]

A man in the stocks, drawn by John Alderdice.

The first Columbia County courthouse, Claverack, New York.

The mysterious deaths of Justus H. Van Hoesen and his wife, Janneke, in 1794 caused excitement and consternation in the city. The *Hudson Weekly Gazette* gave the following accounts: "Death of Mr. Justus H Van Hoesen on the 4th, in his 39th year, Magistrate and merchant. The morning preceding his death he was well, at half past 11 in the evening he was no more"; on February 15, "Persons alarmed at the sudden death of J.H. Van Hoesen and his consort Janneke Van Hoesen who departed this life on Monday. Their deaths were produced, it would appear, by arsenic mixed with Flower of Sulphur, which was taken by themselves and family to preserve health. They both were taken by vomiting at the same time. He died in the evening at 11 o'clock.—Mrs. Van Hoesen lived about five days longer, aged 38 years—leaving 7 orphan children."[10] Suspicions were bandied about, but no one was charged as it was deemed an unfortunate accident. The Van

Hoesens were buried in the Van Hoesen-Hyatt graveyard, located in an orchard on a hillside. The remains were moved to the present cemetery when Allen Street was constructed.

In April of 1786, the state legislature divided Albany County into two counties, of which one would be Columbia County. Most histories conclude that the choice of Claverack as the county seat was a part of that legislation; however, in February 1787 the Common Council learned that there were objections against the legislature "granting the petition ... of the inhabitants ... of the City of Hudson ... for establishing the Court house and Gaol within the city." The council was determined, however, that "the court house and gaol be established in Hudson for the good of the county," and it was willing to relinquish some of the provisions in its charter in order to procure the county seat for Hudson.[11] Seth Jenkins, who represented the city in the meeting to determine the county seat, failed in

THE FLAG HOUSE.

The Flag or Round House, was the greatest, and most popular pleasure resort in this city, three quarters of a century ago, (75 years.) Not only was this renowned "House" used for the purposes described below, but also as a watch tower or signal point for vessels, particularly for steamboats then running on the river. On account of their imperfect construction these boats had no *positive* or *definite* time for their arrival and departure. The wind and tide, with the conditions of the weather, oftimes obstructed and delayed their coming and going according to announced schedule time.

Under these condition a watch was kept from the "observatory" of the Flag House, and when a steamboat came in sight, a horn or bugle would be blown, as a notification of the approaching steamer. The "blast" would notify the whole town, and those desiring to attend or see the landing, would run to Parade Hill and watch the arrival. This was considered a novelty, and one of the most interesting features of the "day's doings" in "ye olden daye."

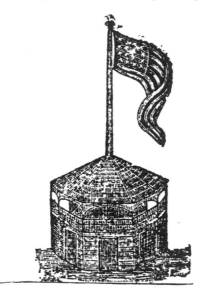

That beautifully situated building commonly called the FLAG HOUSE, having been put in good order, the subscriber informs the public that he is ready to wait upon them.

No pains will be spared to supply the establishment with the choicest delicacies, both eatable and drinkable: and those rarities which Hudson cannot furnish, can be procured by the regular trips of the Steam Boats, from New York. Oranges, Pine Apples, Lemons, Figs, Raisins, Prunes, Grapes, Nuts of various kinds, Ice-creams, &c.: the best of liquors, and whatever may be necessary to enhance their relish, will be at hand.

There is a pleasant apartment on the first floor, fitted up with seats and tables and furnished with Newspapers, where the news can be read and public events talked about, with as much summer comfort, as in any room on the continent.

The charming prospect from this spot; which is unrivalled in beauty by any inland view in America, or any where else, can be enjoyed in perfection from the second floor of the building, to which none but subscribers, and strangers will be admitted, and where a spy-glass will be kept to assist the eye.

The subscriber will steadily execute his intention, that this establishment shall be frequented by none but decent company, and that nothing shall be permitted to take place there incompatible with public decorum.

CORNELIUS MYERS.

N. B. TURTLE SOUP prepared in the best manner, will be furnished on

The Flag House, or Round House. Advertisement in Robert M. Terry, *The Hudsonian: Old Times and New,* 1895.

his mission and Claverack was proclaimed the county seat. Construction began on the first courthouse, which cost $9,000. It was not finished until 1788. Despite the cost, by 1801 the building was found "to be in a state of decay" and $300 was allotted for repairs.[12]

The piece of land at the foot of Main Street had been designated as a parade or mall by the Proprietors. This parcel was turned over to the Common Council forever "for the purpose of a public walk or mall and for no other purpose whatsoever."[13] It became known as Parade Hill from the

The first, original seal of the City of Hudson.
(Courtesy of the City of Hudson.)
Photo by Photo-Art, Claverack, New York.

The "sanitized" version of the city seal, which appeared
unofficially at a later date. (Courtesy of the
Hudson City Clerk's Office, Hudson, New York.)

various hometown military companies that would drill there in their flamboyant uniforms. Several companies existed over the years, and one or two actually served during the War of 1812. They took part in celebrations, such as the Fourth of July, accompanied distinguished personages through town, and made up the funeral corteges for local heroes. But mostly they paraded, to the delight of the local maidens, in their colorful uniforms with an abundance of flowing plumes in their hats. In later years each political party sponsored a military company. The park remained unfinished until the 1830s. It took the name Round House Hill from an octagonal, two-story building that sold refreshments. The second story offered an open view of the scenery, and a flag waved from the roof.

The council decided to change the name of Hudson's longest and widest street. The following notice was chalked on fences (which at that time were mostly red and yellow) on October 11, 1799: "This Street is no longer Main Street, but called Warren by order of the Common Council." No reason has been recorded, and the Warren who was being honored is not known.[14]

A mayor's court was started with the city's incorporation, but it was terminated when justice and police courts came into being. Apparently lost forever is "the Mayor's Seal." The seal had an anchor with the words "Hudson Mayor's Court Seal."[15]

The seal of the City of Hudson was made by Peter Maverick in August of 1785 at the cost of $15.58. Nine men contributed money to pay the expense. The seal was, if nothing else, unusual. The original seal later disappeared from public view, possibly because the frontal near-nudity of the very athletic Neptune offended Victorian sensibilites. The Latin motto translates as "Both the honor and reward of rectitude." (Neptune and the mermaid were removed from the seal in 1979, as well as the Latin motto.)[16]

In the early years after the incorporation, the Common Council busied itself with a long list of regulations and prohibitions. A harbormaster was appointed. His job was to keep the ferry steps clear, to see that ships' bowsprits did not extend into the street, and to prevent spare masts and other equipment from clogging the public thoroughfares.

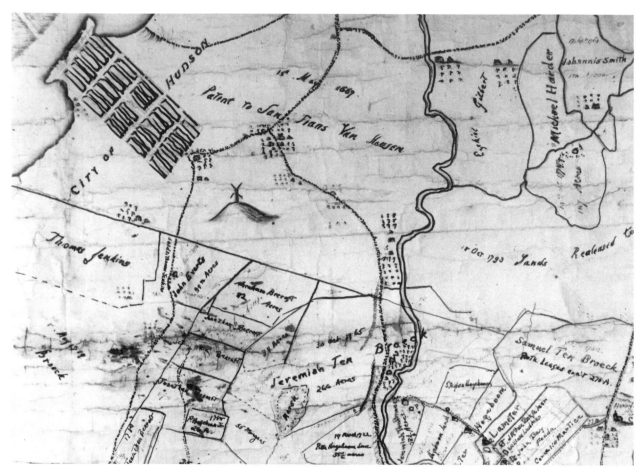

Section of the Penfield Map, 1799, showing Joseph Barnard's windmill atop Windmill (Prospect) Hill. [19]
(Courtesy of the Columbia County Historical Society, Kinderhook, New York.) Photo by Michael Fredericks, Jr.

Forty-one licenses to sell liquor were granted, some for wholesale and others for retail. Several breweries were started. Seth Jenkins established a distillery on Water Street on the east corner of Cross Street in 1785. It grew to become one of the largest in the valley. When Thomas Jefferson visited Hudson in 1791, he noted that the distillery was producing 1,000 hogsheads of rum a year. (At 63 gallons per hogshead, that equals 63,000 gallons of rum per year!)[17] The small stream that flowed into the North Bay had never been adequate to furnish power for the series of mills that cropped up there, but the city's boundaries extended to the center of the Stottville and Claverack creeks in the north, both of which had falls and excellent waterpower, so the Hudson Proprietors built several mills there. In 1796, John Alsop and Elisha Bunker constructed a flour mill on Stottville Creek. It flourished, and

soon two schooners, two sloops, and a scow were employed by the mill to carry cargo out of Stottville Creek to the markets. More mills were begun on both creeks, organized by former Hudsonians such as Jonathan Scott, Benjamin Marshall, and some Macys. The Columbia Manufacturing Society was formed and the area became a thriving cloth manufacturing community.[18] In 1833, the Town of Stockport was formed from sections of Hudson, Stuyvesant, and Ghent, thereby depriving the City of Hudson of this strong manufacturing base and giving the smallest town in the county the ability to tax for its own needs.

Joseph Barnard, one of the early settlers in Hudson, thought that wind power would work for grinding if the city's waterpower was not adequate. In 1789 he built a windmill for grinding flour on the top of the hill above what is now Prospect Hill

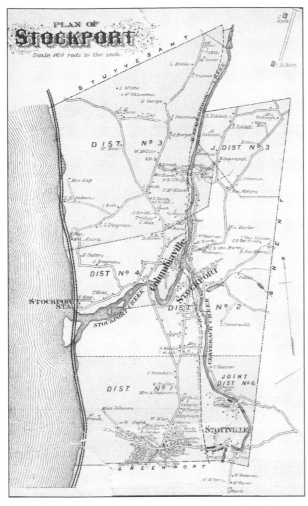

Map of the Town of Stockport, from *Atlas of Columbia County, New York*, Beers, Ellis & Co., 1888.

(originally Windmill Hill). It was a two-story, octagonal building with wings that rose seventy-five feet above the ground. The windmill could be seen for miles. The mill was not successful because the climb up the hill was too steep for a horse-pulled, laden wagon. After a refreshment stand failed there also, the building was torn down. (In recent times hikers from out of town came upon the stone foundations and declared they were ruins from druid worship!)[20]

On the sad run of water that ran from Underhill (named for a man, not a location) Pond and which had defeated so many earlier mills, a new mill was constructed with an enormous overshot wheel. That, too, failed.

The *Weekly Gazette* reported in June 1793 that a severe hurricane, lasting fifteen hours, brought

rain and hail. The wind was from the northwest "and destroyed several buildings in the city and county. Sixty fathoms of the rope walk together with a new building 150 feet in length and two stories high, just completed—intended for a Duck factory—have blown down and destroyed. No lives lost."[21]

Conradt Flaack held the rights to run the ferry between Hudson and Loonenbergh (Athens) for his lifetime, but the council established full authority over the ferry and its fares. Fares could be increased by half as much if the water was low and required the boat to go around the "flats." From early records and prints, it is obvious that the surface of the flats was just below the waterline at high tide. At some time, wild Indian rice was planted on the soil of the flats. As the rice grew and thrived, the rice stalks held the silt and debris that floated by. It took many decades, but eventually the flats became the distinct islands that appear today.[22]

Flaack's canoes, even when enlarged, were primitive at best. When Flaack died in 1790, the council immediately purchased two scows with sails. Teams could enter the scows at either end, and they were manned by four men each. This advertisement appeared in April of 1790: "Henry Lyons advertises an excellent new scow to carry wagons and carts across to Loonenburgh [Athens]."[23] In

The Overshot Mill, formerly located on Mill Street in the northern part of the city, c. 1784.

View of Hudson & the Catskill Mountains, by Jacques Gerard Milbert, *Amerique Septentrionale*, c.1820, Plate 4, No. 12.

1803, with cooperation from the western-side authorities, plans were made to dig a canal through the flats to facilitate the trip. Dig they did, and every spring a freshet would fill it up again. In 1816 a more concerted effort was made to construct a permanent canal, but it was never possible to keep it clear.

In 1816 a horse-powered ferry was built by William Johnson at a cost of $9,000. A trial trip was scheduled with the mayor and Common Council on board. The pilot, a newcomer to the job, managed to collide with another craft, shaking the boat to such a degree that all the officials fell flat on the

Horse-powered ferryboat in use between Hudson and Athens prior to 1859, from J. Van Vechten Vedder, *History of Greene County, New York*, 1927. (Courtesy of Hope Farm Press, Saugerties, New York.) Photo by Robert Ragaini.

One of the log water pipes that carried Hudson's water supply. The pipe is 9.5 feet long,
28 inches in circumference, and 8 inches in diameter. One end is tapered to fit into the next pipe.
(Courtesy of FASNY Museum of Firefighting, Hudson, New York.) Photo by Robert Ragaini.

deck.[24] Later, a steam ferry was used. A car ferry was the means of crossing the Hudson until 1935 when the Rip Van Winkle Bridge was constructed.

The Common Council also involved itself in the operation of what was called "the Lower Ferry." This ferry ran from the shore of the Hudson nearly opposite Catskill (this later became known as Catskill Station) to the village of Catskill. It was run by a Hollenbeck for many years who also had a license to sell liquor. Another Hollenbeck—John W.—kept an old tavern known as "First House" across the South Bay at the foot of Mt. Merino.

One of Hudson's early water pumps. Postcard, 1937.

In 1799 Daniel Penfield bought all the remaining Van Rensselaer Lower Manor holdings, which included what is known today as Mount Merino. Penfield sold the mountain in 1810 to Samuel Jenkins, who advertised merino sheep for sale on the 400-acre farm, giving the site its present name. Jenkins sold the farm to his partner, Beriah Pease, and Oliver Wiswall in 1817.

In May of 1798, a committee was appointed to build a fence three boards high with a gate around the burying ground. The burying ground had been neglected for a long time and needed clearing. It was reached by a road through the woods from the country road (now Green Street) in the vicinity of Schermerhorn Town, "a name by which a collection of buildings in the locality was known."[25]

Providing water to all the residents of the city was, and still is, a major problem. Several water pumps were the first answer. Later, in 1785, water

was brought to the city by log pipes from a nearby spring. The pipes were long logs hollowed out and covered with clay. For $25 each, lot holders could arrange to have water piped to their homes. In 1793 the Common Council bought the Huyck spring, better known as "the Fountain" (located on Route 23B). A corporation was set up to pay the expenses. Hezekiah Dayton was hired to listen for dripping water in basements, indicating a leak.

The last act of the old Congress of the Articles of Confederation was the passage of the Ordinance of 1787 for the settlement of the Northwest Territory, which paid veterans of the Continental Army with grants of land. Massachusetts, Connecticut, New York, and Virginia gave up their claims to the land between the Great Lakes and the Ohio River. States were to be formed in this territory, and scores of pioneering emigrants from the Northeast were expected to settle there.

There were those who envied the City of Hudson's amazing business success, and they believed that they could build a better city on the western side of the river. A group of men decided

The Fountain—the source of Hudson's (and Greenport's) water supply for some time, located in the Town of Greenport, State Route 23B. Photo by Robert Ragaini.

that a site across from the City of Hudson would be the doorway to the west—a canal, perhaps? They envisioned thousands of immigrants pouring through this future city on their way to a new life in the new west. Three Livingstons—Edward, Brockholst and John R.—along with Elihu Chauncey Goodrich, joined their finances and purchased from Albert Van Loon in 1794 a large area of land above the ferry landing. This purely speculative effort was to be a city called Esperanza, and shares were sold to investors.

Roads, called avenues, were laid out and given such unusual names as Bread, Cider, and Beer. House lots were sold, and squares were set out for a courthouse, taverns, and churches. For a little while the future looked bright for Esperanza. It is reported that a brig was built, wharves were constructed, and enthusiastic residents enjoyed their new city. But, as the Proprietors in Hudson found, it cost more to provide the basic needs than was returned by lot sales. The major stockholders in Esperanza became impatient. By 1799 the principal founders had financial problems and there was a partition of their holdings. The success of another speculative venture to the south led to the incorporation of the Village of Athens. Esperanza was merged with the lower village and became part of Athens.[26]

Section of a map of the Town of Esperanza (now part of Athens), Greene County, c. 1850. (Courtesy of the Vedder Research Library, Bronck House, Greene County Historical Society, Coxsackie, New York.)

From the Dung Heap: Plagues and Epidemics

[There are more] *very sickly among us, more now than ever I knew since I lived in this place. The measles prevails very much among the children and the spotted fever after the measles. Jared Coffin's child lives at the point of death. Daniel Clark lost his oldest daughter 2 weeks today. Zepeniah Coffin lost his son about 3 weeks ago. Another Nantucket person that I know of. It seems to be a time of trouble among us. There is few among us that is clear of trouble.*

Letter from Susanna Bunker in Hudson to her father, Shubael Barnard on Nantucket, June 26, 1789 (courtesy of the Nantucket Historical Association)[1]

It may seem strange to devote a whole chapter to disease, but in the time period of this book, death from a variety of epidemics was a common occurrence. The residents of Hudson were frequently in panic because of the spread of fatal epidemics, and death among the young was particularly rampant. Most people understood that some diseases were contagious, but the concepts of germs and bacteria were not understood. Much was blamed on bad air (mal aria), or bad living. The rich, living on the hill, looked down on the poor, living in the low, crowded part of the town, and concluded that the illnesses that spread through the slums resulted from ungodly, depraved living, not suspecting that it was caused by contaminated drinking water.

Diphtheria, smallpox, typhoid fever, and scarlet fever were the common enemies of children.

Consumption (tuberculosis) claimed children and young adults. Because of the lack of adequate medical knowledge, even minor illnesses could be fatal. Infection, malnutrition, and food poisoning were all common, and could become deadly. Occasionally, disaster struck.

In August of 1785, the Hudson Common Council announced that all vessels coming into the port of Hudson were to be quarantined until thoroughly inspected by a team of medical experts because "a contagious disorder prevails in New York City [it was yellow fever], and vessels may be expected from thence, and thereby hazard the spreading of the said disorder in this city." No vessel could come to any wharf, nor could anyone come to shore, land any goods, trunks, or clothing, until a committee inspected it all and determined everything and everybody free of disease. "If any

Dear father   Hudson June the 26 1789

Having this opertunity thought to right hoping these may find the and and the rest af the famly in joying the same steat af helth as these leve me in at this time tha very sickly a mong ous more sow then ever I knew sence I leve In the place the measels prevales very much a mong the children and the spotted fever follers after the measels James Caffins child lise att the pint af Death Daniel Clarks last his oldest Daughter 2 weeks to Day Zepeniah Caffin last his sone about 3 weekes a goe naather nantucket parsen that I knew af It sems to be a time af trubell a mong us their is not a hous a mong us that is clear af trubell I Dont expect to scape a part of trubell latham has ben gone 2 to Day I am left all most a lone and lonly I have a hope to a rise that the will come up hear this somer for hear I am all a lone and lonly I cant rise up and gae to fathers as many can but hear I must set an think a bout you an that all I can Dae sae with love to all frends Conclude and remain thy Dutyfull child

Susanna Bunker

their is iest now a woman in hear with Strahnys graslngs on butter to sell and wont bae time that is all the sry her lived hear is exeedin hase a mong us Tuckey corn fon indco I never have in my life time they Day at Queamons pattern then is ane Pamley Steads

Letter from Susanna Bunker of Hudson to her father, Shubael Barnard, on Nantucket.
(Courtesy of the Nantucket Historical Association, Manuscript Collection 382, Folder 61.)

person lands or unloads without permission, they will be fined and placed in a secluded house until determined free of contamination."[2]

Yellow fever is a disease transmitted between humans by the mosquito Aedes aegypti, generally called "the yellow-fever mosquito."[3] It is mostly a tropical disease, but can occur in more northern regions if the weather is warm enough for that particular mosquito to survive.

Smallpox, sometimes called variola, was a constant terror to the residents of Hudson. Smallpox resembles influenza except that a rash spreads over the body forming pus-filled blisters. These would leave permanent pits, so that the face of a victim was disfigured. Pneumonia was a complication, as though one were needed. Virulent smallpox epidemics could, and did, spread through the city, wiping out the weak—especially children and the elderly. Easily spread by droplets from the nose or mouth, smallpox could also infect by contact with anything that contained small particles of dried smallpox scabs from the victims.[4] (The British were accused of sending infected blankets to their American Indian enemies in 1763, and deliberately spreading the disease among American troops during the Revolution.)[5] Though British scientist Edward Jenner made a smallpox serum from cowpox in 1796, most Americans were vaccinated (it was called "variolation") by scratching material from the pustules of a smallpox victim into the skin.[6] It was hoped this would result in a minor outbreak of the disease. Once infected, whether fully or not, the body was immune to the illness forever. Regardless of the degree of the disease, however, the victim was infectious.

In 1785 the Hudson Common Council forbade inoculation of smallpox except in a "hospital" licensed for that purpose. A fine was imposed for disobeying this order. In March of 1790, the citizens of Hudson sent a plea to the Common Council requesting the privilege of inoculation by themselves in their own homes "because they were so exposed to the disease" when they left their houses. The council suspended the prohibitory ordinance.[7]

Then, in December of 1793, the Common Council announced that "the continuance of the small pox promiscuous inoculation ... is highly injurious to the commercial interests of this place by impeding its communications with the county." In plain English, the council was worried that the prevalence of smallpox in the city prevented farmers from bringing their products into the town. So inoculation was forbidden and fines imposed. "If a person or persons shall be found to have natural or inoculated Small Pox, they shall be sent to a secluded building [called a pest house]." "Harboring" a victim within a home brought a fine. The controversy continued for years.[8] The Common Council was concerned that the contagion would increase as more chose inoculation, thereby spreading it to others.

There was worse to come. The Asian cholera began in India in 1816, was carried to Britain by British troops returning from India in 1831, and then from Britain into Ireland. The great Potato Famine of 1842 sent thousands of Irish immigrants to American shores, and with them cholera. Cholera is caused by the bacterium Vibrio cholerae, which contaminates victims' food and water.[9] Rapid dehydration can cause death in a few days, or even hours. At the time, treatment consisted of tartar emetic, to induce vomiting; opium (legal then), to check diarrhea (supposedly); calomel to increase the flow of bile; and spirits (liquor) for warmth. It is now known that all of these treatments exacerbated the disease. The pandemic of 1832 forced the Common Council to close the port facilities. Persons infected were sent to the pest houses.[10] Hudson lost several skippers to the disease: they were in the wrong port at the wrong time. The residents who could, fled the city.

The Asian cholera returned in 1848 and lingered for several years. Hudson was hit especially hard, with many deaths. By the summer of 1848, the city had all but closed down because of the fear of contagion. "All the churches and stores were shut up like Sunday" was the comment. To add to the woe, it was a particularly hot summer. On Warren

Rachel Weeping, oil on canvas, 1772, by Charles Willson Peale. (Courtesy of the Philadelphia Museum of Art: Gift of the Barra Foundation, Inc.) Photo by Grayden Wood, 2001. The artist's wife weeps over her young daughter, who died of smallpox.

Street on July 6 the temperature registered 103° in the shade.[11]

An epidemic is easy to spot when reading the obituaries. Long lists of the deaths of children are especially significant, because the children were so vulnerable to bacterial illnesses. Typhoid fever was prevalent, caused by drinking water or eating food contaminated with the bacterium Salmonella typhosa. The bacterium can enter water from the feces of a diseased person, and food can be contaminated by a diseased person or a symptomless carrier.[12] Flies, particularly the housefly, *Musca domesti-*

ca ("the queen of the dung heap"), was called the typhoid fly (more on flies later).[13] Fever and headache are the beginning symptoms. In the second week small, raised, pink spots appear on the chest and abdomen. Some people recover, but harbor the disease for years, becoming carriers.

Diphtheria, also called diptherethic croup, was a great enemy to children. It is a bacterial disease and is highly contagious. It begins as a sore throat, but the full infection could close off the windpipe. Death usually followed the throat infection. If not, complications weeks later usually led to heart fail-

AN OLD ADVERTISEMENT.

HUDSON BATHING HOUSE.

THE public are respectfully informed that the new Bathing House is now opened and ready for their reception. Warm Baths can be had on Wednesday and Saturdays from 6 to 9 o'clock, A. M. and from 6 to 9 in the evening and any other hour or day in the week by giving the keeper one hour's previous notice and paying the price of three baths—(Sundays excepted.)

PRICES OF BATHING.

Warm Bath..25 cts.
Cold Bath..12½ cts.
Shower Bath..12½ cts.
Common Bathing place..............................12½ cts.
TICKETS for the Season may be had by applying to the Keeper.
For a family..4s.
A single person..2s.

WM. FOSTER, Keeper.

WILLIAM JOHNSON, } Committee.
RICH'D ROBOTHAM, }

Hudson, Aug. 27, 1816

Hudson Bathing House advertisement in Robert M. Terry,
The Hudsonian: Old Times and New, 1895.

ure or paralysis. Again, a carrier, immune to the disease, harbors the bacteria in the nose or on the skin, spreading them by air or touch.[14]

Scarlet fever received its name from the rash of tiny, red spots that starts on the neck and upper body and spreads rapidly. Predominantly a childhood disease, it is spread by the streptococcal bacterium in droplets coughed or breathed into the air. Sore throat, headache, and fever are early symptoms. Scarlatina was another name for the disease.[15]

Tuberculosis, or consumption, infected children and young adults. It is spread by airborne droplets containing bacterium from the coughing and sneezing of the victims. It is a slow death, as the lungs fill with fluid. Phthisis is an old term for a form of tuberculosis. Bovine tuberculosis came from con-

taminated cows' milk and is not to be confused with brucellosis, a bacterial disease caused by drinking unpasteurized milk.[16]

A genealogical enthusiast may be surprised to discover an ancestor having several wives, each following one another in death. It wasn't until 1866 that Joseph Lister advocated using sterile conditions during operations, following Louis Pasteur's discovery of bacteria in 1858. Until that time, doctors attending at operations and childbirth never cleaned their hands or clothes, and moved from one patient to another without the slightest effort to wash their hands. Puerperal fever, caused by bacteria entering the birth canal, caused deaths that were attributed to "childbirth." The bacteria would cause a sepsis infection within ten days after childbirth, invariably leading to the death of the mother.[17] Cutting the umbilical cord with a non-sterile instrument could cause the same bacterial infection in the baby.

Some other causes of death in the early obituaries have different names today. To die of apoplexy was to have a killing stroke. Brain fever was usually hypertension (high blood pressure), but it could also be cerebral palsy or epilepsy. Death due to dropsy means edema—fluid collecting in the body—caused by congestive heart failure or kidney disease.

Sanitary conditions were appalling. The necessary outhouse (privy) might leak into a neighbor's cellar, where the drinking water cistern was located. The first house plumbed in Hudson was in 1855. It was considered "a very questionable, if not dangerous" improvement.[18] Earlier, before 1850, Martin Van Buren had installed a "closet" in his nearby home, Lindenwald.

The prime villains, however, were the combination of the fly and the horse. An average horse produces fifteen to thirty pounds of manure in a day. Flies would thrive in the stables, the manure pile, and the privy. Window screens were unknown, so flies could move freely from outhouse or manure pile to the food on the table. Cholera, typhoid fever, and other infectious diseases like dysentery and infant diarrhea, were all blamed on the bacteria carried by the common housefly. In dry weather, dung on the streets would be ground into fine, polluted dust particles that blew through streets and windows.[19] The city hired a man to remove the excrement from the streets, but only every three weeks, and only on the paved streets.[20]

The Common Council did remove one cause of contamination. In May of 1805 it forbade the slaughter of cattle within the compact part of the city.[21] Before that time, the numerous slaughterhouses would dispose of the slaughter waste into the bays, to be washed out by the tide.

It was difficult to cure a disease if the cause was unknown, but that didn't prevent the unscrupulous from advertising treatments for all maladies. It was an age of patent medicines and nostrums, all guaranteed to cure. The hidden, high alcohol content

Two-door privy, drawn by John Alderdice.

was bound to make anyone feel much better. Laudanum, a tincture of opium, was the "aspirin" of choice in the nineteenth century.[22] Other "medicines" were more bizarre. This advertisement appeared in the April 1795 *Hudson Weekly Gazette*: "A RATTLESNAKE wanted as a medicine. Any person having one that has not been killed so long as to have lost its virtue ... A generous price for it by sending it to the printer."[23]

One visitor to America in 1846 blamed the prevalence of illnesses on the "vast quantity of decomposed vegetable matter produced every fall."[24] This same traveler warned his fellow travelers to "wear flannel underwear, avoid cold water, and, most important of all, shut out the dangerous night air."[25]

At the beginning of the nineteenth century, women's dress styles changed radically. A narrow,

Common housefly (*Musca domestica*), drawn by John Alderdice.

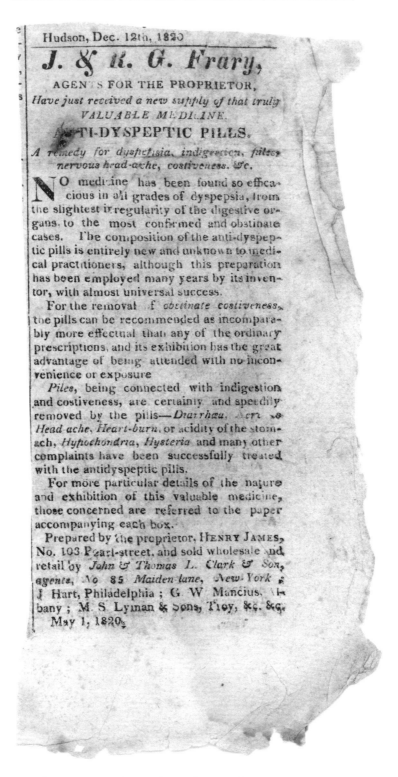

Advertisement in the *Northern Whig*, a Hudson newspaper, 1820.

straight dress, usually made of thin muslin with the waist hovering just below the breasts, was the fad for the next few decades. A single shawl was the outer garment for all seasons, and thin, flat cloth slippers covered the feet. This style of dress was held responsible for the large proportion of women who succumbed to consumption (tuberculosis). An estimated 500 deaths from consumption in New

York City in the year 1818 were attributed to women's dress, or lack thereof.[26] One wag commented that in one year, "Eighteen ladies caught fire and eighteen thousand caught cold."[27]

In *The Balance and Columbian Repository* of July 14, 1807, readers were regaled with a copy of an address given by the vice-president of the Columbia County Medical Society on the subject of fevers. Dr. Thomas Brodhead, obviously enjoying a captive audience, used his lengthy dissertation (two pages long), to uphold his theory that fever was caused by "an increase in the momentum of the blood. The heart and the arteries act with unusual energy, and the blood within them moves with unusual velocity, causing the body to heat." Thus, by his reasoning, typhoid fever was not a fever, because the blood was sluggish, "and therefore should not be treated as a fever."[28]

It took a hardy individual to survive the medical ignorance of those times!

The Sailor's Return, an early print that illustrates the style of women's garments in the early nineteenth century.

Traitorous and Lawless Action 1800–1807

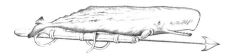

[for] *deceitfully, wickedly, maliciously and willfully traducing, scandalizing and vilifying President Thomas Jefferson and representing him as unworthy of the confidence, respect and attachment of the people of the United States …*

Section of the indictment against Hudson editor Harry Croswell, 1803[1]

The Quasi-War with France was over, but the United States would not be free of foreign troubles for another fifteen years. Residents in Hudson followed the European wars in their newspapers, which carried news of all the battles, albeit belatedly. In 1797, as war clouds gathered, a military tax was levied for the first time on noncombatants (the Quakers). The rate was three dollars per poll,

and there were four polls. The next year the number of polls was increased to twenty-five, and the rate was increased to four dollars per poll.[2]

Napoleon continued his victorious excursions against the European coalition. When Britain found itself alone against his forces, it signed the Treaty of Amiens in 1802. Napoleon, with his control of the Louisiana Territory, was tempted to try conquests overseas, but fared badly in an attempt to conquer Haiti. When a new war between France and Britain broke out in 1803, Napoleon gave up his North American dreams and sold the Louisiana Territory to the United States. Thomas Jefferson, then president, paid $15,000,000 for 830,000 square miles, doubling the size of the nation.[3] (Previously, in the 1783 Treaty of Paris between Britain and the United States, Britain had ceded to the new nation all the territory from the Appalachian Mountains to the Mississippi.)

With the Louisiana Purchase, the new country held nearly three-quarters of what is now the

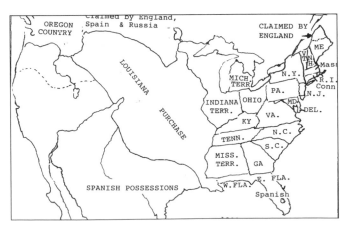

Map of the United States in 1803, including the Louisiana Purchase.

Napoleon at Home, an attempt at public relations by "the scourge of Europe" to present himself as a peaceful family man.

events created effects that filtered down to the residents of Hudson.

John Adams was president of the United States from 1797 to 1801. To his credit, he managed to keep the country out of a declared war with France and, in the process, revitalized the U.S. Navy and the Marine Corps. To his discredit, however, were two rulings that left a blot on his term. He imposed the first tax on the American people—a tax on land. He also allowed the Alien and Sedition Acts to be made into law. These acts curtailed and actually forbade criticism of the government under the guise of preventing foreign influences in political matters.[5] The country was inundated with refugees escaping from the French Revolution and the Irish Rebellion of 1798.[6] The French, particularly, were attempting to influence American sympathies toward France, against the wishes of the then-Federalist govern-

United States. Unfortunately, the boundaries of the purchase were not clearly defined, especially those dividing the territory from the Spanish holdings of East and West Florida and Mexico. Aaron Burr took advantage of the fuzzy line between the Louisiana Purchase and the Spanish province of Texas to begin, it is alleged, an armed excursion into the eastern Spanish holdings. His purpose, it was charged, was to bring the states and territories bordering the east sides of the Mississippi and Ohio rivers into the invasion, conquer Mexico, and set up a new country with himself as president. This conspiracy and the trial of Burr filled the local newspapers. He was acquitted in 1807.[4]

Napoleon crowned himself Emperor of France in 1804 and began successful military conquests of the European continent. When Horatio Nelson defeated the French Navy at Trafalgar in 1805, however, the British controlled the seas. All these

Thomas Jefferson, from *The American Revolution in New York*, University of the State of New York.

ment headed by John Adams. The three Alien Acts put broad limits on alien activities, allowed deportation, and changed the residency requirements for citizenship from five to fourteen years. The Federalists were opposed to the "equality and brotherhood" ideals of the French Revolution, believing, among other things, that government would run best if led by successful, wealthy men. The Alien Acts were repealed in 1800.

The Sedition Acts made it unlawful "to oppose any measure or measures of the government of the United States, counseling or advising such opposition, writing, printing, uttering or publishing false, scandalous, and malicious writing or writings against the United States or the President of the United States, with the intent to defame … or to bring them into contempt or disrepute." Of course, the First Amendment to the Constitution reads, in

Resolutions (passed in 1798) affirming states' rights and nullifying the Alien and Sedition Acts.

This explanation is necessary because Hudson became the battlefield in the right of the press to print material derogatory to anyone or any party. The first years of the new century brought an excess of violent denunciations of political opponents. Newspapers were established for the sole purpose of idolizing their party's leaders and insulting the opposition. In the *Hudson Weekly Gazette*, Peter B. Ten Broeck published that Killian K. Van Rensselaer, Esq. "is a coward, pusillanimous and destitute of the truth."[8] DeWitt Clinton stigmatized a political adversary as "a liar, a scoundrel, and a villain," which led to a duel with injuries, but no deaths.[9]

As soon as Jefferson became president in 1801, the Federalists began a campaign against him and

Header of the Hudson newspaper, *The Balance and Columbian Repository*.

part, "Congress shall make no law … abridging the freedom to speak, or of the press."[7] But, no matter—the Sedition Acts passed, though violently opposed by Vice President Thomas Jefferson who led a party, called the Democratic-Republicans, ranged against the Federalists and based on the principles of democracy and a republican form of government. States' rights was one of the major issues separating the Federalists from the Democratic-Republicans. Jefferson formulated the Kentucky and Virginia

his party equal in vituperation and ferocity to that used by Jefferson's party earlier against the Federalists. Jefferson was furious. Alexander Hamilton's writings predominated in the Federalist press in the larger cities, and the insults were repeated and magnified in innumerable small-town presses. Jefferson soon found virtue in the Sedition Act he had attacked, but that act had expired in 1801 before he took office, so he suggested state prosecution under common law.

Ambrose Spencer (1765-1848), assemblyman, state senator, attorney general, Supreme Court judge. From Peyton F. Miller, *A Group of Great Lawyers of Columbia County*, 1904.

The Hudson Federalists backed Ezra Sampson as editor of their newspaper, *The Balance and Columbian Repository*. In 1802, Harry Croswell was hired as junior editor. That same year, Charles Holt opened a newspaper in Hudson called *The Bee*. Holt had been fined $200 and jailed for three months for libel in Connecticut (for writing about Alexander Hamilton's love life). *The Bee* was a rabid Democratic-Republican (i.e., Jeffersonian) paper, and Holt announced he would "Buzz impertinently in the face" of *The Balance*.[10] Harry Croswell persuaded editor Sampson to let him answer *The Bee* in a publication called *The Wasp*, with Croswell using the pen name Harry Rusticoat.[11] The battle was on! Croswell, in September of 1802, quoting other Federalist newspapers, listed five acts by Jefferson that Croswell claimed violated the Constitution. He also charged that Jefferson paid Callender (editor of the *Richmond Examiner*) to call "Washington a traitor, a robber and a perjurer; to call Adams a hoary headed incendiary; and to slander other virtuous men."

Ambrose Spencer, who had switched from the Federalist Party to the New York (Jeffersonian) Democratic-Republican Party, was the attorney general of the State of New York and a former Hudson attorney. Spencer brought two indictments against Croswell for "seditious libel, for deceitfully, wickedly, maliciously and willfully traducing, scandalizing and vilifying President Thomas Jefferson, Etc." Croswell was arrested and brought before the Court of General Sessions at the courthouse in Claverack in 1803. (It would be two more years before Hudson would become the county seat and the courts would be moved there.)

Most often asked is why Croswell and his *Wasp*, with limited circulation, were indicted when far worse libelous statements were being printed in the large, Federalist city newspapers. Most historians agree that by prosecuting a small-town newspaper, there would be little publicity or public outcry outside the region. If Croswell were declared guilty, then there would be a legal precedent to charge other, larger newspapers.

The record of the Croswell trial could fill a book, and should. At the first trial in Claverack,

Elisha Williams (1773-1833), assemblyman and president of the Bank of Columbia County in Hudson. From Captain Franklin Ellis, *History of Columbia County*, 1878.

Reverend Harry Croswell, D.D. (1778-1858), oil on canvas, 36" x 29", 1839, by Henry Inman.
(Courtesy of Mead Art Museum, Amherst College, Bequest of Herbert L. Pratt [Class of 1895]: AC 1945.12)

Croswell was defended by Elisha Williams, Jacob Rutsen Van Rensselaer, and William W. Van Ness, all top Federalist attorneys serving without a fee. Ambrose Spencer, attorney general of the State of New York, served as prosecutor, with Ebenezer Foote as his assistant. (*The Balance* referred to him as "Spencer's foot.") Claverack legend has it that Alexander Hamilton appeared for Croswell in Claverack. He did not, though he may have offered legal advice to Croswell's lawyers. It was at the second trial, in Albany, that Hamilton represented Croswell, also for no fee. (Hamilton hated Jefferson, and had printed the Callender story in a newspaper that he backed, *The Evening Post* of New York City.)

The trials were travesties of justice. Impartiality on the part of judges was unknown in those days, and the fact that many judges were willing to change their political affiliations in order to be rewarded with high judicial office reflects clearly on their integrity.

Croswell's defense hinged on the truth of what he had printed—that Jefferson had paid Callender to print the insults to Washington and Adams. Under New York State common law at that time, however, printing any derogatory or insulting comment, even if the writer could prove it true, was still considered libel.

At the trial in Claverack, Croswell was found guilty, but his attorneys charged that Chief Justice Morgan Lewis had misdirected the jury. A new trial was granted, to be held in Albany before the New York State Supreme Court.

The defense lawyers planned to obtain a statement from Callender stating the true facts but, unfortunately, Callender was found dead, mysteriously drowned in three feet of water—a suspicious death. He was known to be a heavy drinker, but a coroner's jury determined he had committed suicide. Locally, his death caused quite a stir. *The Balance* dared not suggest what most Federalists believed—foul play.

On February 12, 1804, the Albany trial opened before a four-judge court. Following William Van Ness, Alexander Hamilton spoke eloquently for hours but the court, split two to two, affirmed the Claverack decision. Croswell, however, remained free.

In 1805, Van Ness successfully sponsored a bill allowing that truth may be given as evidence. With that, Croswell was awarded a new trial, but no move was made to reopen the case. (If it were proven to be true that Jefferson paid Callender, there would have been great embarrassment for Jefferson and his party.)

The Wasp ceased publishing in 1803, and in its last issue printed an attack on attorney Ambrose Spencer and Ebenezer Foote. Spencer and Foote sued Croswell and editor Sampson. Sampson settled, but Croswell declared it was the truth that Foote was "a scoundrel and a blockhead." At the

Alexander Hamilton, from *The American Revolution in New York*,
University of the State of New York.

trial, witnesses testified to Foote's character and declared he had been seen cheating at cards. The jury awarded Foote six cents.

Croswell became editor of *The Balance* in 1809. Later, he moved to Albany, fell into debt, abandoned politics, and never voted again. He entered the ministry of the Episcopal Church and was called as rector of the Christ Church in Hudson in 1811. The next year he became rector of the Trinity Church in New Haven, Connecticut, where he served for forty years.

Holt, editor of *The Bee*, printed a severe attack on local lawyer Elisha Williams. Furious, Williams posted three friends near the newspaper office for support, if necessary. Williams then attacked the editor and knocked him down. The city was

appalled. Williams was a man of "high position" and was strongly built. The fact that he found it necessary to provide reinforcements in advance to waylay the man was scandalous because Holt was not only feeble and slight, but also a cripple.

The risks of libel went beyond lawsuits. While Alexander Hamilton was in Albany, Federalist Party leaders discussed Aaron Burr as a candidate for New York State governor. Hamilton made some scathing remarks about Burr that reached Burr's ears. When Burr lost the election for governor, which destroyed him politically, he blamed Hamilton. He challenged Hamilton to a duel and, on July 11, 1804, Aaron Burr killed Alexander Hamilton.[12]

Turnpike Fever
1800–1807

The beginning of the new century brought the beginning of what must be called "Turnpike Fever." Enthusiasm for turnpikes had spread throughout the east. The capital for these endeavors had to be from local sources, because corporate organization was used with shares sold to raise funds.

Buying shares in anything was an American passion. Herman Melville described it well, referring to those who bought shares in a ship: "the stocks were held by a crew of old annuitants, widows, fatherless children, and chancery wards, each owning about the value of a lumberhead or a foot of plank, or a nail or two."[1]

COLUMBIA TURNPIKE.

Capital by Charter consists of 1,000 Shares of $ 25 each.
Passed 29th March, 1799.

Nº 39

Peter Mesick is entitled to Four Shares in the Stock of the Columbia Turnpike Road, having paid Twenty-Five Dollars on each Share.....The dividends payable semi-annually in January and July, and the Stock transferrable by assignment on the back of the Scrip.

By Order of the President and Directors,

Seth Jenkins Treas.

Hudson, July 1st 1819

Alex Coffin Pres't.

—S. W. Clark's print.—

Stock certificate for the Columbia Turnpike purchased by Peter Mesick in 1819.

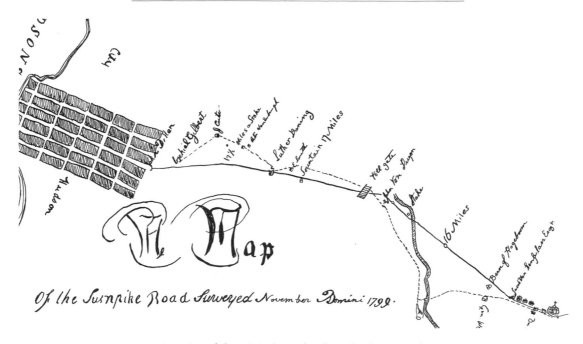

A section of the original map for the Columbia Turnpike.
The broken line indicates the original road from Hudson to Claverack.
Map Book 5, pages 395-98, Office of the Columbia County Clerk, Hudson, New York.

Investing in stocks was, and is, risky, but there was an additional problem with early corporate shares. Most were assessable stock, meaning that if the corporation needed more money at any time, it could levy successive assessments as often as required. Failure to pay the extra assessment meant the loss to the holder of the entire stock.

Roads into Hudson from the country were appalling. Products from the country were essential to the city's shipping industry and the backbone of its prosperity. Good roads had to be provided. The Columbia Turnpike, chartered in 1799, and the Union Turnpike, chartered in 1801, were the first. The Columbia was to run from Hudson through Claverack, on to Hillsdale and into Massachusetts. It was the third toll road chartered in New York State and it was a major highway east.[2] The tolls, paid at tollgates, were expected to provide the funds necessary for maintenance. Many major Hudsonians, such as Alexander Coffin, Thomas Jenkins, and Robert Folger, were some of the original investors. The Columbia operated as a toll road until 1907. The Union Turnpike, now Route 66, ran northwesterly from Hudson to New Lebanon near the Massachusetts state line. It operated until 1908.

The Hudson Turnpike (1801) ran from Hudson to West Stockbridge, Massachusetts. The Ancram Turnpike was the southern route out of Hudson to Ancram. The Hudson-Livingston Turnpike, chartered in 1802, ran on what is now Worth Avenue southeasterly to the "Manor of Livingston." The Hudson Branch Turnpike, beginning in 1805, was the route south from the east side of Hudson, and the Farmers Turnpike, chartered in 1813, was the river road, (Route 9) between Hudson and Troy.

The turnpikes were another great idea that didn't work. Maintenance cost more than the tolls produced. "Shun-pikes" was a name given to the side roads that were used to avoid tolls. It was against the law to avoid toll paying by that means, but many of today's back roads originally were built to bypass a toll road. Eventually, state and local governments took over the complete road system, with tax money replacing the tolls.

Though the histories don't mention it, the city fathers surely spent about eighteen years agitating

OLD TOLL GATE, HUDSON, N.Y.

The first tollgate of the Columbia Turnpike, Greenport, New York. Postcard, 1899.

to have the county seat moved to Hudson. On December 10, 1795, the newspaper published the following: "Notice is given that a bill will be presented to the Legislature of the State for moving the Courts and jail from Claverack to the City of Hudson."[3] Success came in 1805 "after much earnest and persistent opposition." Much to the chagrin of the citizens of Claverack, Hudson was designated the county seat of Columbia County, with a courthouse and jail to be constructed. The community in Claverack had garnered a busy trade as the county seat, especially at court terms. Lawyers, judges, court officials, and citizens involved in trials flooded into the hamlet, which was filled with inns and other services. The courthouse and jail in Claverack was sold for $1,500 to a private individual. The money was to be used toward the building of the new facilities in Hudson.[4]

The city hall in Hudson, originally intended to be the courthouse, had never been finished. The upper floor was used as a school, while the lower stored hay. The Common Council allotted $2,000 to remodel the hall and build a new jail.[5] That new jail is now the building occupied by the *Register-*

Star.[6] (In 1833 a new courthouse was planned and finally constructed.)

A map of the City of Hudson dated 1801 shows the South Bay's northern shore filled with an assortment of businesses. There were tanneries, asheries, and a shipyard. The asheries made potash, the principal export of the United States as late as 1836. The product was used for making glass, soft soap, and gunpowder. Potash was made by leaching water through wood ashes. The liquid, called "clack ley" (lye), was evaporated by boiling it in cast-iron pots. Then, the "black salt," or potash, was chipped off from the inside of the pot. When scorched in ovens until the carbon burned away, it could be used to make cheap glass and yellow soap. If black salt was dissolved in water, recrystallized and re-baked, the white powder resulting was pearl ash, used for the best glass and soap. As forests were cleared for farmland, the ready supply of ashes from the wood was an important commodity for trade.

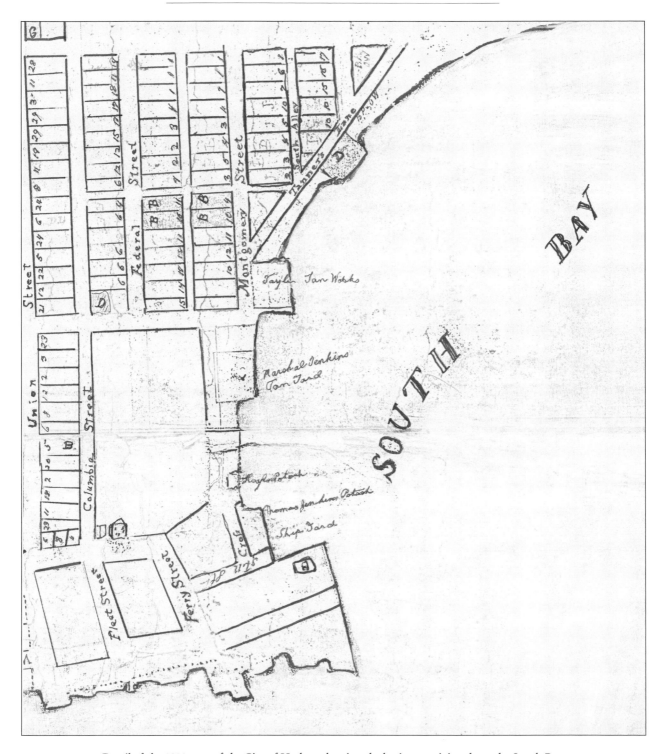

Detail of the 1801 map of the City of Hudson showing the business activity along the South Bay.
(Courtesy of the Office of the Columbia County Clerk, Hudson, New York.)

To serve the burgeoning population, mercantile establishments appeared, located below Fourth Street and mainly on Front and lower Main

(Warren) streets. Thomas Jenkins advertised "the best India and New England rum, salt and dry goods." Thomas Worth had silk and stuff shoes (stuff is a finished textile of wool or worsted material) for sale "at his shop near the market." and

Dennis Macnemara was a "tailor for Ladies and Gentlemen." Also needed and supplied were saddlers, bakers, and boot and shoe makers.

Mr. Robardet advertised that he would open a class for the instruction of dancing, "after the most approved method. ... Scholars would be taken from seven to fifty years of age." Ambrose Liverpool would open a seminary, teaching all English branches, the Latin and Greek classics, plus the principles of several musical instruments.[7]

Orders for millinery and mantuas (loose-fitting gowns) could be obtained from Mrs. Hussey, who promised the best fashions from New York City.[8] Monsieur Hyacinth L'Escure kept "a choice lot of essences near the market house," also cushions and queues of "excellent human hair." He would take his pay in wheat and Indian corn. Monsieur L'Escure was formerly a drummer under General Burgoyne, and was employed as the one and only "barber to the corporation." He dressed in a "long striped calico gown, a ruffled shirt, silk stockings and yellow slippers. His habit was to pace in front of his shop, humming a tune and snapping his fingers."[9]

Liquor was sold by every respectable merchant. Water was not something people drank much of in those early days. The dubious quality of the water made it unpalatable, even if the germs it carried were not yet recognized as a source of illness. Instead, liquor, preferably rum and cider, beer and ale quenched the thirst of these nineteenth-century people. Benjamin Faulkins opened a brewery, giving his product the name Hudson Ale. Two other breweries existed, one near the North Bay, and another on the south side of the city.[10] Nineteen men operated inns within the city in 1787, and more appeared as trade with the countryside increased.[11]

If the impression has been formed that the City of Hudson was a staid, stuffy city solely inhabited by strict and unforgiving Quakers, nothing could be further from the truth. Any excuse for a celebration brought out a large contingent of young "gentlemen" who delighted in partaking of long dinners followed by innumerable toasts. The Fourth of July

was always a good excuse, as was the anniversary of the surrender of Burgoyne at Saratoga. The *Gazette* described a typical Hudson Fourth of July celebration: "Three hundred attended an elegant entertainment at Kellogg's Tavern." The newspaper article then lists the thirteen toasts that were presented, starting with a toast to the United States of America. Toast number eleven was to "the fair sex of America," and the last toast was, "May the liberty and independence of America be forever supported by his sons."[12] After this article, the newspaper generally refrained from enumerating the toasts at subsequent celebrations and merely stated, "Toasts were made." When John Jay visited Hudson in 1792, it was reported that eleven toasts were presented at a dinner in Jay's honor at Kellogg's Tavern, including one toast to the "National Assembly of France and the Friendly Powers of Europe.[13] Clearly, Hudson was a lively city and not all its citizens were restrained and reserved.

The presence of slavery in Hudson is further evidence that the city was not entirely dominated by Quakers. The Society of Friends was firmly opposed to slavery and tried for years to abolish slaveholding in Hudson. They were no more successful in doing so, however, than the Congress of the Confederation, which was trying to frame a constitution for the new nation. The issue of slavery almost destroyed any chance for a united nation and helped drag out the negotiations until 1789, when agreement was finally obtained and George Washington was inaugurated in April.

Hudson had been a city for four years by that time, and slaveholding in the city was extensive. Innumerable advertisements, such as the following, appear in the *Gazette* relating to the sale of slaves or rewards for runaways: [May 5, 1785] "For sale ... a likely negro wench about 30 years of age. Also—a negro child one year and a half old. Enquire Philip H. Bortle, two miles south of Hudson"; "A likely Negro Wench—about 21 years old with a sucking child to be sold. Enquire of the printer or Jacob Temper, Rhinebeck Flatts"; [July 1793] "To be sold;

several negroes for cash [signed] Philip H. Hoffman"; [July 1786] "Robert G. Livingston of Rhinebeck offers $20 Reward for taking the runaway negro man Ben of yellow complextion and a great talker, walks as though he had lost his toes, etc."[14]

On the side of humanity, this notice appeared in the May 12, 1785, issue of the *Hudson Gazette*: "A respectable number of citizens having formed themselves into a society for <u>promoting the manumission of slaves</u> and protecting such of them as have been or may be liberated, the following extract from the proceeding are published for the information of the public. 'The Benevolent Creator and Father of men, having given them all an equal right to life, liberty and property, no power on earth can justly deprive them of either.'"

Advertisement for a runaway slave in *Northern Whig*
(a Hudson newspaper), April 24, 1824.

The Teakettle that Changed the River: Fulton's Folly, 1807

Fulton's Steamboat, from Wallace Bruce, *The Hudson*, 1913. Photo by Robert Ragaini.

On August 17, 1807, a single event changed navigation on the Hudson River forever. Robert Fulton perfected a steam-driven craft that traveled up the Hudson River from New York City to Albany and back again. (As the *Rural Repository* summed up Fulton's accomplishment on August 31, 1849, "the principles of the steam engine he did not invent, he claimed only the application of that machine to water wheels for propelling vessels.")

The vessel was 142 feet long and could move without the aid of wind or current, although one little-mentioned fact is that the craft had sails, and they were used to supplement the engine when the wind was right. Because there was no other craft like it, it was known simply as the *Steamboat*.[1] Pushed by enormous paddle wheels and belching black smoke, "Fulton's Folly" steamed up to Clermont, picked up Chancellor Robert Livingston and his son-in-

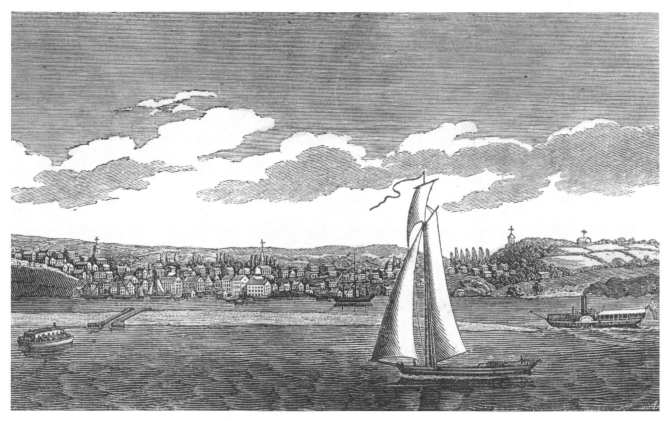

A View of the City of Hudson, drawn and engraved for the *Rural Repository*, c.1824.

law, Edward Livingston, and then proceeded to Albany using the western channel. Spectators lined the shores, and boats filled the river, all gawking at this new phenomenon. The return to New York City was uneventful, except for the excitement of the watchers from the shore. Soon, travel on the *Steamboat* was fashionable.

As the *Steamboat* became popular, the sloop interests recognized a potential rival. A campaign of deliberate ramming, particularly of the paddle wheel, was begun by jealous sloop captains.[2] Finding the right captain for the *Steamboat* was a problem. Two captains were fired before Fulton settled on Samuel Wiswall of Hudson, who proved equal to the task.[3] The *Steamboat's* first pilot was David Mandeville, also of Hudson.[4] When the *Steamboat* was enlarged and rebuilt as the *North River*, the work was performed by Hudson mechanics.[5] Livingston was granted a New York State monopoly on the running of steamboats on the Hudson, and a succession of other steamboats,

such as the *Car of Neptune* and the *Paragon*, led to great success for him and Fulton.

One major disadvantage of early steamboat travel was that, as its popularity increased, whole forests were destroyed in order to provide fuel for the engines. The price of firewood increased as supplies dwindled. It wasn't until the 1840s that anthracite coal was used rather than wood. An early history claims that Daniel Dunbar of Hudson was the first to adapt a steam engine furnace and blower to use coal for fuel.[6]

Livingston's monopoly was declared unconstitutional by the Supreme Court in 1824. A famous name appears for the first time in the steamboat monopoly dispute. Twenty-four-year-old Cornelius Van der Bilt had been sailing his sloop ferries in New York harbor for eight years. He was hired to run a steamboat for a rival firm involved in the monopoly dispute. Considered "a bold and resourceful operator," Van der Bilt went on from steamboats to railroads, to an unparalleled success.[7]

Corsairs and Privateers
1800–1807

It was a signal for the nation to heave to under bare poles; that the ship of state had been turned out of her course and yawed about by a lubbery helmsman until the voyage was ruined and the owners half broken.

Reuben Folger of Hudson on Jefferson's embargo,
from *Random Recollections of Albany*, by Ignatius Jones, 1850[1]

Britain ruled the seas, or so she thought. Her immense navy was the pride of that nation. It took men, lots of men, however, to man those ships, and few were willing to commit to the brutal, dangerous life aboard His Majesty's fighting fleet. Press gangs roamed the streets and countryside, rounding up any able-bodied man, by force if necessary. Dragged unconscious to the ship, they came to as unwilling crew members under merciless officers. With the arrogance born of contempt for their former colonies, British ships would stop American ships, call for all the crew to be assembled, and then pick out those they claimed were deserting British sailors. They usually impressed more Americans than "British deserters," but under the guns of the British ship, no American captain could argue.

The long wars in Europe had produced a demand on the continent for the neutral vessels of the United States to carry food supplies and lumber to their ports. The profits were high enough to risk capture. As Britain and France warred, both preyed on American ships. Sail cargo to France, be seized by British ships; sail cargo to Britain, be seized by French ships. Hudson skippers made fortunes, then lost money and ships to capture.

Between the years 1801 and 1808, twenty-seven vessels were built at the Hudson yards. Of these, twenty-two were ships, ranging from 200 to 413 tons. This high percentage of larger vessels indicates the flurry of activity in the transatlantic trade. Only two schooners were built during this period. Schooners were faster than sloops, they could be larger, and they could have several masts for sails. The schooner *Boston* was 74 tons, and the *Mentor* was larger, at 107 tons. One brig (short for brigantine) was built in 1807; the *Amelia* weighed 129 tons.[2] Were any of these vessels armed? That point is never mentioned, but if they were captained by Quakers, they were not.

In 1807 the British frigate *Leopard* opened a series of broadsides against the American frigate *Chesapeake*, killing three of her crew. The British seized four *Chesapeake* crew members, one of them British. The crippled ship limped back to Norfolk, Virginia. Americans were enraged at the affront. Then the British issued a proclamation that asserted its right to board any merchant vessel to search for British seamen. Napoleon countered by announcing that any vessel submitting to a British search would be seized and its crew imprisoned. Further, he declared that the ports of France and her allies were off-limits to any neutral vessel that stopped at a British port. Jefferson, trying to avert war, brought out the Embargo Act, which prohibited American vessels from sailing to foreign ports, including China and the East Indies, and put severe restrictions on the coastal trade. The New England maritime states were furious, and threats of a civil war were bandied about. The Embargo Act was intended to damage the trade of the two European countries; instead, it ruined America's trade. It even denied the right of American ships to trade at Canadian ports. This led to wholesale smuggling, which was ignored by most coastal officials.[3]

Another problem faced the whaling and shipping interests. After Napoleon sold the United States the Louisiana Territory, the federal govern-

ment began to envision an America covering the entire North American continent. Spain still held Florida and Texas and became irritated by the threats of annexation by America. Not strong enough for armed conflict, Spain retaliated by closing all of its South American ports to American ships. Those ports were often used by whalers for "refreshments" (fresh food supplies for the crews), and the inability to land for supplies or repairs brought misery to the whaling industry. Ports along the coast of Peru had been essential after the long (two or three weeks') sail around Cape Horn. Now, scurvy became a plague.

In 1802 numerous trading sloops were returning to Hudson with reports of being turned away from the French ports on the island of Hispaniola. The revolution begun by Toussant L'Ouverture, a mulatto who overthrew the landlords and planters, continued after L'Ouverture was overthrown in turn. Napoleon sent in troops to quell the rebellion and imprison L'Ouverture. (It was the spread of disease—probably yellow fever—among these troops that would discourage Napoleon from his plan of controlling the West Indies and Louisiana and convince him to sell the Louisiana territory to

Cap't. Sterrett in the Schooner Enterprise *paying tribute to Tripoli, August, 1801*, by M. Corne.
(Courtesy of the Franklin D. Roosevelt Presidential Library.)

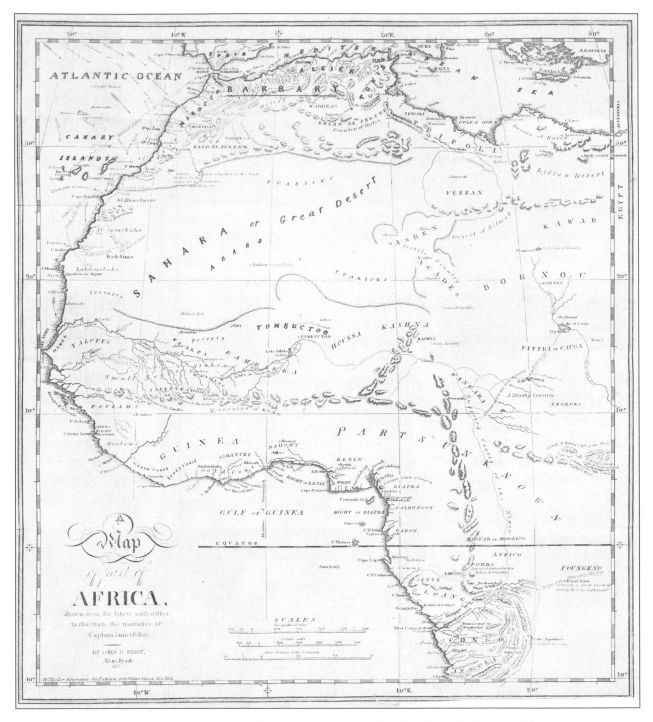

Map of a section of Africa showing where Paddock was captured and the path of his ordeal, reprinted from James Riley, *An Authentic Narrative of the Loss of the American Brig* America, *etc.*, 1818.

the United States.) Revolt followed revolt, and the unstable condition of Hispaniola put a crimp in trade.[4] French and British ships stalked each other and neutral ships throughout the Caribbean.

There was yet another problem that affected Hudson's shipping. "To the shores of Tripoli," a line from the "Marine Hymn," has a definite tie to this tale. Since 1783 the United States and European powers had been paying a yearly tribute to the rulers of the North African countries so that merchant ships could trade safely with European countries on the Mediterranean. These Barbary Coast pirates, called Corsairs, preyed on the ships of Christian nations. (The Barbary Coast comprised today's Morocco and Algeria, as well as Tripoli and Tunis.) The pirates captured ships and held the crews for ransom, or sold the men into slavery if the funds were not forthcoming. In 1793 the Algerine Corsairs sailed through the Strait of Gibraltar and captured four American ships, five brigs, and a schooner, adding 105 slaves to the fourteen Americans that already had waited eight years for their ransom to be paid.

Negotiations had to be carried out with each individual Barbary Coast nation, and the American government ended up paying out more than $2,000,000 in bribes to those countries. The payments were euphemistically called "donations" or "presents." A yearly tribute also was expected, and in 1796 a thirty-six-gun American frigate was another "donation." The American government's reasoning behind paying this extortion was that the overall profit on exports to the European countries on the Mediterranean far exceeded these payments.[5]

Into this mess sailed Judah Paddock of Hudson. He and his brother, Laban, were well-known sailing masters of the city. Judah, who had

shipped to the West Indies, Liverpool, and Russia, once had aided a Russian ship, for which he had received a sword from Catherine of Russia in appreciation. On the 8th of January 1800 he sailed from New York harbor in the converted whaler *Oswego* bound for Cork, Ireland, with a cargo of flax seed and barrel staves. After the cargo was sold, Paddock headed for the Cape Verde islands to pick up a load of salt and hides to bring back to the States. Somehow, his navigational skills went awry and the ship was wrecked on the Barbary Coast.

Paddock and his crew of seventeen men found themselves on a coast of barren sand with high mountains in the distance. After retrieving as much food and water from the wreck as possible, they set out across the desert for St. Cruz, a port city that Paddock believed to be a five-day walk away. After three days, eight of the crew, tortured by thirst, elected to return to the ship where at least there was water. Captain Paddock and three others continued on across the desert, where they were attacked by a band of Arabs who robbed them of all their belongings, including $600 in gold that Paddock had secreted in a pocket. The robbers then drove Paddock and his men by lash across the desert.

An Arab Camp, reprinted from James Riley,
An Authentic Narrative of the Loss of the American Brig America, *etc.*, 1818.

The American seamen suffered from heat and unbearable thirst during the day, and freezing cold during the desert nights. Paddock estimated that between April 14 and April 19 they walked at least 140 miles over burning sands and craggy mountains, "… with the sun nearly vertical, scorching, like fire, over our emaciated frames, having not more than four ounces of food to eat, excepting the raw barley, and not more than one quart of water each, except the stinking water in the pond." The pond, he noted, could be smelled a quarter of a mile away.

Eventually they were sold to another tribe, except for two black crew members, one of whom was Paddock's personal servant, Jack. Those two had to remain with their original captors and were never seen again. Paddock and the third crew member were sold several times to passing tribes, but conditions did not improve. Finally, Paddock convinced his captors that ransom would be paid if he were taken to St. Cruz. Delays occurred and the horrendous ordeal dragged on, but Captain Paddock eventually reached the U.S. Consulate and his freedom was purchased. The consul congratulated Paddock on the short stretch of his captivity—only six weeks! Most captured seamen spent years in captivity.[6]

Early historians like to include a serendipitous event to this story. Back in Cork, Captain Paddock had purchased some flowered fabric (tabinet) for his wife. After the wreck, Paddock's servant, Jack, secreted the fabric in his pack unbeknownst to Paddock, who had ordered the fabric discarded. As Paddock was about to sail for home after his captivity ended, an Arab peddler appeared and displayed merchandise for sale. Paddock was amazed to see the two pieces of tabinet, but he had no money to buy them. They were purchased by another man who wished to give them to Paddock after learning about his ordeal, but Paddock refused them. One year to the day after he had left his home in Hudson, Paddock was unpacking his trunk when he found the tabinet hidden at the bottom.[7]

Commodore Preble's Squadron Fires at Tripoli, **August, 1804. (Courtesy of the Franklin D. Roosevelt Presidential Library.)**

Two for One, reprinted from J. Ross Browne, *Etchings of a Whaling Cruise, 1846.*
(Courtesy of Belknap Press of Harvard University Press, Cambridge, Massachusetts.)

Judah Paddock wrote a narrative of his shipwreck and ordeals, recording the "sufferings of the Master and the crew while in bondage among the Arabs; interspersed with numerous remarks upon the country and its inhabitants, and concerning the peculiar perils of the coast." Preceding the text of the 1818 edition are printed letters from Ambrose Spencer, Elisha Jenkins, Robert Jenkins, and Ezra Sampson—all local men of high repute—attesting to the veracity of Paddock's story. John Clark, second mate of Paddock's ill-fated ship, also testified to the truthfulness of the tale. There may have been good reason for these testimonies. Just prior to the publication of Paddock's account, Captain James Riley wrote and published a narrative of the wreck of his brig, *Commerce*, on the coast of Africa in 1815. He, also, tells of the "sufferings of the officers and crew, who were enslaved by wandering Arabs of the Great African Desert, or Zahahrah," etc. The two accounts are very similar.[8]

In 1802 the Tripolitan dey (ruler) demanded additional sums for the "protection" of American ships. The United States refused and placed a blockade on Tripoli. Jefferson levied a special import tax to provide revenue to send several squadrons to the Mediterranean. Stephen Decatur led a daring raid that blew up an American ship captured by the Corsairs.[9] An expedition of 500 men, including U.S. Marines, captured the Tripolitan city of Darma in 1805, ending the piracy and the demands for ransom. The Barbary Coast "war" had lasted four years and succeeded in establishing peace for the next ten years, as well as proving that the U.S. Navy and its Marines were a force to be respected. The Marines were back in 1815 to put a stop to further Corsair raids.

Reflecting the dangerous situation on the high seas, only four whaling or sealing vessels are recorded having left the port of Hudson from the years 1800 to 1804. There are no reports of any whale ships sailing from Hudson after the return of the *Thomas* in 1804, until the *General Scott* sailed for the Pacific in 1815. Starbuck lists the *Nanina* as a Hudson whale ship, but it was owned by a New York City firm and sailed from New York. Following is a list of voyages from 1800 to 1804:

Cap't. Bunker's Sloop, the **North River,** by W.H. Bartlett.

1802	*Uncle Toby*	Ship	Master and voyage unknown[10]
1803–04	*Uncle Toby*	Ship	Swain, master; Pacific[11]
1803	*Juno*	Ship	Paul Bunker, master;[12] Pacific; sealing. Sailed with the sloop *Betsey*. There is a tale of the crew of the *Juno* meeting with other sealers in the Falkland Islands and having a "Ball" aboard the *Juno*, with music from a flute, drum, and violin.[13]
1803	*Volunteer*	Brig	Jenkins, master; Patagonia; last reported with 300 Bbls. Whale and some sealskins[14]
1803–04	*Thomas*	Ship	Folger, master; South Seas; 900 Bbls. Whale[15]

This sad piece of information, originally appearing in *The Bee*, was found in *The Balance* on November 24, 1807: "On Friday, the 6th, the brig *Catherine Ann*, Captain Pitts of Hudson, was 35 hours out of New York City in a snow storm. The brig sprang a leak. Captain Pitts, the crew and passengers got aboard a [life] boat and left the vessel. The mate, a Mr. Ashley and a crew member remained and climbed to the top of the mast, where they remained for three days until they were rescued. The fate of the Captain and the rest is doubtful, and it is feared they all perished. Among the missing is the son of Doctor Joshua Porter of this city, a son of Judge Cantine of Red Hook, and a son of Captain Martin, part owner. The Brig was owned by the Captain, and bound for Charleston.[16]

Sloops had become more luxurious as they competed for Hudson River passengers. All claimed finer accommodations and a faster voyage, but all were at the mercy of the wind and tide. Packet sloops became the norm early in the nineteenth century. Their schedule of stops on a particular day, rather than the random voyages of before, became popular with travelers. In 1806, two very large, elegant sloops were built expressly for carrying passengers between Hudson and New York City. (They were not built in Hudson, however.) They were both named the *Experiment*, and weighed thirty tons. Captains Bunker and Paddock, who had retired from ocean voyages, navigated the two vessels. A traveler on one of the *Experiments* commented: "It was fitted up finely, and accommoda-

tions were very comfortable; for passage, five dollars including a bed-place [berth], and three meals a day with spirits. About nine o'clock we left the wharf which was crowded with people to see us depart and having a smart breeze, soon left the city of Hudson behind us."[17]

Another captain doing the Hudson to New York City run was Robert Folger, who also had abandoned the sea and entered the river trade. He commanded several small vessels on the river run. One was the "fast-sailing" sloop *Sally*. After steamboats became popular, sloops gave up the passenger business and were used only for freight.

A ticket issued to William Ludlow to carry aboard the *Experiment* a servant girl and wine, October 8, 1809.

Winds of Change:
The City of Hudson, 1808–1829

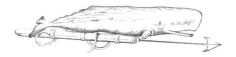

While our western wilds are whitening with the bones of our murdered women and children—while the Indian war-hoop and the British drum are in unison saluting the ears—while the brave American tar, the intrepid defender of our rights and redeemer of our national character—is impressed by force into a service he detests ...

Martin Van Buren in his Republican appeal
to the electorate to support the war, 1813[1]

Action between his Majesty's Ship Shannon *and the American frigate* Chesapeake, *off Boston Light House on the 1st. of June, 1813.*
Published by Virtue, Emmins & Co., 1859.

Winds of War

The residents of Hudson knew trouble had come. More and more of their vessels were seized or returned to port with their cargoes, unable to run the blockades. Still, they defied Jefferson's embargo. One indication of how seriously they viewed the situation was the order by the Common Council in 1808 to build a powder house within the

In 1808 the Embargo Act was replaced by the "Non-Intercourse Act," which was said to sanction smuggling.[3] James Madison, the new president, played France and Britain against one another, but favored France. Several more ineffectual acts followed, but war fever grew in America. Britain was accused of inciting the Indians to war on Americans; but, secretly, the U.S. government had its eyes on Canada. There was hope to annex Canada and Florida.[4]

Preparations for War to Defend Commerce. The frigate *Philadelphia*, launched November 28, 1799, was captured after shipwreck by the Tripolitans. Stephen Decatur blew it up in the harbor of Tripoli in 1804. (Courtesy of the Franklin D. Roosevelt Presidential Library.)

compact part of the city for the safekeeping of powder and firearms.[1] Jacques Milbert, in his diary that included a description of Hudson, wrote that Mount Merino was "crowned by a fort."[2] The histories don't comment on a fort there, so we may speculate that it was a "lookout" type of structure.

America was strangely divided by the coming war. The Northeast, which had suffered the most from British depredations, opposed the war. Some New England governors refused to let their militias cross state boundaries, and there was talk of secession.[5] The west, where there was concern that the Indian raids encouraged by the British would slow expansion, was for war. A large segment of the population was opposed and even held antiwar rallies.

America was not prepared for war. The standing army numbered only 6,700 men, to be augmented with state militias and volunteers. Officers were mostly inexperienced or downright incompetent. The navy was better, with experienced sailors fresh from the Barbary Coast battles, and it was augmented by American privateers who knew their way around a gunfight at sea. The most important plus on the American side, however, was that Britain was already at war with France.

War against Britain was declared in 1812. The Americans attempted to invade Canada from Detroit, but the American general allowed his baggage to be captured and he surrendered. An attempt to invade Canada via the Lake Champlain route was frustrated when the New York Militia arrived late and then refused to cross the border. The Americans were defeated again, this time on the Niagara, when the New York Militia refused to support the regulars.[6]

The tide turned toward the American side when Oliver Perry defeated a British fleet and cleared Lake Erie of the enemy. William Henry Harrison pushed into Detroit, found the British gone, and pursued them into Canada. This separated the western Indians from their British supporters. But an American army at Sackett's Harbor, New York, and another on Lake Champlain failed in all attempts to move on Quebec.

In 1814 Britain planned to invade the United States at Niagara and Lake Champlain in the north, and at New Orleans in the south. A good offensive

Perry's Victory at Lake Erie, anonymous nineteenth-century oil painting. Perry is transferring his flag from the *Lawrence,* which had been battered by the British, to the *Niagara.* (Courtesy of the Franklin D. Roosevelt Presidential Library.)

Victory at Lake Chaplain, engraved and published by Benj. Tanner, July 4, 1816.
(Courtesy of the Franklin D. Roosevelt Presidential Library.)

by the U.S. Army, aided now by more experienced officers and men, crossed into Canada and destroyed the British advance guard. The battle in the north was won when the British fleet on Lake Champlain was destroyed. On September 12, 1814, the British marched back into Canada.

Fourteen thousand seasoned British troops, fresh from victory over Napoleon in Europe, were rushed to America. The British troops descended on Washington unopposed and burned the White House, the Capitol, and most of the city. Baltimore, known for its harboring of privateers, was next. Guarding the harbor was Fort McHenry, which was bombarded day and night. Francis Scott Key saw the American flag flying through the smoke "by the dawn's early light." His poem, set to an old ballad, became our national anthem.[7]

Both sides wearied of the conflict. On Christmas Eve, 1814, Britain and the United States signed the Treaty of Ghent, ending hostilities. Two weeks after the peace treaty was signed, the Battle of New Orleans was fought. This was the British southern expedition that the British believed would give them control over the west. British General Sir Edward Pakenham, brother-in-law to the Duke of Wellington, carried a commission making him governor "over all the territory fraudulently conveyed by Bonaparte to the United States." But Pakenham died in the fierce Battle of New Orleans, won by "Old Hickory" Andrew Jackson. It was the greatest American victory of the war. Pakenham's body was shipped back to London in a cask of rum.[8]

There were no real winners in the War of 1812. Worse, the war need never have been fought. Four days before the American proclamation of war, Britain repealed all of its orders that had caused the problems between the two countries. Fifty British ships left for America filled with goods and carrying the papers declaring an end to the seizure of American ships and the impressments of American sailors. Jefferson's embargo had worked, crippling the British manufacturing trade. But the news arrived too late to stop the war.[9]

Battle of New Orleans. (Courtesy of the Franklin D. Roosevelt Presidential Library.)

Hudson men served in the War of 1812, but it is difficult to determine from the lists given in the local histories which veterans were from Hudson. It is known that the citizens of the city were roused to patriotic fervor when General Winfield Scott and 700 men arrived in the city near the beginning of the war. They encamped overnight on an open green on the easterly side of the present courthouse. The Wigton Artillery (a Hudson Republican Party-sponsored militia who dressed in black cocked hats, blue coats faced with red, and white or blue pantaloons) and the federal company, the Hudson Greens (who wore green coats and pantaloons, and black hats with green feathers), were ordered off to the war and stationed in New York City. The Hudson Greens, commanded by Captain Barnabas Waterman, were part of Lieutenant-Colonel Jacob R. Van Rensselaer's Light Infantry Battalion. They saw no action. William A. Spencer, a Columbia County native and a son of Hudsonian Ambrose Spencer, fought as a midshipman in the naval battle on Lake Champlain and was wounded in action.[10]

The effects of the War of 1812 and the Embargo Act that preceded it, with the near-total cessation of shipping during the blockades, left Hudson with few oceangoing vessels arriving or leaving its port. This led to the loss of its designation as a port of entry. From 1815 on, all Hudson ships would register at the port of New York City. Gone were the customhouse and the federal appointments for custom officers.[11]

Commerce, Licit and Illicit

The Proprietors' Association had deeded all the streets, highways, and public lands to the city's Common Council some years before. Finally, in May of 1811 the association decided to turn over its records to the city and cease its existence.

Hotheaded Cotton Gelston objected fiercely. He threatened to burn the books rather than turn them over, but he was prevented by three men present. A few books were burned, but most were saved, and the Proprietors' Association came to an end.[1]

Not daunted by the signs of financial ruin appearing in Hudson from the crippling of international shipping, the Columbia Furnace was organized in 1814 by Kellogg and Briggs, becoming the only foundry on the river between New York City and Albany. In 1816 it was advertised as the Hudson Air Furnace. Later it was owned by Starbuck and Gifford, and then by Elihu Gifford.[2]

Elihu Gifford was not only a prominent Hudson businessman, he also had the distinction of being the father of the artist Sanford R. Gifford. Sanford was one of eleven children of Elihu and Eliza Starbuck Gifford. The family's fortune allowed Sanford to dedicate his life to painting, and he traveled extensively in America and Europe. He had a studio in New York City, but always returned to his father's home in Hudson on the corner of Columbia and Sixth streets (now a parking lot), where he had his studio on the top floor. At his death in 1880, one of his many paintings of the local area was found in his studio. It was titled *A Scene along the Claverack Creek*. Sanford Gifford's funeral in Hudson was attended by some of the leading American artists of the day, including Frederic E. Church. Gifford is considered one of the more notable artists of the Hudson River School, and his meticulous yet luminous paintings command a high price today.[3]

Changing its products with the times, Gifford's foundry continued to flourish. Eventually it became Gifford and Wood, and it is now W.B. McGuire Co., on Hudson Avenue. Elihu Gifford ran the business at 31 Columbia Street, which would give the impression that it was located near the river. In earlier days, however, Columbia Street only extended from Seventh Street to the Columbia Turnpike. What is known now as Columbia Street was the famous (or infa-

Elihu Gifford, reprinted from Captain Franklin Ellis, *History of Columbia County*, 1878.

mous) Diamond Street, which stretched from Front Street to Seventh.

Diamond Street earned a widespread reputation for blatant prostitution. The onslaught of travelers, traders, and sailors into Hudson presented a requirement for "diversions" not filled by the usual, lawful businesses. This need was met by the early establishment of brothels in the city.[4] These first, shanty-built bawdy houses were on the third block of Diamond Street, a section of the city deemed unlivable by the gentry because it was surrounded by slaughterhouses, tanneries, and oil works. The Quaker leaders turned a blind eye to the situation, considering it a necessary evil. Possibly they reasoned that since prostitution had been around since Biblical times, its existence was inevitable. Surely, they may have reasoned, this evil was better when confined to a small, remote area than having the young maidens and wives of the gentry insulted, or worse. Fights occasionally spilled over into the more refined sections of town, but when they did, punishment was swift.

Commemorative pin for the Hudson-Fulton Celebration, 1909, when the lower section of Diamond Street was named Fulton Street. Photo by Robert Ragaini.

The first "scarlet ladies" probably moved to Hudson from New York City after the Revolutionary War. They were soon joined by unhappy wives, bored young girls, and penniless or wanton females. The "institution" flourished, and soon much of Diamond Street, which became less isolated as the city grew and spread, had its unique reputation. By 1843 the city fathers were at least embarrassed. The recorder, who was the legal officer of the Common Council, commented in July of that year about the houses of ill fame with which "our city is disgraced." To "suppress the vice," however, a witness was needed to come forward to testify to the existence of the establishment or to having experienced its "function."[5] No one came forward to testify. In 1859 an ordinance was passed for the "suppression of vice." A fine of twenty-five dollars was placed on the convicted owner of a brothel, and a five dollar fine on an apprehended prostitute, vagrant, etc. This paltry sum was easily paid.

Liquor and gambling joined prostitution and soon became so entrenched in the city's financial prosperity that such establishments were located throughout downtown Hudson. Through the years Hudson's political candidates would champion the vision of a "pristine" city free of vice, but once they were in office the matter was dropped. There was even a period when a quasi-legality existed, with a council-appointed doctor periodically examining the girls.

In the early 1900s, during the Hudson-Fulton celebration, the city paid a dubious honor to Robert Fulton by renaming the lower section of Diamond Street—south from north Third Street to Front Street—Fulton Street. It was probably an attempt to remove some of the odium attached to that section of town. In 1926 Fulton and Diamond streets were combined and renamed Columbia Street, leaving out-of-towners looking for "some action" perplexed.[6]

The era of prostitution brought Hudson to the forefront of wide-open cities. The reputation of "the block" and the easy availability of gambling and liquor spread by word of mouth. This situation continued until 1950, when then-Governor Dewey organized a secret raid by state troopers to break up the vice. The troopers rolled into the city under the cover of darkness and raided all the "houses" and gambling sites.[7]

As a financial panic spread through the United States in 1819, the Bank of Hudson failed. It had been organized in 1808. The 1819 panic brought more trouble to Hudson—wholesale prices dropped 50 percent, purchasing power all but ceased, and bankruptcies became common. The panic was, fortunately, as short-lived as it was sudden.

Jacques Milbert kept a diary of his observations as he traveled and sketched the Hudson River port towns. Sometime around the 1820s he visited Hudson, carefully portraying two scenes of the city near the river and writing about his impressions. He mentions walking from the steamboat landing up to the city along "a ramp cut in the rock." His descrip-

tion of the rock "with shellfish encrusted in it" indicates limestone. What is not known is if the rock cut led upward from the river to South Front Street, or if it was on South Front Street itself. Workmen did have to blast to open that street, but no such rock channel exists today.[8]

In 1822 George Robinson established a brewery, one of many that had been created since the founding of Hudson. This one was destined to continue for a long time, however, although under another name. Robert W. Evans bought the brewery in 1856. It grew in size and fame, becoming the C.H. Evans & Co. Brewery, world-famous for its "Evans Ale." It was the next century's ill-advised experiment in prohibition that finally spelled the end for this extraordinary business.[9]

The City of Hudson suffered yet another financial blow with the failure of the Bank of Columbia in 1829. The bank had been chartered in 1792—the

View near Hudson. Hudson River Portfolio (1820-1826), No. 15. Engraved by Hill, after a watercolor by William Guy Wall. **This is today's South Third Street.**

third chartered bank in the state. Thomas Jenkins had been the first president and Seth Jenkins a member of the board, and under their guidance the bank had flourished. After Thomas Jenkins' death, a great scandal erupted involving Elisha Williams, William Van Ness, Jacob R. Van Rensselaer, and the new Federal Bank of America. Accusations of bribes were bandied about, and an investigation was ordered. When the bank failed in 1829, it brought severe losses to many private individuals and city and county businesses, and created panic and depression throughout the county.[10] Captain Laban Paddock wrote in his memoirs in 1853 that the bank, "Failed in 1825—with capitol of $150000. lost. President [Elisha Williams] retired with a fortune of $300000."[11]

The General Disappoints

In 1824 the French hero of the American Revolution, Marie-Joseph-Paul-Yves-Roch-Gilbert du Motier, Marquis Lafayette, decided to revisit the United States. He was sixty-seven years old at that time. When it was learned that his plans included taking a steamship up the Hudson River and stopping at various places along the way, the valley went into a Lafayette fervor. Special commemorative dinnerware was created, banners were made, and elaborate plans to welcome "America's Hero" were set in motion.

Hudson's Common Council announced it would prepare to fire cannons as he passed, if the

"Landing of Gen. La Fayette," a commemorative platter, c. 1824, celebrating the arrival of La Fayette in New York City. (Courtesy of The Home, a retirement residence, Union Street, Hudson, New York.) Photo by Robert Ragaini.

general was unable to stop at the city.[1] A committee was set up to arrange for his possible entertainment, and that committee grew larger weekly as more and more people wanted to be involved in the festivities (or, more likely, to be in a position to shake his hand), but no one really knew if he would pause in Hudson. But, as with all committees, its plans got bigger and more elaborate, for Hudson should never take second place to any other city.

As Lafayette traveled up the river, cannons were fired in salute as he passed, even during the night. How anyone aboard his steamship got any sleep is a mystery. He had left New York City on September 15 aboard the steamship *James Kent*. "The gentlemen had to sleep on the decks" because so many ladies insisted on being on the trip, but Lafayette had a cabin for himself.[2]

Meanwhile, the Common Council appealed to the committee "to make suitable and necessary plans" for receiving Lafayette "should he be able to visit." Lafayette had stops in such places as West Point, Newburgh, Poughkeepsie, and Staatsburg, where he participated in processions, receptions, banquets, speeches (innumerable), and toasts. He had to shake hands with all the surviving veterans of the Revolution, plus thousands of others. When he arrived at the Livingston estate of Clermont, a ball and supper was served in the Orangery.[3]

Somehow, Hudson must have discovered that Lafayette's schedule did not include a stop in their city. The whole city had been decorated beyond description, a large banquet had been planned, ladies had acquired new gowns, and excitement was at the highest level. All this, when originally they were to be content to fire off a few cannons! So, with typical Yankee nerve, Mayor Reed and his party, two militia companies, the Hudson Brass Band, Brig. Gen. John R. Van Rensselaer and suite, as well as Brig. Gen. James Fleming and suite, all piled into the *Richmond* to steam to Clermont and escort Lafayette to Hudson.

This comment came from Clermont: "In the evening, we were a little disturbed by a delegation from Hudson, requesting that Lafayette should be

The Marquis La Fayette, from Bayard Tuckerman, *Life of General Lafayette*, London, 1889.

given up to them, as if he had become a State prisoner. They wanted their share of the nation. General Lewis, who was a member of the committee who had him under their protection, was steady in their refusal, and secured for the veteran a quiet sleep, which he greatly needed." Apparently, all the Hudsonians went back to their steamboat.[4]

The next day Lafayette landed in Catskill for a procession and a reception of Revolutionary War veterans. About noon on the 17th of September, Lafayette arrived in Hudson. He was drawn through town in a carriage pulled by four black horses, the streets crowded with cheering people. Arches of flowers and evergreens were everywhere, and a statue of the Goddess of Liberty bearing the Stars and Stripes crowned the end of the street. At the courthouse, filled with "elegantly dressed women," Lafayette heard a long speech, gave a short speech, and shook hands with sixty-eight veterans, local military officers, and the ladies. Mr. Allen's tavern, the site of the banquet, had a "throne" for the guest of honor, decorated with a wreath and "poetical welcome." (Earlier, in New

York City, a triumphal wreath held by a fake eagle had fallen on Lafayette's head.) The enthusiasm died when it was discovered that Lafayette could not stay. He had a glass of wine, bade farewell to the crowd, went back to the river, and boarded the *James Kent*, steaming off for a reception and dinner in Albany.[5]

Fury was the next emotion. Politics were blamed for the fiasco. The city fathers believed that Albany was jealous of Hudson, and had deliberately lured Lafayette away from the city. After all, Albany only won by one vote over Hudson to become the capital of the State of New York. The bill for the festivities came to $502.23, paid by the Common Council.

Lafayette's tour continued until September 9, 1825. His adventures took him up the Mississippi and Ohio rivers. His boat on the Ohio was shipwrecked and he was rowed to shore in a small boat, sleeping on the ground that night. When he was in

Virginia in August, it was so hot that one of the horses pulling his carriage dropped dead from the heat. Considering the discomfort of travel in those days, the uncertainty of the food, and the insistent demands on his time, it is a wonder that Lafayette survived his American tour.[6]

Bypassed by Progress

Another enormous celebration occurred in November of 1825 when the Erie Canal was completed. From Buffalo to New York City, cheers and cannon fire erupted from every community along the way as the flotilla passed by. Prior to the War of 1812, the New York Legislature had considered a man-made waterway to the west. Funds were authorized in 1817. Despite the fact that there were no professional engineers available, tremendous locks and aqueducts were designed, and an undeter-

Excavation at Lockport, from *Cadwallader Colden's Memoir*, 1825. (Courtesy of the New York State Library.)

minable amount of earth and rock was moved. Two canals were being constructed at the same time: the Champlain Canal, connecting the Hudson with Lake Champlain, was finished in 1823; and the Erie Canal. Seventy-five miles of the middle section of the Erie Canal were finished in 1819, and in 1825 the canal was completed.[1]

The momentous celebration began in October of 1825. "Clinton's Big Ditch" was a financial success, despite the prediction by naysayers of total ruin for the state. As the *Seneca Chief*, a packet, moved out of Lake Erie and into the new canal, a battery of cannon fire began, with communities along the route as far as New York City firing as they heard the fire from the community above. It took eighty-one minutes for the firing to extend to New York City. Hundreds of vessels, strewn with flags, accompanied the *Seneca Chief*, which carried two kegs of water from Lake Erie to be poured into the Atlantic Ocean on arrival. At Albany they entered the largest lock, where they were lowered to the level of the Hudson River. As the flotilla moved slowly down the Hudson River, the shores echoed with cheers and cannon fire. At Hudson the engines were stopped and the boats drifted by as more cannons were fired in salute from the shores. It was probably one of the most exciting events of the century, or of any century, for that matter. At New York City a great ceremony with speeches, fireworks, and a parade celebrated the connecting of the west to the Atlantic.

While the city fathers of Hudson were standing on Parade Hill, cheering with all the rest, did any one of them get a chill down his spine, suddenly realizing what the opening of the Erie Canal meant to their city? All the products from the farms and forests of the west could now be shipped easily through the canal and on to New York City, and then out to other ports. It would be a supply of raw material beyond anything the territory feeding Hudson could ever amass. The Erie Canal marked the end of Hudson's reign as a major shipping port.[2]

Another canal that also would have an effect on the city of Hudson was completed in 1828. For years there had been unsuccessful efforts to find "pit coal" in Columbia County. Coal was the fuel of the future, but anthracite coal was far away in inland Pennsylvania. In 1828, however, a canal system was completed that connected the coal fields of northeast Pennsylvania with the Delaware River. The Delaware and Hudson Canal left the Delaware River close to the northwest corner of New Jersey, crossed New York State and ended at the Rondout (Kingston) on the Hudson. From there, sloops and barges could deliver coal to the river ports.[3] The canal's importance to the City of Hudson lay in the future, when a more successful railroad line was run from the port of Hudson to Massachusetts, carrying up to 250,000 tons of coal per year. At that time, the rail system would operate a slip (wharf) and storehouse near the South Bay to facilitate the coal transportation.[4]

Native Sons and Daughters

One of the city's most macabre events occurred in 1817. Margaret Houghtaling, alias Peggy Dinsmore, was found guilty of murdering a child in her care. She was indicted on September 10, 1817, tried on the 12th, found guilty on the 13th, and sentenced to be hanged on the 15th. October 17, 1817, was the date set for the hanging, and the city "began to fill up early in the morning; they came from the east and the west, the north and the south." In a recollection by B. F. Jenkins printed in a local newspaper, Jenkins states: "I saw her taken out of the jail and placed in a cart, with her coffin for a seat. The gallows was erected on an elevation north of the city, near the ropewalk. I was too young then to estimate the numbers, but I should say there were thousands there. … All was quiet until after the execution, and then it was turned into a gala day, and it was late in the night before the city became quiet." He ends his account with this chilling statement: "There was some doubt [as to the guilt] in the case

The grave of Lieut. William H. Allen, northwest corner of
Cedar Park Cemetery. Photo by Robert Ragaini.

of Margaret Houghtaling—I have heard that the mother of the child confessed that she committed the crime herself."[1]

In December of 1827, a sad ceremony took place in Hudson. The remains of Lieut. William H. Allen, a Hudson native, were brought to Hudson for reburial. He had been an active seaman, and had lost his life rescuing some merchant vessels and their crews off the coast of Cuba while in command of the vessel *Alligator*. He was buried originally in Matanzas, near Havana, Cuba, in 1822, but arrangements were made to have his body moved to Hudson. The casket was delivered by steamboat to

the city, where a procession moved with it to the burial grounds. Bells tolled in the city, and guns were fired from Parade Hill. The Allen streets in Hudson are named in honor of this man.[2]

In 1828, Columbia County failed to carry the vote for Martin Van Buren as governor by a mere 136 votes. He did win the statewide vote, but apparently many in Columbia County did not want their native son, their former surrogate, attorney general, and senator. In his run for president of the United States in 1840, Van Buren carried the winning ticket in the county by a mere 188.[3]

War and Whales: The Port of Hudson, 1808-1829

Were it not that such a nation as Britain existed, this act of treachery might be correctly styled unparalleled; but British history is full of incidents of such black ingratitude. Such conduct, even in our enemy, cannot fail to call forth the indignant feelings of every American who has a drop of patriotic blood flowing in his veins.

The Bee, 1814, on the fate of the *Nanina*[1]

The effects of the Jefferson embargo were evident on Hudson's maritime activity by 1808. The Embargo Act stated that no vessel was allowed to leave for any foreign port, and no vessel could sail

Catch Me if You Can, c. 1810-1812. British frigate pursues two-masted American privateer, which apparently is replacing British flag with U.S. colors and flying flag from top mast that says, "Catch Me if You Can." (Courtesy of the Franklin D. Roosevelt Presidential Library.)

in the Atlantic Coast trade unless heavy bonds were given by the ship's owners. Many sailors and whalers were left without occupations. The war cast a pall over Hudson's shipping industry. Unemployment reached desperate proportions. There could have been, however, one redeeming feature to the shipping slowdown. It should have directed the city to concentrate more on manufacturing, as did many other, similarly affected seaports. But even after losing its port of entry status, Hudson's focus still was on its port.

The warring European nations were in desperate need of goods, particularly grains as their countrysides were destroyed by war. The promise of a high profit sent many Hudson seamen to chance the blockades and possible capture in order to secretly ship foodstuffs to France.[2] They also chanced encounters with enemy ships as they continued with their U.S. coastal trading. Others became privateers, though perhaps not carrying the letter of marque that designated an official privateer. This letter, written by a government official, granted the shipmaster the right to seize the subjects of a foreign state or their goods. The seized vessel would then become a "prize," and the captor the official owner. No good, Quaker shipmaster would intentionally set out to overpower any foreign vessel by force of arms, but smuggling was a different matter.

At the beginning of the War of 1812, the discouraging news of U.S. Army losses was balanced by the brilliant exploits of the U.S. Navy. The American frigate *Constitution* ("Old Ironsides") defeated the British *Guerriere* in a sea battle in 1812 that humiliated the British leaders, who believed the U.S. Navy to be inferior.[3] When the British *Shannon* captured and boarded the American frigate *Chesapeake* in 1813, the dying American Captain Lawrence's words to his crew, "Don't give up the ship," became the rallying cry for the navy and the nation.[4] But it was the 492 privateers commissioned by the federal government that brought the most harm to British ships. The privateers captured over 1,300 British ships with an estimated value of $9,000,000.[5]

Action between the *Constitution* (later called *Old Ironsides*) and the *Guerriere*, August 19, 1812.
Jeakes, Sculp't., published by G. Webster.
Captain Isaac Hull of the *Constitution* sank the *Guerriere* 800 miles east of Boston.

"Don't Give Up the Ship," c. 1813, the dying words of Captain James Lawrence aboard the crippled *Chesapeake.*
The words became the rallying cry of the War of 1812. (Courtesy of the Franklin D. Roosevelt Presidential Library.)

Shipbuilding continued in Hudson, but the size of vessels changed, reflecting the end of the long, transatlantic voyages. In the next twenty-one years until the end of shipbuilding in Hudson, just seventeen vessels were constructed. Two were ships, nine were sloops, two were schooners, and in 1827, two barges, one towboat, and one scow were built. The ship *Iris*, of 251 tons, was constructed in a Hudson yard in 1810. The *William Wallace*, of 228 tons, was constructed in 1822.[6]

The two barges were constructed in a yard located on the South Bay. Captain Judah Paddock, remembered for his adventures on the Barbary Coast, had begun a freighting business between New York City and Hudson. When Paddock died in 1823, the business was taken over by John Power,

Advertisement in the (Hudson) *Northern Whig* newspaper,
August 18, 1821.

who was well experienced in river traffic. It eventually became the Hudson Tow-Boat Company, organized in 1830.[7]

Passenger and freight sloops were still busy between Hudson and New York City. During the 1820s at least five sloops advertised for passengers and freight. The sloops *Telegraph* and *Thrasher* were running alternatively every week on Saturdays.

The sloop *John Hancock*, which boasted superior accommodations for passengers, sailed alternatively on Thursdays, under Captain U. Coffin. The *Sultan* and the *Gen. Livingston*, "staunch and fast sailing" sloops, were owned by Judah Paddock and Company. They sailed every Saturday afternoon from "the south side of the Ferry Slip."[8]

In this time period, there was but one Hudson steamboat, called the *Bolivar*, which began the Hudson-New York run in 1825. It was not successful. Most of the successful steamboat activities of the city began after 1830.[9]

The sealing brig *Nanina* has been listed in Starbuck as a Hudson ship; however, it really belonged to the firm of Murray & Son of New York City. The reason it is mentioned here is because the major characters in the following adventure had originally been from Hudson, moving away shortly before the *Nanina* sailed. The *Nanina* became a *cause célèbre* in the Hudson newspaper, *The Bee*.

The *Nanina* weighed 232 tons, and carried the frame of a shallop (a small open boat, usually two-masted, used chiefly in shallow waters) of 20 tons, called *The Young Nanina*. The shallop was to be used to cruise among the islands in pursuit of seals. The *Nanina* left New York City harbor early in April of 1812, heading for a sealing voyage to the Falkland Islands. The captain was Charles Barnard. His father, Valentine Barnard, was a figurative captain, agreeing to go along to bring the *Nanina* home while the rest of the crew was sealing. Valentine Barnard had left Nantucket in 1773, moving near Hudson. His son, Charles, was born in Hudson in 1781. Charles moved away in 1804, with his father following in 1809. One of the three co-partners was Barzillai Pease. Pease was born in Easton, New York, in 1773. He later moved to Hudson, and then to Coxsackie.

To quote Starbuck on the *Nanina's* misadventures: "While whaling and sealing, [they] came across a British ship *Isabella*. Barnard agreed to rescue [the] crew and passengers in exchange for some of *Isabella's* cargo, but the *Nanina* and crew were infamously betrayed into the hands of the English authorities. Tidings reached the hands of the naval commands, and they were rescued." This terse account does not begin to tell the story.

The narration by Captain Charles Barnard of his ordeal in the Falkland Islands and elsewhere is one of treachery, betrayal, and suffering. (His narrative, published in 1829, was edited and re-published in 1979. The book is entitled *Marooned*, and is a great read.) While sealing in the Falkland Islands in April of 1813, Barnard came upon the British ship *Isabella*, wrecked on Eagle Island of the Falklands while on a journey from Australia to London. Stranded on the island were forty-seven women, children, and men, including some Royal Marines. The *Isabella* had been wrecked on February 13, 1813, and the captain, Higton, had dispatched a boat with seven men aboard and a three-month supply of provisions to try to reach South America and bring help. Captain Barnard offered to bring the survivors aboard his brig, the *Nanina*, and carry them to the United States. He made the mistake of informing the British that their two countries were at war.

The seas around the Falkland Islands are treacherous, and the winter was fast approaching, so Barnard decided to move the *Nanina* to a safe harbor near the *Isabella* and wait until more favorable weather arrived. Some of the islands had great quantities of wild pigs, seals, and a variety of large birds, including penguins. Barnard knew that fresh provisions would be needed for such a large number of people, so he proceeded off on a hunting expedition in a small boat with four men—one member of his crew and three Britons from the *Isabella*—as well as his dog, Cent, a great hog-killer. After slaughtering a number of hogs, they returned to the anchoring site only to find that the

Nanina was gone. Captain Barnard had left aboard the *Nanina* his father, his co-partner, and Captain Durie of the 73rd Regiment of the Royal Marines, who had been on the *Isabella*.

After navigating their small boat for days in freezing weather and angry seas, moving from island to island hoping to find the *Nanina*, the five men were exhausted and hungry. They survived on wildfowl and seal. They had one gun, but the captain wanted to save the powder for starting fires, so they killed their prey with rocks and clubs. By July, as their situation became more desperate, one of the British soldiers, Samuel Ansel, confessed that he had been part of the conspiracy to take over the *Nanina*, a plan that originated as soon as the British survivors learned that the United States and England were at war. The *Nanina* was now a British "prize."

The five men continued to move from island to island in their little boat, hoping eventually to reach the wrecked *Isabella* where they might find enough supplies to make their situation more comfortable. They killed seals to make clothes from the skins. By

unraveling the fabric from a sail, they had thread, and they were fortunate enough to have a sail needle with them. At an albatross rookery they were able to obtain a supply of eggs for food.

On the 10th of October, Captain Barnard was out hunting alone. When he returned, he found the boat, the four men, all the supplies (including his flint for making fires), and even his dog, gone. The others obviously expected Barnard to die alone on the island, but his narrative explains in detail how he went about obtaining food, building a shelter, making a club for killing seals, and finding a stone that produced sparks to replace the missing flint. He also discovered a large bed of peat, which served as fuel for heat and cooking. Captain Barnard then began to build a stone house with a fireplace and a roof made from sealskins.

After the ninth week of Barnard's solitude, the four men returned in the boat with Barnard's dog. The four had taken the boat to the wrecked *Isabella*, where they found a note stating that a search had been made for them and, as they were not found,

Return of Captain Barnard's Companions, reprinted from Charles H. Barnard, *Embracing an Account of the Seizure of his Vessel at the Falkland Islands, Etc., 1812-1816.* (Courtesy of The New Bedford Whaling Museum.)

Arrival of the ships *Asp* and *Indispensable* at New Island, rescuing Barnard and his companions, reprinted from
Charles H. Barnard, *Embracing an Account of the Seizure of his Vessel at the Falkland Islands, Etc., 1812-1816*.
(Courtesy of The New Bedford Whaling Museum.)

they were presumed dead. Barnard learned later that
the search had been perfunctory, and they were left
to their fate despite his father's pleas. Barnard also
learned that Ansel had planned his marooning and
was not to be trusted; however, the five men learned
to live together and share the work.

Finally, two British ships appeared and
anchored in a nearby harbor. The men were rescued,
but Barnard's long journey back to his home was
circuitous and filled with more adventures and dis-
comforts. His rescuing ship, the *Indispensable*, continued whaling, sailing around the Horn and into
the Pacific. Anxious to find a ship sailing to the
United States, Barnard left the whaler. Over the
next year he traveled by a variety of means and had
a long layover in Peru, a shorter stay in the
Sandwich (Hawaiian) Islands, and finally ended up
in Canton, China, where he found a vessel returning
to Rhode Island. Barnard landed at Martha's
Vineyard on October 23, 1816, after an absence of
four years and six months.

At home he learned from his father that the
Nanina had been taken over by the British as soon

as Barnard had left to go hunting. Barzillai Pease
was chosen to pilot the brig through the islands,
apparently without any reluctance on his part, leaving the impression that Pease may have been a willing member of the conspiracy to take over the
Nanina. Valentine Barnard, Pease, and the rest of
the *Nanina* crew were held prisoner by the British
on the *Nanina*, which sailed for Rio de Janeiro. On
arrival there, the minister and consul granted them
permission to leave and they sailed for America on
the ship *Bingham* of Philadelphia.

The *Nanina* eventually was sailed to London,
where in June 1814 "said ship, her Tackle, Apparel
and Furniture and the Goods, Ware and
Merchandizes ... belonging at the time of the
Capture and the Seizure thereof ..." was confiscat-
ed and condemned as a good and lawful prize.

The Bee carried a copy of the protest made on
October 5, 1813, by Valentine Barnard, Andrew
Hunter, Barzillai Pease, and Edmund Fanning to
Philip Rutter, acting commercial agent at the port of
Rio de Janeiro. The newspaper notes that "this
account is furnished us by Captain Barzillai Pease

of this city, who is one of the unfortunate sufferers, and who arrived here a few days since."

By 1821 Charles Barnard was off on another sealing voyage.[10]

Hudson's whaling business was dying. Below are the only reported whaling ships from Hudson from 1808 until 1830:

1815–17	name unknown		David Paddock, Pacific; "Full"[11]
1815–17	*General Scott*	Ship	Robert Jenkins, Pacific; 450 Bbls. Sperm. "Went sealing and whaling. Made a poor voyage because of inexperience."[12]
1817	*Diana*		Coffin, Pacific; last reported with 760 Bbls. Sperm, 140 Bbls. Whale[13]
1817	*Eliza Barker*	Ship	David Paddock, Pacific; 1,950 Bbls. Sperm, 150 Bbls. Whale. "Boarded by a Privateer and the officers and crew robbed of their clothing ... 1818."[14]
1818–19	*Harriot*	Brig	Nathan Hildreth, Brazil Banks; lost on the coast of Brazil with 800 Bbls. whale oil[15]

The Dying Whale, drawn by Francis Allyn Olmstead, reprinted from *Incidents of a Whaling Voyage*, 1839-1840, Tuttle Publishing, Boston, Massachusetts.

Though the *Essex* was a Nantucket whale ship, a mention of her story is necessary because two of those involved in the tragedy have ties to Hudson's history. Matthew Joy of Hudson was second mate on the *Essex*. The Joy family was of Nantucket Quaker stock and had moved to Hudson in 1800 when Matthew was six years old. He was a Hudson Quaker until 1817, when he returned to Nantucket to marry Nancy Slade. She was a Congregationalist, so Matthew was disowned by the Quakers for "marrying out." (Quakers are not to marry non-Quakers.) After two years of marriage, he signed aboard the *Essex*, which sailed from Nantucket on August 12, 1819. When he came aboard, it was noticed that he was of a "weakly and sickly consti-tution," which probably meant tuberculosis. There were twenty men aboard, but only eight survived the ensuing ordeal, and Matthew Joy was not one of them.

The *Essex* was rammed by a sperm whale and sank on November 20, 1820. The men took to the three whaleboats, the captain, first mate, and second mate each in charge of a boat. In the three months that followed, the boats traveled 4,500 miles. The men were starving, thirsty, and exposed to sun and storms.[16] Joy's health rapidly deteriorated, and on January 10, 1821, he died. They "sewed him up in his clothes, tied a large stone to his feet, and, having brought all the boats to, consigned him in a solemn manner to the ocean."[17]

Three of the crew were rescued from a desolate Pacific island in April of 1821. First Mate Owen Chase, boatsteerer Benjamin Lawrence, and cabin boy Thomas Nickerson were picked up by the London brig *Indian* on February 18, 1821. Captain Pollard and sailor Charles Ramsdell were rescued by the Nantucket whale ship *Dauphin* on February 23, 1821. From the stories told by the survivors, the men in the boats endured unbelievable misery, starvation, and finally cannibalism. (For the full account, read Nathaniel Philbrick's *In the Heart of the Sea, the Tragedy of the Whaleship Essex*.)

At the time of this tragic event, Nantucket was sending seventy whale ships to sea.

First Mate Owen Chase soon married Matthew Joy's widow, Nancy Slade Joy. Boatsteerer Benjamin Lawrence, another survivor, will enter Hudson's history in 1832 as the captain of the Hudson whale ship *Huron*.[18]

Trials, Tribulations, and Catastrophes 1830–1850

Booms and Busts

This history of early Hudson has reached its last chapter, the years 1830–1850. In a spasm of activity, the city attempted to take control of its future, but events—some self-made, others beyond its control—contrived to drive a once-flourishing city into mediocrity. The strange return to whaling, and the building of the Hudson Berkshire Railroad

Southeastern view of the City of Hudson, New York, from Academy or Prospect Hill.
Engraving by Barber & Howe, *Historical Collections of New York*, 1841.
The principal street of Hudson, one mile in length, occupies the central part of the engraving.

107

consumed the city. At the same time, the historic sections of the city that played such an important role in its early success were being erased, as if to block out forever those past days. Two great fires, two disfiguring railroad lines, and the loss of over 15,000 acres of land transformed Hudson into a different city, with a different future.

Improvements to the city proper were the subject of interest as the financial situation improved slightly. Sidewalks had been of wood, stone, or nonexistent. In 1830 an effort was made to have uniform walks, but that would take a long time. Storm sewers were laid down in two parts of the city, alleviating some of the runoff that carried filth to other neighborhoods. Two years earlier, some fifty posts and lamps were erected "at the most convenient places" to provide some street lighting.[1]

In 1830 a city newspaper printed an article decrying the poor condition of public buildings in Hudson. The most ire was directed at the courthouse. This was the large, brick, two-storied structure built in 1786 as a city hall, and then appropriated as the county courthouse in 1805. This is the 1830 newspaper description: "A large, unsymmetri-

cal, decaying pile, from the exterior surface of which the paint has been obliterated long since, the ceilings of which are cracking, and the timbers trembling like the limbs of an ague patient ... If something is not done speedily, the trouble of demolishing it will be saved; it will come down of its own accord; the very swallows whose countless tribes have tenanted the belfry for years, are forsaking it. 'Twill make a wonderous gap in the legal profession should it fall at term time."[2]

Finally, in 1833, the county decided to build a new courthouse and jail. Hudson offered to pay $7,000 for the old court building, appropriate $3,000 toward the new building, and help defray the cost of purchasing the South Fourth Street acreage. By 1834 these proposals were adopted at what was to be a total cost of $19,000. There was tremendous opposition to the project, to the point where there was a movement to create a new county to be formed from the southern Columbia County towns and the northern towns of Dutchess County. Columbia County assemblymen were urged to join the supervisors in opposing the attempt to divide the county. The county stayed intact, and a new

The third courthouse, torn down in 1900. Photo by Frank Forshew, Hudson. Rowles collection.
There is no known image of the second courthouse, formerly on the site of the
present Presbyterian church on Fourth and Warren.

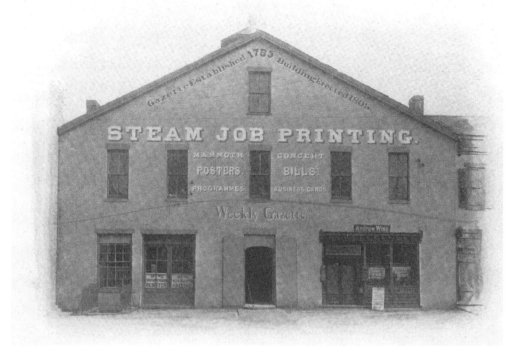

The building that was the second jail, a city hall, and finally the offices of the *Register-Star* newspaper.
Photo by Frank Forshew, c. 1860. Rowles collection.

courthouse, with a jail, was constructed. The total cost came to $26,211.51.[3] When the new courthouse and jail was completed in 1835, the old jail was remodeled for use as a city hall and municipal offices. It remained the city hall until 1855, when a new hall was constructed (today's Opera House).[4]

The county also bought a farm and buildings in Ghent to use as an almshouse and poor farm. That

This building began as an almshouse in 1818, then became a private insane asylum in 1830, a female academy, a private residence, an orphan asylum, and is now the Hudson Library. This 1900 postcard shows the building as an orphan asylum, known then as the Children's Home of Columbia County.

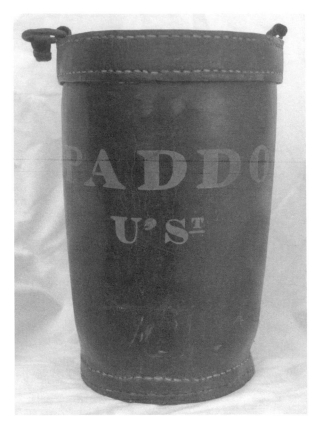

Leather fire bucket inscribed "M. Paddock, U' St."
(Union Street). Photo by Robert Ragaini.

house" until 1830. Dr. Samuel White then occupied it and ran it as a private insane asylum. In 1841 an advertisement stated that "during the first ten years of its existence about three hundred patients were admitted, most of whom left cured." The opening of an asylum in Ithaca spelled its doom. A few years after, it was a female academy, and then the private residence of George H. Power. Mrs. Robert McKinstry was instrumental in forming the Hudson Orphan and Relief Association in 1843. There were two previous buildings for the purpose of housing orphans before the board purchased the Power building and converted it into an orphanage in 1879. It is now the Hudson Area Library.[6]

When the bookstore and office of the *Hudson Gazette* was destroyed by fire in 1793, Hudsonians had no fire equipment or firefighting organization. Aware that a disaster could occur, plans were made to purchase a "fire engine." Meanwhile, hearths and chimneys were inspected every two weeks. Leather buckets marked with the owner's initials were to be at hand by the front doors. Houses having three or more fireplaces were to have two buckets. These buckets, filled with water, were passed hand-to-hand to empty on the fire. They were then passed

total was $15,000.[5] In Hudson, the stone "Alms House" was built in 1818 and remained as a "poor

Drawing of the fire of 1838, by William H. Clark. (Courtesy of FASNY Museum of Firefighting, Hudson, New York.)

back to be refilled. A four-pump-section action engine of 180-gallon capacity was purchased. It could throw water 300 feet. Soon, two engines and two fire companies followed. Buckets were still used, this time to fill the fire engines. A man was appointed to ring the bell on the Presbyterian church if there were a fire. Hooks, chains, poles, ropes, and six fire ladders were added in 1799. A third fire company was organized in 1802, with

another engine. There was still the problem of buildings to house the engines, a problem that persists today.[7]

In 1825 a fire began in Cherry Alley and, with a southerly wind, crossed Warren Street and almost reached Diamond Street. First Street was laid out in the ruins. There were five fire engines in use in the city in 1825: four were small, but the fifth, a homemade original, weighed 4,000 pounds.[8]

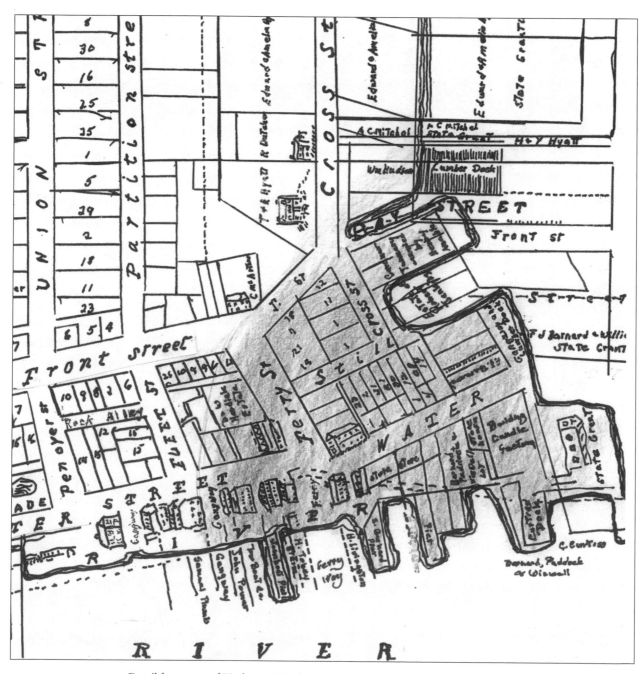

Detail from map of Hudson, 1839, showing the area destroyed by the fire of 1844.
(Courtesy of the Office of the Columbia County Clerk, Hudson, New York.)

The old Academy building (burned down) on a hilltop
near the western boundary of the cemetery. Postcard, 1907.

At about 5:00 PM on August 7, 1838, a spark from the smokestack of the steamboat *Congress* set the Plumb storehouse on fire. A strong northwest wind spread the fire, consuming seventy houses, in addition to stores and other buildings, and left 100 families homeless. The square bounded by Water, Front, Fleet, and Ferry streets was in ruins. The square surrounded by Ferry, Front, Still, and the South Bay, plus all the buildings between Cross Street and the bay and the lumber yards, also were consumed by the flames. The square bounded by Front, Second, Partition, and Cross streets (except for three houses) was destroyed. Franklin Square, a public park, was laid out on the vacant ground. The loss came to over $150,000, on which there was insurance amounting to just $50,000.[9]

On June 28, 1844, a second great fire took place in Hudson, in very nearly the same area that had been destroyed in the 1838 fire. About 5:00 PM, flames were discovered that seemed to have come from the steamboat *Fairfield* docked nearby. Destroyed were two lumber yards, an oil factory, a warehouse filled with wood, the old still house, which contained a large amount of hay, and about thirty other buildings in the area of Franklin, Ferry,

and Water streets. Also ruined were three wharves and a vessel filled with flour. The loss was estimated to be about $175,000, on which there was insurance of $65,000.[10]

The common school system was established in Hudson in 1841. The building of schoolhouses (and outhouses) was required, and three brick buildings were constructed, one for each of the three school districts in the city.[11] Private educational institutions had been in Hudson for years. These included the Hudson Academy, the Misses Peake's Hudson Young Ladies' Seminary, the Hudson Female Academy, the Lancaster Society and School, and the Hudson Select Academy. The latter was known as the "Shad Academy" from the efforts to have a tax levied on Hudson River fishing near the city to finance the school.[12]

Waterpower from waterfalls was all but lacking in the City of Hudson. At the northwest boundary of the original city, however, the Claverack Creek makes a descent of fifty-three feet, with three successive falls. The Stottville Creek (Major Abram's Creek), formed from the joining of the Kinderhook and Claverack Creeks, was deep enough in early times to allow sloops to navigate. In 1809 Robert

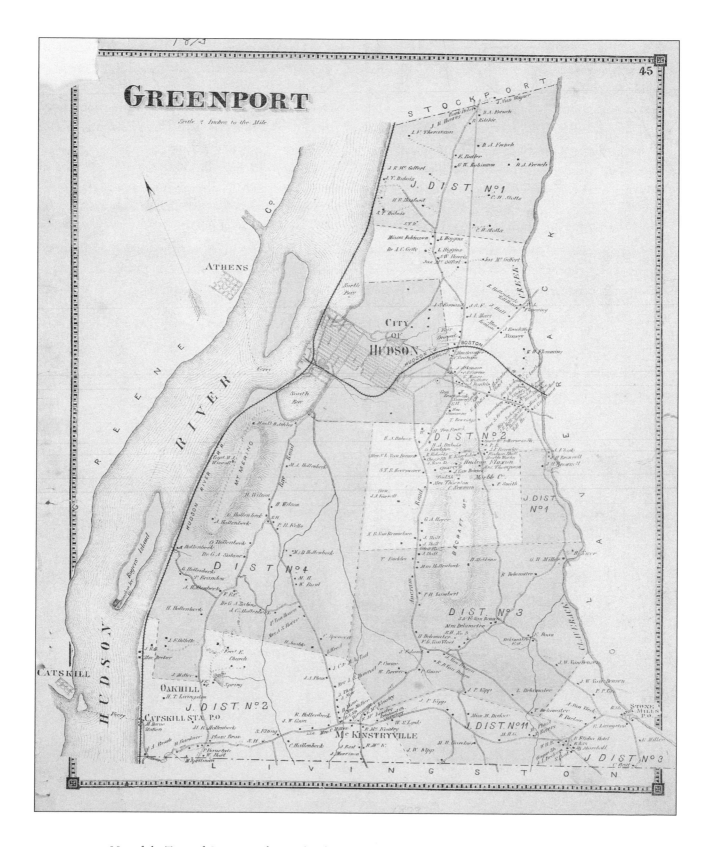

Map of the Town of Greenport, from *Atlas of Columbia County, New York*, Beers, Ellis & Co., 1878.

Jenkins, Seth Macy, and others of the Hudson entrepreneurs formed the Columbia Manufacturing Society and purchased the mill site in what is now Columbiaville for producing cotton goods. Workers' homes and more mills led to a thriving village. The Columbia Manufacturing Society was "peculiarly empowered," having all the powers and functions usually accorded an incorporated village. These powers continued even after the society disbanded in 1824. The financial prosperity of the whole area, which included many busy mills surrounded by housing and businesses related to the workers' needs, led to the decision to form this section into a separate town. In April of 1833 the Town of Stockport was officially set off from the City of Hudson and parts of the towns of Stuyvesant and

Ghent. This left Hudson with a great loss of not only its tax base, but its only real site for water-powered manufacturing.[13]

In May of 1837, after "some serious discussion," the Town of Greenport was formed out of all the area surrounding the present City of Hudson. Spreading from the river and the Livingston line on the south, circling the city with the Claverack Creek as the eastern boundary, and ending on the north at the Stockport line, the new town had a total of 12,224 acres. It left Hudson with 1,600 acres, about 2.5 square miles. Basically the new Town of Greenport signaled the end of growth for Hudson.

The reason given for the separation from the city was taxes. Residents living outside of the compact part of the city objected to paying taxes for the

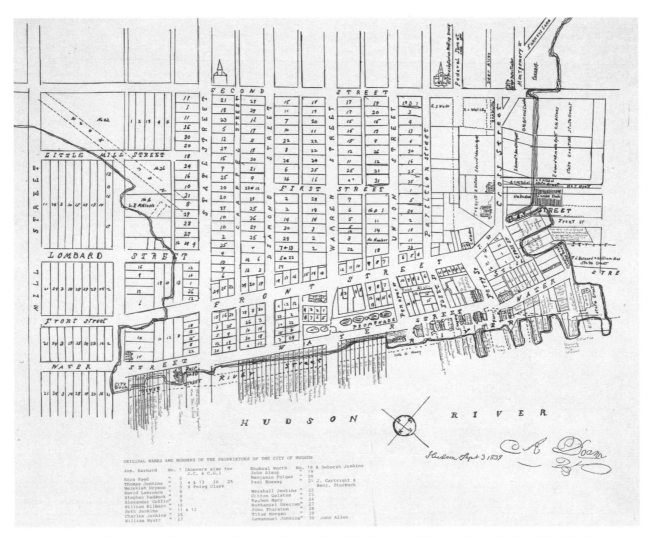

Map of the City of Hudson, 1839. (Courtesy of the Office of the Columbia County Clerk, Hudson, New York.)
Map Book 1, page 69.

View of Hudson and the Catskill Mountains, W.H. Bartlett, c.1840.

upkeep and improvements (streets, lighting, water, etc.) necessary in the city. Since Hudson officials did not mount a campaign to ward off this legislative authorization, it is possible that the city was happy to be rid of the expense of maintaining this outside area. With the exception of the turnpikes, the city was responsible for a myriad of country roads, plus schooling and safety. The year 1837 was a financially precarious one, and both Hudson and Greenport were relieved by the "divorce." Greenport residents claimed a great reduction in taxes. Hudson, in retrospect, would have fared better had it not given up quite so much land.[14]

As if to make up for the loss of land from the formations of the two towns of Greenport and Stockport, the city was busy reclaiming the marshy land of the North and South bays. In the 1839 map of the city, a multitude of state grants cover the northern shore of the South Bay. Extending from the shoreline into the bay, these grants allowed the

grantee to fill the property for his use. Along the North Bay's southern shore, streets and building lots were already established. Eventually, as riverside dockage was no longer needed, the space between the wharves was filled in, extending the surface ground by many feet into the Hudson River. What is seen today in these areas is a far cry from the landscape of the original city.

In December of 1835, the Hudson Aqueduct Company petitioned the legislature to raise funds to replace with metal pipes the wood pipes bringing water into and through the city. This was roundly opposed by the citizens (who would have to pay the extra amount), because new wooden pipes had been laid not too long before. The measure finally passed in 1841.[15]

The beginnings of antislavery sentiment started in Hudson in 1835, when attempts to hold a rally were unsuccessful. In April of 1838, a large meeting was held at the Baptist church in Hudson,

View of Warren Street showing the Worth Hotel (demolished). Postcard, 1906.

addressed by several speakers of the Anti-slavery Society. The meeting was headed by Alexander Coffin, then ninety-eight years old. It never influenced votes in the county. The highest number of votes cast locally for an antislavery candidate was less than the number of the original officers of the local society, which does not speak well for their commitment.[16]

News came to the city faster in 1846 when the telegraph wires reached the local newspaper office.[17]

The Hudson River Bank was organized in 1830 with Oliver Wiswall as president. (This bank is not to be confused with the current Hudson River Bank and Trust Company, which began as the Hudson Savings Bank in 1850.) The Farmer's Bank began in 1835 with Elihu Gifford as president.[18]

Other businesses sprang up in Hudson during these years, grew, developed, and changed with the times or stumbled and fell by the wayside. The first hotel of importance was built in 1839 by a stock company. It had a variety of names and owners in its early years: Boutwell's Tavern, Bryant's, Columbia, and Begley's Hotel. It was given the name Worth House in 1858 when it was bought by Cornelius H. Miller. The three-story, eighty-foot-by-forty-foot building was a "stage house" where steamboat travelers would catch a stagecoach for travel to inland sites, such as Lebanon Springs. This hotel would not be mentioned here except for a

comment in Miller's *Sketches of Hudson*, published in 1862. In his comments on the reasons for Hudson's decline, he states that Hudson suffered "not so much from the lack of enterprise, as from unsuccessful enterprise." As examples, he mentions the Hudson and Berkshire Railroad, the whale fishery, and the erection of the Hudson House. The hotel did not get off to a successful start.[19]

The rope works in Hudson had changed hands several times. In 1836 the firm was owned by Folger and Coleman. A newspaper article printed the following: "Railroad ropes are manufactured in this place by Messrs. Folger and Coleman. It is the only establishment of the kind in the country. More than one hundred and fifty tons are turned out annually. The ropes are often one and one half miles in length; more than two hundred men would be able to carry. Ten miles of these ropes are used on the Portage Railroad, in Pennsylvania, per annum." In order to make such gigantic ropes, the walk had been extended to 750 feet. The Portage Railroad referred to was a series of inclined planes with cable cars, designed to carry canal boats up and over a section of the Allegheny Mountains. Canal boats traveled from Philadelphia by river and canal, then were hauled up one side of the incline and down the other side.[20]

In 1848 the Hudson Stove Works was established by Charles McArthur. The works came under the firm of Hunt, Holmes and Co., eventually producing 2,000 stoves a year, including ranges, cook, and parlor stoves. It was located on the site of the old distillery.[21]

A stock company was formed for the Hudson Iron Company, constructed on the edge of the South Bay. The buildings covered two acres of land, and the debris and cinders from this company filled in ten or twelve more acres of the bay. The iron came from the ore bed in West Stockbridge, which the company purchased. The Hudson and Berkshire Railroad carried the ore to the site. When the ore ran out, the firm shut down and the buildings were torn down.[22]

When the news came over the wires that gold had been discovered in California, a great many young Hudsonians were ready to try a new occupation (if it can be called that). A stock company was formed by fifty men who would each invest $500 for transportation and other expenses. By December of that year, the first group had left Hudson for the long voyage around Cape Horn by ship to California. They sailed from New York City on January 13, 1849. A second group left in February.[23]

One final business begun in these years, organized as a stock company in 1850, is significant today because there is a cleanup commencing of the material left behind. The Hudson Gas Company began with capital of $50,000. Located on Water Street, the gasworks was planned to serve the needs of a population of 15,000. By distilling coal, a superior illuminating gas was produced. (It was also very combustible.) At the time, citizens were delighted to have such a convenience piped into their homes, but the resulting coal tar left after the process now has to be removed from the soil.[24]

Railroad Frenzy

They call the 1830s the time of railroad agitation. It would be more accurate to call it a frenzy. This infancy period of American railroads was fraught with missteps. Ingenuity and time solved the problems, but not before a great deal of money was lost. Tracks and steam engines were constantly being improved as loads became heavier. The first wooden tracks were topped with an iron bar or strap. The ends of these had a tendency to come

The Hudson Iron Works, with Athens in the background, reprinted from Benson J. Lossing, *The Hudson: From the Wilderness to the Sea*, 1866.

The First Railroad Train on the Mohawk and Hudson Road, oil on canvas, 1892-1893, by Edward Lamson Henry (1841-1919)
(Courtesy of Albany Institute of History & Art: Gift of the Friends of the Institute
through Catherine Gansevoort [Mrs. Abraham] Lansing.)

loose and curl up under weight. That the loose end might crash up through the floor of a passenger car did not add to the appeal of railroad travel.[1]

The T rail, made entirely of iron and required in New York State after 1847, solved the problem but proved to be too expensive for most fledgling companies.[2] Piles were considered the most economical base, particularly over uneven ground, and always over marsh and water. These, too, had to be abandoned, as did the granite blocks that replaced them. Wooden sleepers in gravel, with rails placed on logs or beams, with cross ties, were the most successful in the 1840s.[3]

The British track gauge of four feet eight inches was carried over into the United States, but the Americans began experimenting with their own railroad engines and different track widths. Soon the disparity in track widths made consolidation of different lines impossible. Private companies, thinking to prevent other companies from using their lines, used nonstandard gauge; eventually they had to shoulder the additional expense of changing over to standard gauge. Eleven different track gauges continued in use in the northern states up until the Civil War, causing all kinds of delays when there was a need for speedy transport of supplies.[4]

The earliest steam engines for trains were never quite satisfactory. They were so weak, in fact, that teams of horses were kept in readiness for contingencies and to get through snow. The original British locomotives were too heavy for American tracks, so Americans invented and surpassed the British with increased steam pressure, better ability to hold the track on corners, and the implementation of the equalizing beam, but some problems continued. Cinders flew into the windows when the train rounded a curve. Heating consisted of a wood stove in the center of the car: sitting too close brought overheating, while sitting too far away meant never being warm. And those closest to the stove were apt to be spattered with tobacco spit, aimed at or bouncing off the stove. Of all the vices catalogued by foreign visitors to America, the masculine insistence on chewing tobacco and spitting was the most prevalent and the most repulsive.[5] This uniquely American perversion was not limited to railroad cars. "Floors, rugs, streets were covered with expectorations."[6]

As early as 1826 there was talk of a railroad from the Hudson River to Boston. The Massachusetts Legislature voted $11,000 to survey such a route from "near Albany" to Boston.[7] After some enthusiastic meetings of interested residents, a route from Hudson to Stockbridge, Massachusetts, was bandied about. Both states deliberated. New York considered two routes: one from Troy to the Massachusetts line; and another of two branches, leaving from Albany and Hudson, respectively, meeting in Chatham, and then continuing on to the Massachusetts line via West Stockbridge, and from there eastward to Boston.

The middle and southern Berkshire citizens were resolved not to wait for the final decision on the route. Fearing much lost time as the route and the construction of the railroad was bickered over in meetings, these southern Massachusetts residents felt that "a short and inexpensive line" might be

Oliver Wiswall (1780-1863),
mayor of Hudson, supervisor and assemblyman.
(Courtesy of the City of Hudson.)
Photo by Robert Ragaini.

built to hasten their access to Hudson River shipping. West Stockbridge was especially eager.[8] The marble quarries of Stockbridge were desperate for a short route to the river to carry their product to the rapidly building cities of the east coast. Hudson sent delegates to the interested Berkshire towns

and, combined, they petitioned the New York and Massachusetts legislatures in 1828 for permission to incorporate. New York incorporated the Hudson and Berkshire Line that same year, but Massachusetts held off until 1831.

It was in May of 1835 that subscriptions for stocks were formally opened for the Hudson and Berkshire Railroad. Some $746,550 was raised, and the company was organized with such Hudson notables on the board as Oliver Wiswall, Rufus Reed, Robert A. Barnard, James Mellen, Elihu Gifford, and Ambrose Jordan. By May of 1837, the thirty-two miles of the line were under grading. (The Western Railroad of Massachusetts, to which this line was to be connected, was not opened until four years later.)

One of the problems that doomed this line was the erratic route, the fault of the local directors who used the railroad to further their own businesses. The original plan had the line laid from the Hudson River at the North Bay, skirting the city and running directly, as much as the topography would allow, to Chatham.[9] But those directors who had businesses on the south side of the city, and Elihu Gifford, whose foundry was on Columbia Street, prevailed. The line began on the north side of the South Bay, extended eastward, cutting another hunk out of Universalist Hill (Willard Place), until reaching a point near today's Seventh Street. There it turned northward, damming two small streams near upper Union Street. This formed a body of water called, appropriately, Railroad Pond. After several curious boys fell in and drowned, it was filled in. Straight along the present Seventh Street it ran (and still runs) northward, heading for director Elihu Gifford's thriving Foundry and Machine Works.[10]

Many motorists driving through Hudson today are dismayed and annoyed when traffic is stopped to allow a train to pass pulling several railcars across upper Warren Street and Route 66. These cars are going only a few miles along the former Hudson and Berkshire Line to the Archer Daniels Midland plant in Greenport, near the site of the former Lone Star Cement plant. The cars are filled with grain to be processed into flour at the Archer Daniels Midland plant, where the tracks end. All flour leaves the plant by truck, so railroad cars heading southwest from the city are empty.[11]

Early in 1800 Ezekial Gilbert had a large "country residence" standing in the vicinity of the present St. Charles Hotel. He gave the city a portion of the land in front of his property to be used as a public park. Through this parcel came the Hudson and Berkshire Railroad on its way to the Gifford works. (In 1878 money was raised to restore the then-treeless, cobblestoned desert to a park. That must have been a year for aesthetics; Promenade Park was improved that same year.)[12]

The continuing route of the line headed east past Claverack. Centerville was so appreciative of Director James Mellen's ability to bring the railroad to their community that they changed the name of their little hamlet to Mellenville.[13] From there the line traveled north to what was then known as Chatham Four Corners. Then it meandered up toward Canaan, heading for West Stockbridge at the northeast corner of the Town of Austerlitz. The

road was open for travel to West Stockbridge on September 26, 1838.

The other fatal flaw with this railroad line was the poor construction of the tracks. Steam-powered locomotives were not considered when the tracks were laid. The plans and estimates by the engineers were "Based on animal power for moving trains—better adapted to the transportation of the endless variety of loading which a dense and industrious population requires." This type of line, using horses or oxen, was called a tramway.[14] The thin, iron track (five-eighths of an inch thick), laid on wooden stringers, was prone to curl and break. When they whipped up, they were called "snake heads."[15] Later, light steam locomotives were used for pulling, but often horses were used to help. Steam engines needed water, so the tank had to be kept filled as the water was used. There were few water tanks along the way, so passengers were enlisted to form bucket brigades from the nearest water source.

The line extended to Pittsfield, where it met the Western Railroad from Boston in October of 1841. The other branch, re-chartered as the Albany to

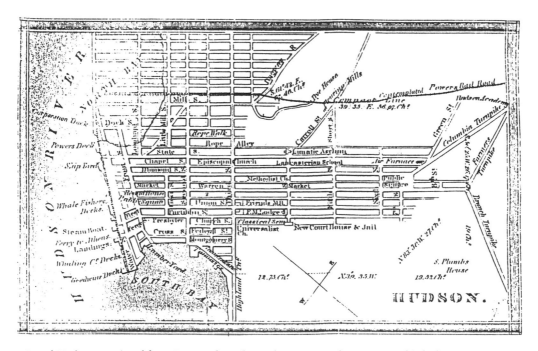

Map of Hudson, reprinted from *Letters about the Hudson River and Its Vicinity*, third edition, published by Freeman Hunt & Co., 1837. (Courtesy of Albany Institute History & Art Library: SPC 974.73, LET) Special thanks to Ruth Piwonka.

West Stockbridge in 1836, was constructed under the Western Railroad of Massachusetts. It was built with heavy iron rail (using the Hudson Berkshire as an example of what not to do). This line reached Chatham in December of 1841. They had planned to use the Hudson-Berkshire tramway eastward, but found it "too frail and dangerous," so they constructed their own line, finishing in 1842. Now, Hudson was linked to Albany and Boston.[16]

From *Columbia County at the End of the Century* comes this statement: "The Hudson and Berkshire Company did not prosper and those persons who had generously aided in building the road lost their investments." It was mortgaged by the state in 1847 on the condition that a stockholder assessment raise $50,000. This was to be used to lay T rails, which was done in 1848. The line was leased until 1854, when the state foreclosed.[17]

The value of this rail line, and of all rail lines in general, was recognized by 1854, for the rails offered a swift and inexpensive means to carry products. In

View of the upper park. The railroad tracks run across the foreground. Postcard, 1907.

the case of the Hudson and Berkshire, coal was the important and essential product. The line supplied coal from Pennsylvania, brought by barges on canal and up the river to Hudson, where it was shipped by rail to the far reaches of Columbia County and into Massachusetts. Grains and, more importantly, hay were sent from depots all over the countryside to Hudson, and then by barge to the cities where they

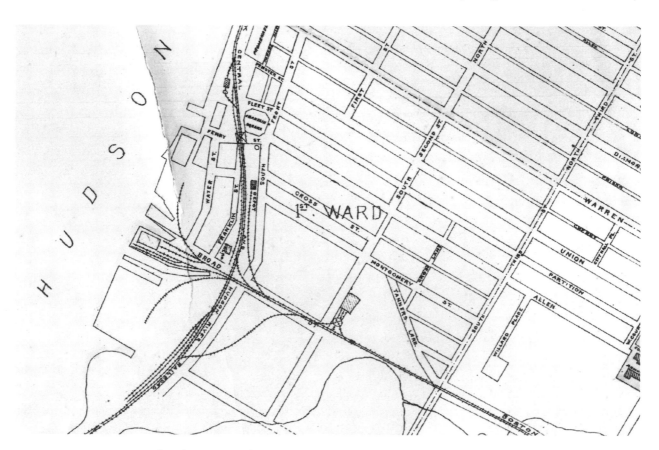

Map of Hudson, c. 1870, showing the final route of the Hudson-Berkshire Railroad.

COAL! COAL!

WILLIAM PARMENTER,

Nos. 63 & 65 Diamond Street,

Nearly opposite the Brewery,

HUDSON,

Keeps constantly on hand a general assortment of

LACKAWANA & CUMBERLAND

COAL,

of all the various sizes.

He is prepared to furnish his friends, and all who may
favor him with a call, at as

REASONABLE RATES

AS ANY OTHER YARD IN THE CITY.

Thankful for past favors, he would respectfully solicit a
share of public patronage.

☞ *Particular attention paid to Screening Coal.*

WILLIAM PARMENTER.

Hudson, Oct. 1851.

Advertisement in *Directory of the City of Hudson, 1851-52.*
Coal was the product that eventually brought
prosperity to the railroad.

were needed. (Horses, still the primary means of
transportation in those days, had to be fed.)

The Hudson and Berkshire line was bought by
the Western Railroad of Massachusetts, the present
B&A. The line's name was changed to the Hudson
and Boston, and then to the Hudson Branch of the
B&A. In 1959 permission was granted to close the
line, and the removal of the tracks began in 1960.
Today, the tracks only run as far as the ADM plant
in Greenport.

Plans had been around for years for a railroad
from New York City to Albany. In the 1830s there
was considerable agitation to have such a railroad
established as far east of the Hudson River as possible to avoid competition with the steamboat and
sloop freighting businesses. Such a route, they said,
would open the Berkshires and western counties of
Connecticut, where greater resources could be

found than on the banks of the Hudson.[18]
Understandably, the people of Hudson advocated
the river route and met with other towns on the
river to push for it. Meetings in Poughkeepsie in
1842 and in 1846 argued that the river was closed
and "hermetically sealed" during one-third of the
year, thereby justifying the need for the shore location. In February of 1848, the directors of the
Hudson River Line decided on the river route, and
stock was sold.[19] The work began in 1848, but lack
of funds and cholera among the workers slowed
construction. On January 31, 1849, the railroad was
opened to Poughkeepsie, but by then no more work
was planned, no contracts were awarded, and no
more money was available.[20]

In June of 1850, stocks and bonds were issued
and work was resumed, this time from Albany
south. In the first survey, the line was planned to
tunnel under the lower part of the City of Hudson,
with the railroad passing under Warren, Front, and
First streets. (The great rocky section that extends
from bay to bay would contain the railroad tunnel.)
The citizens opposed this idea, however, electing to
give up a great part of their valuable waterfront for
this modern convenience. The route chosen is the
one in use today.[21]

Hudsonians went into culture shock when the
workmen engaged in building the railroad arrived
on the scene. Hundreds of rough, brawling, and
unkempt (by local standards) laborers poured into

The Hudson River Railroad near Hudson, c. 1855,
from Thomas Hunt, *History of the Town of Clermont.*
Photo by Robert Ragaini.

the city. The citizens were appalled and compared it to a foreign invasion. The predominantly Irish workers filled the stores, had free-for-alls in the taverns, caroused in the streets, and generally made life miserable for the locals. The staid and decidedly prejudiced city folk conjured up imaginary threats of a Catholic takeover of their churches. As it turned out, the workers were equally unimpressed with the city, and none stayed after the work was completed.[22]

In June of 1851, the Hudson River Line opened from Albany to Hudson, where passengers then had to take steamboats to Poughkeepsie or on to New York City. Finally, in October of 1851, the line was completed all the way from Albany to New York City. As the first locomotive passed through Hudson, there was a great celebration.

Labor Unrest

The 1820s brought radical changes to the average working man in Hudson and throughout the Northeast. It was a decade of discontent among the laboring class, who began to realize the lack of equality that the new industrialism was creating. In 1826 in New York State, all white men twenty-one or older were given the right to vote without the previous restriction of property ownership. There was the hope that by using the vote, conditions would improve for the workers, who were overworked and underpaid.

Before 1800 most necessities were either home-produced or made by a craftsman that specialized in a certain product. The example used here will be shoes, because that became the root of the labor problems in Hudson, but any handcrafted item would serve as well.

A shoemaker was called a cordwainer, from the word "cordwain," a Spanish goat leather made in Cordova (a cobbler only repaired boots and shoes). Most shoes in this early period were "bespoke work"—custom-made to the client's foot. If the shoemaker became successful, he would hire

BOOTS & SHOES.
R. B. LAWTON & SON,
No. 3 South Front St., Hudson, N. Y.

Would respectfully tender their sincere thanks to their patrons and friends for past favors, and would inform them that they still continue to manufacture BOOTS & SHOES at their stand, No. 3 South Front St., next door below A. Gifford's crockery store, where they would be pleased to see all who may be in want of anything in their line.

R. B. L. & Son would take this opportunity to inform the public that the stock manufactured is domestic; the workmanship is neat and durable. NO EASTERN WORK is sold in their store. They have now and will continue to keep on hand, a large assortment of Boots and Shoes manufactured under their own inspection, that will be sold at prices, which, in view of their quality, will astonish those who inquire, more agreeably than the Hudson River Dutch were surprised at the sight of Fulton's steamboat. Let those who doubt, call and examine prices, and they will then be able to form an opinion of the truth of what we say.

R. B. LAWTON,   }   R. B. LAWTON & SON.
ALONZO LAWTON.   }

Hudson, Oct. 1851.

Advertisement in *Directory of the City of Hudson, 1851-52.*

apprentices, young men who lived with his family and learned the trade. A contract bound the apprentices to the "master" for a certain number of years, and at the end of that time, the apprentice became a journeyman, free to work anywhere.

In the new century, cordwainers were making extra shoes and boots in standard sizes and styles, called "shop work." The master cordwainer sought outside markets for the products made by his hired journeymen, thus becoming a retail merchant. Soon, master shoemakers were seeking outside workers to do piece work—anything to make production cheaper. For the skilled journeyman, lower wages became a problem as the now-retailing shoemaker, in order to be competitive, had to make his shoes for less. The transportation revolution created new markets for shoes, and journeymen found they were no longer artisans, but simply wage earners, and with decreasing wages as well.[1]

The dissatisfaction spread to other handwork trades, such as printers, carpenters, and tailors. They banded together, attempting to force their employers to improve wages and working hours. When these organized journeymen refused to work, they were hauled into court for trying to "extract great sums of money from their employers."[2] With the advent of suffrage in 1826, workingman's parties appeared, fielding or supporting political candidates. They united in supporting and re-electing Andrew Jackson as president in 1832. They advocated free education and laws for protection against defaulting employers. They condemned imprisonment for debts, licensed monopolies (such as banks), and lotteries that impoverished the poor, and sought the restriction of competition from prison labor.[3]

As part of an 1823 prison reform act, convict labor was used to finance prisons with the sale of such things as shoes, which sold for 40-60 percent less than a cordwainer's product. When cordwainers in Geneva, near the Auburn prison, tried to strike, they were found guilty of being "injurious to trade and commerce." Newspapers, writers, politicians,

included. For an extra fee the drawing of their house could be improved. The Shoemakers' Trial and their subsequent acquittal exemplified everything the businessmen abhorred. It amounted to mob rule, in their eyes.)

A general Union of Cordwainers of the United States was formed in 1836. At the same time, the working shoemakers of Hudson formed the United Society of Journeymen Cordwainers of the City of Hudson. Rates of wages were agreed upon; to work for less meant expulsion from the union or a fine. Employers not paying the rates could be fined, and no member of the society would work for them. In September of 1835, the cordwainers refused to work for Eli Mosier, Nicholas Kittle, George Algar, and

John W. Edmonds (1799-1874), judge and justice of the New York Supreme Court. From Peyton F. Miller, *A Group of Great Lawyers of Columbia County*, 1904. Edmonds espoused spiritualism in later years.

Ambrose L. Jordan (1788-1865), assemblyman and attorney general famous as a superb orator. From Peyton F. Miller, *A Group of Great Lawyers of Columbia County*, 1904.

judges, and clergymen cried that the "workers' movement will destroy business,"[4] which may be why none of the local histories mention the Shoemakers' Trial in Hudson in 1836. (In the nineteenth century, reading material was expected to inspire the reader to higher goals or to emulate the lives of illustrious leaders. It was the privileged class that bought the histories, and also paid a fee to be

Solomon Shattock, who had not hired union workers and paid less than regular wages. Mosier complained, and eight journeymen cordwainers were indicted under a statute for combining "to raise their wages, etc. to the great injury of trade and commerce."[5] With the common-law precedent set in the Geneva trial, it appeared that the Hudson shoemakers were to be sacrificial lambs to the labor movement. The trial began in June 1836 at the

Court of General Sessions in the new courthouse in Hudson.

The prosecution (District Attorney J. Sutherland and Henry Hogeboom) claimed that labor societies "restrain the free circulation of wealth throughout the county, and should be put down before it spreads throughout the nation." The defense (John W. Edmonds, assisted by Ambrose L. Jordan) noted that Mosier's lowering of wages in winter caused hardships for the workers and that he had conspired with other bosses to lower wages. Both sides produced witnesses, and then Edmonds summarized for the shoemakers. He claimed that the Supreme Court had erred in the case in Geneva and told the jury that they, the jury, were the judges of what was to be the law. In the summary by the district attorney, Sutherland expressed shock at such an insult to the highest tribunal in the land and repeated the charge that the defendants were guilty of actions injurious to the interests of trade and commerce.

Judge Wilcoxson in his charge to the jury reviewed the statute of the Geneva verdict, but admitted that if the jury found the statute to be wrong, they had the right to set aside the decision. He added that if the Hudson journeymen were found to have the right to combine, then journeymen throughout the country could control the labor of every mechanical industry. If so, would this injure trade?[6]

The jury was out but twenty minutes and then dispersed, arriving back at court the next morning. The verdict was read: "The jurors find the prisoners not guilty."[7] This decision sent a shock wave through the business community, not only in Hudson, but throughout the Northeast. In Philadelphia a jury found plasterers not guilty, also in 1836. The joy was short-lived, however. The Panics of 1837 and 1839, followed by a deep depression, marked the end of the early labor movement.

It must be pointed out that this movement was not composed of common laborers or factory workers, who would later predominate in union activities. These were the artisans whose markets were changing and would continue to worsen as the factory system became prevalent. The belief that voting rights would lead to an equality in standards of living was quickly dispelled, but in 1842, a decision by a chief justice in Massachusetts affirmed the right of workers to organize and to strike to secure the "closed shop."

A Feudal System Collapses

"Looking back at all the military preparation, it is often remarked that it was wholly unnecessary. It may have been so. It is difficult to tell what length of outrage the misguided tenants, calling themselves Indians, under the lead of wicked men, might not have gone, had not the force been arrayed against them." (Stephen Miller, *Sketches of Hudson*, 1862)[1]

Providing enormous tracts of land to a few individuals was an inducement to colonization in the early Dutch history of the Hudson Valley. The landowner, the *patroon*, had to promise to settle farms on his property at a time when few settlers had any desire to move to the wild, dangerous wilderness. The bait for the tenant was a large farm with some livestock. The downside was that the tenant could never own the property. The rent was minuscule—some grain, a day of labor, etc.—but the tasks of clearing and improving the farm without the possibility of ever having complete ownership became an irritant.

Disagreements concerning the boundaries of Massachusetts and Connecticut with New York started the first troubles between landlords and tenants, which became known as the Anti-Rent Wars. Both the Livingston and Van Rensselaer patroonships saw outbreaks of conflict. Victory in the American Revolution, with its promise of freedom, fanned the agitation, leading in 1791 to the shooting of the sheriff of the district, Cornelius Hogeboom. Hogeboom had ridden to Nobletown (Hillsdale) to auction off a farm that was in arrears on rent. A mob, dressed as Indians and in calico, converged on the scene, and in the melee the sheriff was shot and

ATTENTION!
ANTI-RENTERS!
AWAKE! AROUSE!

A Meeting of the friends of Equal Rights will
be held on *[handwritten] Second Tuesday - February at Court House*

in the Town of *[handwritten] Hudson —* at / O'clock.

Let the opponents of **Patroonry** rally in their strength. A great
crisis is approaching. Now is the time to strike. The minions of Patroonry are at
work. No time is to be lost. Awake! Arouse! and

Strike 'till the last armed foe expires,
Strike for your altars and your fires—
Strike for the green graves of your sires,
God and your happy homes!

☛ **The Meeting will be addressed by PETER
FINKLE and other Speakers.**

Broadside: a call to an anti-rent meeting, c. 1840. (Courtesy of the New York State Library.)

killed. The murderer was never found, and the other conspirators were tried and acquitted.

Extreme anti-rent activity next occurred in Albany and Rensselaer counties, and then spread back to Columbia County. In 1844 a group of tenants met in Taghkanic and formed the Taghkanic Mutual Association. Its members pledged not to pay rent or purchase any land without the consent of the majority of members. There were also groups of tenants called "Indians" under the direction of "Big Thunder" (Smith Boughton) and "Little Thunder" (Mortimore Belding), both of Rensselaer.

The duty of the "Indians" was to prevent law officials from serving processes for sales of property in arrears of rent. The "Indians" wore calico, with feathers and animal skins attached. They were summoned to meet by the blowing of the tin horns used to call workers for meals. Tar and feathers threatened any that opposed their views.[2]

A group of 300 "Indians" prevented Sheriff Henry Miller from serving papers in Copake in December of 1844. He was taken to a tavern, relieved of his papers, which were burned in front of him, and then he was sent on his way. This event caused quite a stir in Hudson.[3] "Big Thunder" next announced a meeting of the Van Rensselaer tenants to be held in Smoky Hollow (Hollowville) on December 18. A massive crowd gathered, and during the activities a young man by the name of W. H. Rifenburgh was shot and killed.[4] When the news reached Hudson, the sheriff and others hurried to Smoky Hollow, arrested "Big Thunder" and "Little Thunder," and brought them back to jail in Hudson. Threats immediately reached the city that an armed invasion would be launched to rescue the prisoners. Panic reigned in Hudson. Mayor Cyrus Curtiss added to the fears by stating "no policy of insurance will cover losses by fire when caused by invasion, insurrection, or civil commotion."[5] As rumors of thousands of "Indians" gathering in the outskirts of the city spread terror, a militia composed of the Hudson Light Guard and volunteers, plus four pieces of artillery were set in readiness. Mayor Curtis asked Governor Bouch for troops to defend the city. Five hundred rifles and proper ammunition were sent from Albany, and a battalion of 500 men formed the Law and Order Association to assist.

On Christmas Day the Albany Burgesses arrived, followed by the Emmet Corps, Van Rensselaer Guards, Washington Riflemen, Albany Republican Artillery, and also a German company of cavalry from New York City. All these men were quartered in private and public houses in the city, and the overflow had to quarter in the ships wintering at the docks (this in the dead of winter). Hudson was an armed camp for nearly a month.[6] Occasionally troops were called out to make an arrest in the countryside. The city went from being under siege to being an exciting festival of flashy uniforms and flirting females. Balls were given for the officers, and city notables entertained at their homes.[7] Finally the troops returned to their own homes, leaving behind quite a few unhappy women (particularly the ladies of the "Block"). Hudson's men were relieved to see them go because they thought the troops arrogant and condescending. The bill for the military assistance came to $24,000.

John Van Buren (1810-1866), attorney general and son of Martin Van Buren. From Peyton F. Miller, *A Group of Great Lawyers of Columbia County*, 1904. Critics called him "Prince John."

All this time Hudson had been suffering from a blockade by the anti-renters, who allowed no food to enter the city, nor any newspaper not in sympathy with their cause. Fortunately, supplies still could be brought in by water.

In March of 1845, Boughton was brought to trial for robbing Sheriff Miller of his papers. The city filled with anti-renters. The citizens were sure that if a guilty verdict came in, there would be a riot. Very little is written about this first trial, other than the difficulty of finding enough impartial persons to make up a jury. Quite possibly the outcome—the jury could not agree on a verdict—was so repugnant to the writers of the time that they chose not to dwell upon it. Boughton was to be retried, and the judge promised freedom on bail, but neglected to make the arrangements. Finally, Boughton was released in July. Anti-rent sentiment had grown even more bitter. Murder, insurrection, and the need for armed troops caused Columbia County authorities to recall Smith Boughton to stand trial again in September.

Smith Boughton went to trial in September of 1845 with all the cards stacked against him. The judge, John W. Edmonds, who had defended the shoemakers in 1836 and had pleaded so eloquently for the rights of the common man, now had a debt to pay for his February appointment as judge of the first circuit. John Van Buren, the prosecutor and newly appointed state attorney general, needed a conviction to assure his political future. Edmonds ruled that every man from the anti-rent areas was to be excluded from the jury—to protect them from reprisals was the excuse. Theodore Miller joined John Van Buren as an attorney for the prosecution, and Ambrose Jordan and James Storm were the attorneys for the defense.[8]

Feelings ran high between John Van Buren and Ambrose Jordan from the beginning. Judge Edmonds would later write that he found the senior defense counsel arrogant, disrespectful, and assuming, and so did "Prince John" Van Buren. On the third day of the trial, angry words erupted between Jordan and Van Buren, with Jordan stating the following of Van Buren: "Though his father had brains to temper his wild ambition to some degree, the son has none to temper his, and it breaks out everywhere in puerility and slush." Van Buren retorted that "it is quite out of place for a man who stands here in this court with the contributions of murder and arson in his pockets to criticize me for any cause whatever." "A dark, withering frown mounted the menacing features of Jordan," according to *The Bench and Bar*. "His nostrils expanded; vivid gleams of anger flashed from his large, expressive eyes, and in the twinkling of an eye he planted a heavy blow upon the face of Van Buren. It was returned with the rapidity of lightning and with staggering effect; thence grappling with each other, a terrible struggle ensued." The sheriff rushed to separate the two. Judge Edmonds ordered them to their seats and had the sheriff take them into custody. He remanded them to jail for twenty-four hours. Van Buren apologized and pleaded to pay a fine rather than go to jail. The judge insisted imprisonment was necessary "as an example to others." Jordan suggest-

ed that they be confined in the same room so they could fight it out. The judge ignored that idea, and the district attorney spent his imprisonment in the judge's parlor, while Jordan served his in the office of the sheriff. One history has them both actually in jail, but that must be doubted. They were, however, confined to the limits of the courthouse.[9]

Van Buren sent his resignation as attorney general to the governor, but it was refused and he and his family remained good friends of Edmonds. (After the trial, Jordan and his family refused ever to see or speak with Edmonds again. In fact, the judge was refused permission to attend Jordan's funeral. "It would be deemed an insult," the family said.)

It took a long time to seat a jury. The trial hinged on identifying Boughton as the man who took the sheriff's papers. The summations were long and wordy. The judge's charge to the jury was far from impartial. It included telling the jury that the tenants should expect no relief "until the base and guilty were denounced and punished." He said that the farmers should not expect laws impairing the obligations of contracts, and his parting shot was to

Samuel J. Tilden (1814-1886), New Lebanon, Columbia County, native best known for losing the disputed presidential election of 1876. Tilden was instrumental in breaking Boss Tweed's Tammany Hall ring. This portrait c. 1845 is from Peyton F. Miller, *A Group of Great Lawyers of Columbia County*, 1904.

advise the jury that circumstantial evidence was often more reliable than positive evidence. The jury disagreed for some time, but the judge demanded that they come to a verdict. The next morning that verdict was announced—guilty.

A crowd of 5,000 people filled the courthouse and the courthouse park to hear Judge Edmonds read the sentence. Among other things, he charged Boughton with high treason, rebellion against the government, and insurrection against the supremacy of the law. "As a warning to others, the sentence of the Court is that you be confined in the State prison in the county of Clinton, at hard labor, for the term of your natural life."[10]

Soon anti-rent sympathy increased and political parties courted the votes of the farmers. In the election of 1845, an anti-rent Whig majority was elected by more than 7,000 votes, the call for a state constitution carried, and the anti-renters elected fourteen legislators.

A committee, headed by Samuel Tilden of New Lebanon, recommended taxing the landlords, limiting all agricultural leases to ten years, and transferring the lands to the tenants on equitable terms at the death of the landlord.

The landlords fought valiantly. On May 13 both houses of the New York State Legislature voted to tax the landlord on income from long-term leases and outlawed the seizure and forced sale of tenant property for non-payment of rent, but despite a new statute prohibiting agricultural leases of more than ten years, and restraints (the quarter sale) on the sale of property, *all existing leases remained unchanged.*[11]

John Young, the anti-rent candidate, won the governorship by a majority of votes over the incumbent Silas Wright. Young pardoned all the jailed anti-renters in 1847, including "Big Thunder," Dr. Smith A. Boughton. Boughton returned to his home in Alps in the Helderberg

The birthplace of William Jenkins Worth, Union Street, Hudson. Photo by Robert Ragaini.

Landing of the American Forces at Vera Cruz, Mexico, March 1847.
(Courtesy of the Franklin D. Roosevelt Presidential Library.)

Mountains of Rensselaer County, where he resumed his medical practice. He retired in 1880, declaring he would "settle down to domestic tranquility so acceptable in old age," and died in 1888 at age seventy-eight.[12]

At the Claverack Lower Manor, many of the farms had already been sold to the occupying tenants by John Van Rensselaer. Van Rensselaer sold the remainder to Daniel Penfield, who then sold to John Watts. At Watts' death, most lands passed to John Watts De Peyster of Tivoli, who referred to himself as the last lord of the manor. (It was he who gave the statue of St. Winifred in the Promenade Park to the City of Hudson.) The anti-rent dispute simply petered out. Some farmers were still paying rent well into the 1920s, but most obligations had been cleared legally. The annual rent of grain, fowl, and a day's work may still exist in the deeds of some farms that have never been sold.

From Shore to Shore

William Jenkins Worth rode back to his birthplace of Hudson in 1844 to receive a sword from the grateful citizens of the city. He had moved up in rank in the military, distinguished himself in the Niagara and Florida wars, and been appointed superintendent of the Military Academy at West Point.[1]

Later, during the early skirmishes prior to war with Mexico, Worth served under Zachary Taylor, but lost command of his division when outranked by another general. Worth, in a huff, left the army, tendered his resignation in Washington, but allowed that if there was a war, he might return. There was, and he did. He led his troops well, fought valiantly, and became an American hero.[2]

What sets the Mexican War apart from other conflicts was the behavior of the American com-

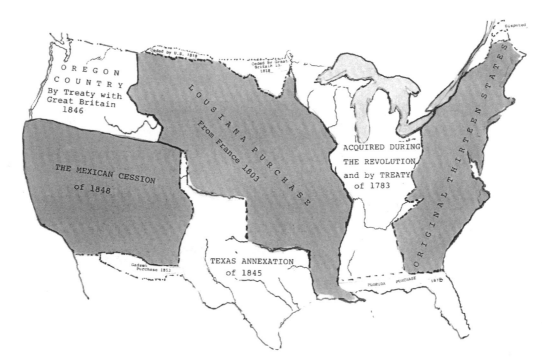

How the nation grew. Map of the United States, 1854.

manding officers. The infighting among the generals was as fierce as the actual combat, resembling a Gilbert and Sullivan operetta. Worth's resignation in a fit of pique is just one example. Incessant jockeying for position, incriminating letters to Washington, and prima donna behavior plagued the leadership. At the end of the war, a group of generals, Worth included, traveled to Washington to blame each other for failures. They threatened courts of inquiry, even courts-martial.[3]

Worth died of cholera on May 7, 1849, at San Antonio. He is buried, not in Hudson, but under a large granite obelisk in the middle of Broadway and Fifth Avenue at 25th Street in Manhattan. Fort Worth, Texas, and Lake Worth, Florida, are named for him. In November of 1849, the Worth Volunteers (a military organization) and the Common Council traveled to New York City for General Worth's funeral.

The war with Mexico is not a large part of the story of Hudson, but its outcome had huge implications for the future of the country. The 1848 treaty that ended the conflict established the Rio Grande as the southern boundary of Texas, whose

territory included most of Colorado, all of Utah, Nevada, New Mexico, Arizona, southwest Kansas, and parts of Wyoming and Oklahoma. California also was included, though most in Washington thought it without value except for its Pacific ports. Then, gold was found at Sutter's Mill in 1848.[4]

In June of 1835, the United States and Britain reached agreement on the Oregon Territory. Ceded to the United States were what are now the State of Oregon, as well as Washington, Idaho, and Montana. America had spread from shore to shore.[5]

Tragedies at Sea and on the River

Hudsonians were outraged when the news reached the city that the grandson of Hudson native Chief Justice Ambrose Spencer had been hanged in December of 1842, accused of mutiny while aboard the U.S. brig of war *Somers*. Ambrose Spencer had moved to the city in 1785 and soon became influential as one of the leading attorneys in Hudson. He

Loss of the Steamboat Swallow while sailing from Albany to New York on Monday evening, April 17, 1845.
Published by N. Currier, c. 1845. "When opposite Athens, she struck a large rock, caught fire, broke in two pieces
and sank, by which melancholy occurrence it is supposed that nearly forty lives were lost."

became state attorney general, a judge of the Supreme Court, and then chief justice. One of his six sons, John Canfield Spencer, was born in Hudson, studied law in Albany, and was admitted to the bar in 1809. He was appointed secretary of state in 1839, secretary of war in 1841, and secretary of the treasury in 1843.[1]

Eighteen-year-old Philip Spencer was the son of Secretary of War John Canfield Spencer. Philip had signed on as a midshipman aboard the *Somers*. The captain, Alexander Slidell MacKenzie, was arrogant and dictatorial, and disliked Philip immediately for "political reasons." Captain MacKenzie was told of a rumor that Spencer was plotting a mutiny with other crew members "to seize the ship for pirating the Spanish Main."[2] Three men, including Spencer, were chained and tied up in canvas bags overnight. The next morning the captain judged the men guilty of mutiny. Despite the protests of the crew, the men's heads were covered with black

hoods, ropes were tied around their necks, and they were hoisted above the deck until dead.

At first Captain MacKenzie was hailed as a hero when the story leaked to the press. Claverack native Col. J. Watson Webb wrote in the *New York Courier and Inquirer*, "The Captain's quick thinking saved the port of New York from a corsair that might have ruined the commerce." Spencer's father questioned the account, and soon public opinion changed to condemning MacKenzie's action. James Gordon Bennett of the *Herald* wrote: "Capt. MacKenzie and his officers acted under a species of insanity produced by panic and lively imagination. Theirs was human intellect run mad." MacKenzie was charged with three murders. Two noncapital charges were dropped, and he was found not guilty of murder.[3] The trial caused an uproar in the nation's capitol. Public outcry drove Congress to tighten requirements for the selection and training of naval officers. Shortly after, the United States Naval Academy was opened.[4]

The ship *Somers* became known as a haunted ship. The three condemned men were said to be seen and heard wailing in the shrouds. That ended when the *Somers* capsized and sank with all aboard in 1846.[5]

In the western channel of the river just above Athens, a small island rose above the water sprouting a few trees. Its true name was Doopers Island, but boatmen called it "Noah's Brig," after a raftsman who mistook it for a brig under sail. After shouting for the island to move, the raftsman threatened to run it down if it didn't get out of the way. It didn't, and he did. Neither boat nor island was damaged.[6]

On the night of April 7, 1845, three steamboats left Albany at 6:00 PM for a nonstop trip to New York City. The *Rochester*, the *Swallow*, and the *Express* were charging a twenty-five-cent fare for the trip—all part of the great competition that was plaguing the steamboat industry. The night was dark and heavy snow squalls buffeted the river. The *Express* left Albany before her scheduled time, fueling the rumors of a race (a dangerous sport that grew from the competition to have the fastest trip to New York City). The *Swallow*, at full speed, took the lead, followed closely by the *Rochester*, with the *Express* in the rear. Obviously racing now, the *Swallow* steamed ahead to keep its lead.

Shortly after supper, about 8:00 PM, the head pilot of the *Swallow*, William Burnett, joined Captain Squires in the pilothouse. In the swirling snow they saw ahead what looked like the spars of two sailing vessels. They steered the ship between them. The *Swallow* ran full speed onto the rocky island of "Noah's Brig," her bow driven thirty feet up onto the rocks. The boat then broke apart at the forward bulkhead and all the aft part immediately sank.

Of the 300 persons on board, some were in their cabins in the aft section. They were drowned in their bunks. The boat immediately caught fire after the collision, but the flames were extinguished as the boat sank. Passengers jumped into the frigid water, some lucky ones finding refuge on the island that caused the wreck.[7]

The church bells rang frantically in Hudson and Athens, calling for help. Small boats from both sides of the river raced to the scene, the cries for help rising from the surface of the water in every direction. The cries ceased quickly because of the intense cold water; soon they were "all hushed in death."[8] Joseph Reed, the rowboat ferryman between Hudson and Athens, was one of the first to arrive at the scene, followed by the other two steamboats in the race—the *Rochester* and the *Express*, who helped with the rescue.

A few days later, attempts were made to raise the boat, and a few bodies were recovered from their cabins. It was originally predicted that forty persons had lost their lives in the wreck, but "eight days after the said catastrophe, but thirteen bodies have been recovered."[9] On May 22 it was reported that "the body of Gen. Walker's son, who was lost on board the Swallow, drifted ashore at Athens last week." Some passengers had boarded the other two steamboats and continued their trip to New York City, which would account for confusion over the number of dead.[10]

It was claimed the inebriation of the pilot caused the accident. The *Express* subsequently banned intoxicating beverages on board, though all concerned were sure that racing was the true cause.

The rocky island, thereafter known as "Swallow Rock," was eventually dynamited out of existence. Some of the rock was used to line the channel in the flats in the river between Hudson and Athens.[11]

Hard Times

Kinderhook native Martin Van Buren was sworn in as president of the United States in March of 1837. Americans were, he stated in his inaugural address, "a great flourishing and happy people," and "we ... had achieved a level of prosperity not

Martin Van Buren (1782-1862), from Peyton F. Miller, *A Group of Great Lawyers of Columbia County*, 1904. This Kinderhook, Columbia County, native was elected president of the United States in 1836.

found elsewhere in the world."[1] In only a few short months those words would haunt him.

The financial depression that devastated the nation began in 1837 and lasted for years. The result was the end of Hudson as a large, thriving city with great plans for the future. The whaling industry would be affected by a shortage of funding, but also by a fall in whale oil prices. The oil might demand a high price when the whale ship left port, but two or three years later when the ship returned to port, the price may have dropped to such a low level that the profits were gone. This price fluctuation, the difficulty in obtaining satisfactory officers and crew, and some unfortunate voyages led to the end of Hudson's whaling in 1843 just as the depression was ending.

The 1830s had been a time of frenzied speculation. There were investments in turnpikes, canals, railroads, other assorted businesses, and land in the new western territories—all financed with state bonds or loans from banks. Andrew Jackson, the first president elected as a true representative "of the people," was admired as a frontier man, a man of action. He detested monopolies and the central-

ization of governmental power. With the counsel of his friend Martin Van Buren, he vetoed the bill to recharter the Second Bank of the United States in 1832. This brought about the "Bank Wars," when credit was curtailed. His Specie Circular in 1836, requiring land purchases be paid for in coin rather than bank notes, led to a shortage of money and the ruin of credit. Shortly after, all the banks in the nation had to close. Specie payments resumed in 1838 and business improved. Then the situation repeated itself, with the depression worsening. By 1842 many stocks had dropped by 50 percent. Agricultural and real estate prices dropped and most construction on new homes and public transportation ceased.[2] In 1843 the crisis showed signs of lessening, and in a few years the American economy began growing again, but for Hudson, the damage had been done.

The City of Hudson was on a downward slide. The last two whale ships of the fleet of twelve were sold in 1845. (see "Off to the South Seas") Ignatius Jones, in his *Recollections of Hudson* describes his thoughts on the city in 1847: "The population of the town, though greatly diminished, struck me as having undergone a still greater change in character than in numbers—what struck me still more forcibly, was the all-pervading air of listless indolence, and the Sabbath-like stillness of the place. ... Hudson was, indeed, for many years one of the most beautiful and flourishing towns on the noble river whose name it bears—but the days of its prosperity have long since passed away. Its population has decreased, its wealth diminished, its business sources have dried up, and almost every vestige of its former glory has disappeared."[3]

In 1839 Alexander Coffin died at the age of ninety-nine. He had been one of the original Proprietors and was active in city affairs all his life. He was made postmaster of Hudson in 1802, and held that position for twenty-three years.

Outside events certainly contributed to Hudson's decline, but once the intense energies of the Proprietors ceased, Hudson foundered. One early writer referred to it in 1862 as "a finished city."[4]

Off to the South Seas:
The Strange Return to Whaling
1830–1850

The Cachalot (sperm whale) is not only better armed than the true whale (Greenland, or right whale) in possessing a formidable weapon at either extremity of its body, but also more frequently displays a disposition to employ these weapons offensively, and in a manner at once so artful, bold, and mischievous, as to lead to its being regarded as the most dangerous to attack of all the known species of the whale tribe.
Frederick Debell Bennett, *Whaling Voyage Round the Globe,* 1840[1]

In 1829 the following statement came from a newly formed organization in the city of Hudson: "Why may there be no hope to rival those eastern cities which the whale fishery has built up? We possess equal advantages, equal enterprise. Under present circumstances the hope is entertained that Hudson will again flourish as in its infant days."[2] Pure hubris is the best definition for this statement. In the more than ten years since the last whaler sailed from Hudson, the whale ships were gone and the experienced masters and mates had moved to prosperous whaling ports where all the paraphernalia needed for long voyages could easily be procured, including ship gear and victuals.

Lower jawbone of a sperm whale on display on the south side of Warren Street between Fourth and Fifth streets in the second half of the nineteenth century.

ARTICLES MADE OF WHALEBONE

J. A. SEVEY,

40 Essex Street - - - Boston.

1. Whip Makers' Bone.
2. Whip Makers' Bone (Patent).
3. Parasol Makers' Bone.
4. Umbrella Makers' Bone.
5. Gross Dress Bone.
6. Samples to sell by.
7. Dress Bone in Boxes.
8. Round Dress Bone.
9. White Dress Bone.
10. Corset Makers' Bone.
11. Corset, showing Place of Bone.
12. Corset Clasps.
13. Hip Busk Bone.
14. Cap Makers' Bone.
15. Hat Makers' Bone.
16. Whalebone Hats.
17. Ribbon Weavers' Bone.
18. Suspender Makers' Bone.
19. Neck Stock Makers' Bone.
20. Bonnet Makers' Shurs.
21. Whalebone Canes.
22. Whalebone Riding Whips.
23. Whalebone Rosettes.
24. Ribbon Bone.
25. Billiard Cushion Springs.
26. Fishing Rod (New Style).
27. Fishing Rod Tips.
28. Landing Rods for Nets.
29. Divining Rods.
30. Drill Bows.
31. Ferules.
32. Busks.
33. Back Supporters.
34. Fore Arm Bones.
35. Probangs.
36. Tongue Scrapers.
37. Pen Holders.
38. Plait Raisers.
39. Paper Folder and Cutters.
40. Painters' Graining Combs.
41. Boot Shanks.
42. Shoe Horns.
43. Bone Fibre Shoe Brushes.
44. Fibre of Whalebone.
45. Fibre Curled for Beds.
46. Brush Makers' Bone.
47. Flue Brushes.
48. Caterpillar Brushes.
49. Whalebone Shavings for Beds.
50. Policeman's Clubs.
51. All Bone Whips.
52. Twisted Whip Handles.

53. Rio Corset Bone, all lengths and sizes.

Copyright, by J. A. SEVEY.

Advertisement for articles made from whalebone (baleen).
(Courtesy of the New Bedford Whaling Museum.)

More importantly, there was the problem of finding a crew of up to thirty men who were reasonably intelligent and could follow orders. The industry was suffering from the inability to sign on capable men who would tolerate the conditions and toil on a whale ship. Factories and the new western territories offered safer adventures and occupations.

It is true, however, that the demand for sperm oil had reached an all-time high. Even rural households demanded the bright spermaceti candles or the smokeless whale oil to fuel their household lamps. New, improved lamps, such as the Argand, increased the demand.[3] Whalebone (baleen) was needed in great quantities for corset stays, hoop-skirts, umbrella and parasol ribs, whips, etc. Sperm oil was indispensable for lubricating moving parts of machinery, so factories, steamboats, and rail-roads added to the demand. More and more small harbor towns were fitting out whale ships to take advantage of this demand.[4]

In 1828 Nantucket had a fleet of sixty vessels, with thirty-one leaving port in that year. In the same year New Bedford sent out forty-nine ships. These figures are important, particularly in calculating the loss to the stockholders in the case of a wrecked vessel or a poor (unprofitable) voyage. The loss of one ship, or an empty hold, though a burden, was not as severe a loss if there were forty other ships to take up the slack. When there were

few ships, or the stockholders had invested all in one ship, the loss was terrible.

So Hudson started its second phase of whaling with great enthusiasm, but with the cards stacked against success. (In looking back on the city's history, it seems that many of its misfortunes came from forging ahead too quickly without considering the pitfalls.) The Hudson Whaling Company was conceived in 1829, but was not incorporated by the state until April 30, 1833. Laban Paddock was the president, and capital was raised in the amount of $300,000. On September 10, 1833, the *Hudson Gazette* reported: "On Wednesday last the whale ship *America* left the city on her way to the Pacific on her second voyage. We cannot refrain from drawing a comparison between spirit and enterprise which now actuates all citizens and the apathy which existed 5 years ago, when it was first proposed to enter the whaling business. At that time

The South Sea Whale Fishery, "a representation of the ships *Amelia Wilson* and *Castor* off the island of Bouro with their boats and crew in the various processes of fishing, showing the manner the Spermaceti Whales are caught, the mode of cutting them into the ship and boiling the oil upon the deck." Published by W.J. Higgins, marine painter, London, 1825. Note: *lower left*, the head of a large whale in the agonies of death; *lower right*, a boat destroyed by a wounded whale.

Whaling in the Ice, by Louis Ambroise Garneray (1783-1857), c. 1845.

when the subject was mentioned no money was to be found, few men willing to embark in the business and those few unwilling to risk much. By dint of perseverance the projectors of the scheme succeeded in drawing all together and the *Alexander Mansfield*, which was considered to be unseaworthy was purchased for $2000.00. This small beginning produced an itching in others to own whale stock and ship after ship until 11 fine substantial vessels belong to this city. Now instead of the old exclaim that there is no money the difficulty is to find ships and fit them up as fast as they are wanted,

scarcely is one ship purchased and brought up to our docks before money is raised for another."[5]

Following is a list of Hudson's whale ships and their voyages from 1830 to 1845. The usual sequence of listing the sailings by year has been changed to reflect the story of each vessel. An abbreviated list by year will follow. Most of the information is from Starbuck's *History of the American Whale Fishery*, augmented by Lund's *Whaling Masters and Whaling Voyages*, local histories, and contemporary newspaper articles.

S = BARRELS SPERM OIL	W = BARRELS WHALE OIL	WB = LBS. WHALEBONE
Alexander Mansfield	Ship	Purchased for $2,000 as unseaworthy, 320 tons
1830 (June)–1831 (March 31)	George A. Bennett, master South Atlantic: 123 S; 2,200 W; 1,000 WB[6]	
1831 (June 30)–1832 (Feb. 26)	Francis Neil, master South Atlantic: 2,000 W	Agent unknown[7]

"The Hudson Whaling Company has been extremely fortunate in its undertaking. The ship *Alexander Mansfield* has arrived in New York with a cargo of 2200 barrels of oil taken in the short voyage of 8 months." (*Poughkeepsie Telegraph*, March 7, 1832)

1832 (June 2) – 1833 (April 22)	Joseph Taber, master South Atlantic: 120 S; 1,480 W	Barnard, Curtiss & Co., agent[8]
1833 (June 5)–1835 (July 21)	R.E. Starbuck, master Chile: 1,500 W	Barnard, Curtiss & Co., agent[9]

"One of the vessels of the Hudson Whaling Co. *The Alexander Mansfield* arrived in New York week before last with 1500 barrels of whale oil on board and 50 barrels sperm oil. The ship has been out 2 years." (*Poughkeepsie Telegraph*, July 29, 1835)

1835 (Nov. 5)–1837 (April 20)	R.E. Starbuck, master Pacific Ocean: 25 S; 975 W	Barnard, Curtiss & Co., agent[10]
1837 (June 25)–1839 (March 21)	Robert L. Douglas, master Pacific Ocean: 200 S; 900 W	Barnard, Curtiss & Co., agent[11]
1839–1840	Robert L. Douglas, master Pacific Ocean	Barnard, Curtiss & Co., agent[12]

The *Alexander Mansfield* last sailed in 1839. It was condemned at Tahiti in 1840, but shipped home 1,000 barrels of sperm oil. "Not long ago, she had left Papeete Bay, bound on a cruise, when, after being at sea for a few days, it was accidentally discovered that the stern timbers of the ship were falling to pieces. … The *Mansfield* was formerly a Liverpool packet, sailing from New York many years since, an exaltation that would hardly be surmised from the appearance of the dingy looking hulk lying condemned at Papeete." (Francis Allyn Olmstead, *Incidents of a Whaling Voyage*, 1841)[13]

America	Ship	About 500 tons
1830 (Aug. 3)–1833 (April 23)	Shubael Cottle, master Pacific: 3,200 S	S.C. Macy, owner[14]

"The *America* was principally manned by young men from the city of Hudson and its vicinity. She has been absent 32 months and returns with a cargo of 3,200 barrels of Sperm oil, averaging 100 barrels taken each month. Her cargo is estimated to be worth $80,000." (*Poughkeepsie Telegraph*, May 8, 1833)

1833 (Sept. 11)–1837 (Jan. 27)	Folger, master Pacific Ocean: 800 S	Barnard, Curtiss & Co., agent[15]
1837 (Aug. 14)–1839 (May 2)	William H. Topham, master Indian Ocean: 200 S; 3,300 W	Barnard, Curtiss & Co., agent[16]

This is the voyage referred to when Charles Wilkes commented on the "uncombed and dirty crew" of the *America*. (see "Scurvy" in Appendix B) It was thirty-five days out of New Zealand with 3,800 barrels of oil. (Granville Allen Mawer, *Ahab's Trade*, 1999)

Whaling in the Pacific, by Oswald Brierly, c. 1850.
(Courtesy of the New Bedford Whaling Museum.) Note the tension on the steering oar.

1839 (Sept. 19)–1842 (Jan. 5)	William H. Topham, master Pacific Ocean: 1,000 S; 2,600 W	Barnard, Curtiss & Co., agent[17]

Sold to Stoningham, 1842.

Henry Astor	Ship	Built in New York City in 1820

1831–1835 (Jan. 18)	Charles Rawson, master Pacific Ocean: 2,200 S[18]	

"News has been received from the ship *Henry Astor*. She had on the 26th of September last, being ten months out, 900 barrels sperm oil. (*Poughkeepsie Telegraph*, 1832)

1835 (July 25)–1839 (Aug. 5)	Charles Rawson, master Pacific Ocean: 1,000 S; 700 W	Robert A. Barnard, agent[19]

Sold to Nantucket, 1839. During the Gold Rush the *Henry Astor* was used to carry men to California.[20]

Martha	Ship	369 tons

The ship *Martha* is difficult to track in the beginning. Ellis states that the *Martha* made "one or more trips between New York and Holland in 1833." From the *Hudson Gazette*, June 12, 1833: "The Ship *Martha* which arrived from the South Atlantic in February last, was sent to Holland with her cargo, has arrived in New York having made a most excellent voyage. As soon as her cargo is discharged she will be brought up to the city and immediately fitted out for the Pacific." The *Martha* is listed as belonging to Hudson in 1831, but Lund also listed a *Martha* belonging to New York City in 1832–1833 with a William H. Young as master, which may or may not be the same ship. The first positive report linking the *Martha* and Hudson comes in the *Hudson Gazette*, September 7, 1833: "The *Martha* will be ready in about a fortnight."[21]

1833 (Sept. 25)–1837 (April 17)	Timothy W. Ridell, master Pacific Ocean: 1,400 S	Alexander Jenkins, owner[22]

"News from the arrival in New York of the whaleship *John Wells*, that the *Martha* was in Talcuhana with 1500 barrels." (*Hudson Gazette*, March 8, 1837)

1838–1839 (April 23)	Weldon, master	Alexander Jenkins, owner[23]
	Indian Ocean: 150 S; 1,500 W; 13,000 WB	
1839 (July 30)–1841 (March 5)	Weldon, master	Alexander Jenkins, owner[24]
	Indian Ocean: 300 S; 2,800 W	
1841 (July 30)–1844 (April 5)	Weldon, master	Alexander Jenkins, owner[25]
	Indian Ocean: 400 S; 2,400 W; 24,000 WB	

Sold in 1845 to Sag Harbor, the *Martha* was Hudson's last whaler. Ellis states that the *Martha* was sold in September 1837 at Bothwell's City Hotel. This is obviously not true. More likely the ship that sold in 1837 was the *Washington*, listed next.

Washington	Ship	
1831 (May 6)–1834 (Jan.)	Samuel Barrett, master	
	Pacific Ocean: cargo not listed[26]	
1834	William Clarke, master	

"The whaleship *Lydia*, burned to the water's edge, on December 31, 1835, latitude 11° 15´ south, longitude 84° 80´ west. The crew abandoned the ship and was picked up by the *Washington* of Hudson, and taken aboard by Captain William Clark, *another Nantucket man*." (Stackpole, *The Sea Hunters*)[27]

The name *Washington* was a popular one for a whale ship, so it is hard to track Hudson's *Washington* after she disappeared from Hudson's fleet. Nantucket and Greenport, New York (Long Island), both had a *Washington* sailing from their ports after 1836.

Huron	Ship	290 tons
1832 (June 7)–1836 (May 1)	Benjamin Lawrence, master	Robert A. Barnard, agent[28]
	Pacific Ocean: 1,250 S	

"The Hudson whaleship *Huron* arrived at that place on Tuesday the 3rd. Inst., having on board 1250 barrels of Sperm oil." (*Poughkeepsie Telegraph*, May 11, 1836) The captain of this voyage was the Benjamin Lawrence who was a boat steerer on the ill-fated *Essex*. (see chapter "War and Whales") In 1840 Lawrence retired from the sea to a farm on Nantucket. (There are tales that he retired to Hudson, but they are false.)[29]

1836 (July 3)–1838 (Jan. 21)	Nye, master	Robert A. Barnard, agent[30]
	South Atlantic: 800 W	
1838 (Sept. 26)–1840 (May 28)	Samuel Barrett, master	Robert A. Barnard, agent[31]
	South Atlantic: 900 W	

Sold to Sag Harbor, 1840.

Meteor	Ship	
1831-1832	(Reuben?) Clasby, master	Barnard, Curtiss & Co., agent[32]
	300 S; 1,800 W	

The ship was under the command of Captain Clasby and was sailing around the Cape of Good Hope, bound for the Indian Ocean. The captain had taken command of a whaleboat when they lowered for a whale and the harpooner had successfully fastened. As the whale moved away from the boat and the line uncoiled, Clasby's leg became entangled and he was pulled overboard and drowned.[33] Mate George W. Bennett brought the ship back to New York City with 300 barrels of Sperm and 1,800 of Whale.[34] Because sailors are very superstitious and are particularly hesitant to sail on an unlucky ship, the *Meteor* was sold that year.[35]

Helvetia   Ship   333 tons

"The Hudson Whaling Company have purchased another ship the _Helvetia_ of about 350 tons burthen to be used in the whaling trade. This is the eleventh ship of that Company." (_Poughkeepsie Telegraph_, August 21, 1833)

1833 (Sept. 28)–1837 (March 18)   Cottle, master   Robert A. Barnard, agent[36]
                                   Pacific Ocean: 2,400 S; 150 W

"The whaleship _Helvetia_, Cap't Cottle from the Pacific arrived at New York on Saturday last with a cargo of 2400 barrels sperm and 150 barrels whale oil and some whale bone. ... the _Helvetia_ as full as she can hold cargo worth $70,000." (_Hudson Gazette_, March 29, 1837)

1837 (Oct. 19)–1839 (June 16)   Cottle, master   Robert A. Barnard, agent[37]
                                   Pacific Ocean: 350 S; 2,350 W; 21,000 WB
1839 (Oct. 4)–1842 (April 26)   Chandler Brown Gardner, master   Barnard, Curtiss & Co., agent[38]
                                   Pacific Ocean: 400 S; 2,000 W

Sold to New London, 1842.

James Monroe

"The _Hudson Republic_ says 'The fine ship _James Monroe_, of 400 tons burthen was purchased last week by Capt. Alex. Jenkins, on behalf of himself, the Messrs. Butts, McArthur and several other gentlemen of this city, and came to the wharf in this city Friday last. This is the tenth ship now owned in this city, either engaged in, or destined for the whale fishery. ... The _James Monroe_ ... will be fitted out during the winter and sail early in the spring. We are progressing finely. Long may our enterprise and industry continue and meet return from the prolific deep commensurate with its merits.'" (_Poughkeepsie Telegraph_, January 30, 1833)

1833 (June)–1834 (Sept. 1)   Coffin, master   Alexander Jenkins, owner[39]
                                   Africa: 150 S; 1,000 W
1834 (Nov. 10)–1835 (July 3)   Plaskett, master   Barnard, Curtiss & Co., agent[40]
                                   Pacific Ocean: 1,650 S

Hudson Whaleship Beaver, watercolor on paper by Isaac Power, c. 1840. Privately owned.

The *James Monroe* leaves the Hudson charts after this voyage. A *James Monroe* ship appears at Fairhaven, Massachusetts, in 1844.

George Clinton	Ship	427 tons
1834 (Aug. 16)	Samuel Barrett, master Pacific Ocean	Robert A. Barnard, agent[41]

"We find the following item of bad news under the head of the New York papers: 'Disaster.... the whaleship *George Clinton* of Hudson, Cap't Barret, Master, from the Pacific Ocean, with a full cargo of sperm oil bound to this port went ashore on the night of Thursday last, in a thick fog, at Little Egg Harbor. When boarded, no person was found on board, the Captain and crew having previously left her. We cannot obtain further particulars.'" (*Poughkeepsie Telegraph*, January 31, 1838) 1,450 barrels of sperm oil were saved. No other *George Clinton* appears in the later whaling lists.[42]

Beaver	Ship	480 tons
1833 (June 8)–1836 (Aug. 3)	Jared Gardner, master Pacific Ocean: 1,900 S	Barnard, Curtiss & Co., agent[43]

"Captain Gardner sailed from Hudson in the whale fishery from the year 1785, and he was still in the trade as late as 1837 … making at least fifty-two years of service." (Ellis, 1878) Gardner also sailed for Nantucket and New Bedford.[44]

1836 (Nov. 15)–1840 (May 1)	William J. Rogers, master Pacific Ocean: 1,100 S; 1,400 W	Barnard, Curtiss & Co., agent[45]

This was the voyage in which Captain Rogers was accused of putting a crew member ashore on a cannibal island when the man complained about the threat of scurvy. (see "Scurvy" in Appendix B)

1840 (Jan. 31)–1842 (May 16)	William J. Rogers, master Pacific Ocean: 270 S; 1,930 W	Barnard, Curtiss & Co., agent[46]

After this voyage the *Beaver* disappears entirely from whaling records in the United States.

Edward	Ship	274 tons
1833 (Jan. 10)–1835 (March 12)	Ray, master South Atlantic: 900 S; 120 W	Seth G. Macy, agent[47]

"The *Edward*, [has been] purchased by one of our enterprising ship owners, [Capt. S.G. Macy] and is fitting out in New York and will depart in the course of a few weeks for the Pacific." (*The Hudson Republic*, January 30, 1833)[48]

1835 (June 14)–1836 (Aug. 3)	Alexander Gardner Coffin, master South Atlantic: 140 S; 700 W	Seth G. Macy, owner[49]
1836 (Sept. 21)–1838 (April 11)	Daggett, master South Atlantic: 100 S; 1,600 W	Seth G. Macy, owner[50]
1838 (July 10)–1840 (Sept. 1)	Daggett, master South Atlantic: 200 S; 1,300 W	Seth G. Macy, owner[51]
1840 (Dec. 4)–1845 (April 3)	Daggett, master Pacific Ocean: 800 S; 800 W; 8,000 WB	Barnard, Curtiss & Co., agent[52]

Note that the change of ownership sent the *Edward* off into the Pacific, while Macy had the safe, short Atlantic voyages. The *Edward* was sold to New Bedford in 1845.

YEAR	Alexander Mansfield	America	Martha	Washington	Beaver	Meteor	Helvetia	James Monroe	Huron	Edward	George Clinton	Henry Astor
1829	X	X										
1830	X	X				X						
1831	X	X	X	X		X						X
1832	X	X	X	X	X	X			X			X
1833	X	X	X	X	X	Sold	X	X	X	X		X
1834	X	X	?	X	X		X	X	X	X	X	X
1835	X	X	?	?	X		X	X	X	X	X	X
1836	X	X	?	?	X		X	X	X	X	X	X
1837	X	X	X	Sold?	X		X	X	X	X	X	X
1838	X	X	X		X		X	X	X	X	Sank	X
1839	X	X	X		X		X	X	X	X		Sold to Nantucket
1840	Condemned at Tahiti	X	X		X		X	Sold to Fairhaven	Sold to Sag Harbor	X		
1841		X	X		X		X			X		
1842		Sold to Stoningham	X		Fate Unknown		Sold to New London			X		
1843			X							X		
1844			X							X		
1845			Sold to Sag Harbor							Sold to New Bedford		

Chart of Hudson's whale ships during its revival of whaling, showing years in service.

In *Whaling Masters and Whaling Voyages Sailing from American Ports*, by Judith Navas Lund, the author lists the schooner *Scituate* from Hudson, 1837–38, with David Thane as master. The *Scituate* does not appear in any local sources, nor in Starbuck; however, Ellis mentions, "Hudson also owned a brig and a schooner, which were engaged in foreign commerce from 1835 to 1838, and probably later." Also listed in Ellis are the vessels *Aurora* and *Splendid*. Nothing is known about the *Aurora* except that a Coleman was captain. It does not appear on any whaling records.[53] There were two *Splendids*, both ship rigged, belonging to Edgartown, Massachusetts, and Cold Spring Harbor, New York. The *Splendid* mentioned as being in Hudson was dated 1845, the year the last whale ships were sold from Hudson. A John Drury is named as captain. It is doubtful that it was a Hudson whaling vessel.[54]

The Barnard, Curtiss & Co. referred to under "agent" was a firm that served many functions for the Hudson Whaling Company. They were the agents attending to the sale of the whale oil. The large sperm oil and candle factory that they constructed on Water Street refined the oil and made spermaceti candles. (see "Spermaceti Candles" in Appendix B) The buildings burned down twice,

Barnard & Curtiss Sperm Oil and Candle Factory, located near the present railroad station on Front Street. *The Rural Repository*, c. 1841.

and when Hudson's whaling died out, the firm moved to Brooklyn.

Hudson bought "used" ships, mostly merchant ships fitted out for whaling. Some were ancient in ship age, and many structural problems might show up when the strains of whaling weakened the timbers. Captains, and probably first and second mates, were imported from the major whaling ports. Experienced boatsteerers (harpooners) were an absolute necessity. Good harpooners could make

whaling in the 1830s. The Newburgh Whaling Company began in 1831 and sent the first of its three ships out in 1832. By 1840 that company was out of business. In 1832 the Poughkeepsie Whaling Company began selling stock, and three ships whaled for that port. By 1838 the firm was in receivership. The Dutchess Whaling Company also was formed in Poughkeepsie in 1832. Its seven ships (they bought two Poughkeepsie Whaling Company ships) sailed until 1838, when the company was dis-

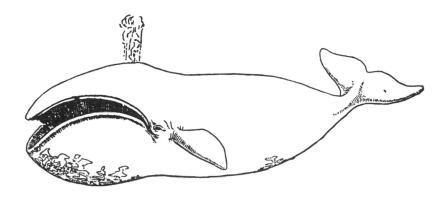

Bowhead whale, hunted almost to extinction by the demand for its baleen (whalebone).

or break a voyage, and it was not an ability that came with a few weeks practice.

The census of 1840 offers the following figures for the whale fishery in Hudson: soap and candles—twelve operatives, $12,000 capital, 164,000 pounds, 46,000 tallow candles, 60,000 sperm and wax candles manufactured; fisheries—37,075 gallons spermaceti oil, 277,200 gallons whale and other fish oils, $147,800 value of whalebone and other products of the fisheries, 304 men and $330,000 capital employed.[55] The Hudson whalers brought a large supply of whalebone (baleen) into the city, but so far no business has been discovered that would have used that material. There was a whip factory over the border in Connecticut, but no local corset maker would have used the amount of baleen that was brought back. (See "Whales" in Appendix B for a list of other uses of whalebone.)

Poughkeepsie and Newburgh were two other Hudson River port cities that became involved in

solved. In that same year the North River Whaling Company was conceived in Newburgh, but it never got beyond incorporation. One of the Dutchess Whaling Company's vessels, the *Newark*, went out as a "temperance" ship and included a library—a dubious attraction for a typical whaling crew.[56]

The early local histories attribute the loss of the whaling industry to the discovery of petroleum. Petroleum did knock out the market for whale oil, but the first oil well wasn't drilled until 1859, in Titusville, Pennsylvania. In the early 1830s camphene was distilled from turpentine (a product of the resin of pine trees). Used in lamps, camphene was an ill-smelling, volatile illuminant, requiring a new type of lamp to keep the flame from the fuel.[57] Kerosene, distilled from coal oil and used as an illuminant, also offered competition for lubricant and wax.[58]

Actually, the high point in American whaling came in 1846, when 731 whaling vessels plied the

HUBBEL, CLARK & CO'S

LINE BETWEEN

HUDSON AND NEW-YORK.

Messrs. HUBBEL, CLARK & CO., having supplied the place of the Fairfield with the favorite Steamer

COLUMBIA,

Capt. C. F. KING,

Will continue to run between HUDSON & NEW-YORK, for Passengers and Freight, as follows:

Leave HUDSON every
MONDAY, WEDNESDAY, AND FRIDAY,
At 6 o'clock P. M. on the arrival of the Cars. Leave NEW-YORK, foot of Harrison-st., every
TUESDAY, THURSDAY, AND SATURDAY,
At 5 o'clock P. M., touching at intermediate landings each way, and arriving at Hudson in ample time for the Cars going east.

The COLUMBIA is a first class boat, and one of the most commodious and comfortable on the river.

This line connects with the Hudson and Berkshire Railroad to Chatham Four Corners, Edwards, West-Stockbridge, Stockbridge, Lee, Pittsfield, and South Adams, and all the Western part of Massachusetts.

BARGE No. 1,........ Capt. H. HILLER,
BARGE No. 2,........ Capt. J. T. HAVILAND,
Leave Hudson every Wednesday, and New-York every Thursday.

☞ SALT and PLASTER constantly on hand.

HUBBEL, CLARK & CO.

Advertisement in *Directory of the City of Hudson, 1851-52.*

world's oceans.[59] In 1845, finally, Britain's duty on sperm oil was reduced, and in 1851 the duty was removed entirely, opening a new and prosperous market. The first bowhead whale was taken off the Siberian coast in 1843, opening a new phase in whaling. The great mouth of the bowhead, full of baleen, answered the needs of the new female craze for corset stays and hoopskirts. This demand led to the near extinction of the bowhead, while the dangerous Pacific Arctic ice claimed over 150 whale ships.[60]

Hudson's whale fishery died because the idea was flawed to begin with. In trying to revive the glory days of the 1700s, Hudson only managed to financially distress its citizens and discourage investments in new industries that would have brought prosperity to the city.

The leaders of the City of Hudson showed considerable restraint when entering the steamboat business. This may have been because of a shortage of capital, which was mostly tied up in their whaling industry, but more likely Hudson's businessmen recognized that they could not compete with the Albany and New York City lines. There was great competition to design the most elegant, luxurious vessel. By 1847 there were over 100 "floating palaces" on the river with orchestras playing day and night. The steamboat lines had given up the passenger "safety barges" for timorous passengers, because towing slowed the vessels.[61] Speed was the most important factor, and races between the competing steamboats became commonplace. The safety of the passengers took second place to the need to outdistance other boats. The competition became so acute that there were times when the fare for a trip from Albany to New York City was only fifty cents (for transportation alone—food, drink, and a berth were extra, and very expensive).

The Hudson Tow-Boat Company was formed in 1830, with the *Legislature* being the first steamboat of the firm. The original intention was to carry merchandise from Hudson to New York City, but they also had tow "barges" fitted up for passengers as well as freight. The Hudson Tow-Boat Company's boats alternated the route once a week, with each trip averaging fourteen hours. In 1833 the *Legislature* was making triweekly trips to New York City with barge #1 "open for the accommodations of boarders in New York." In 1836 the firm became the Hudson and New York Daily Steam Transportation Company, with three barges, adding the *General Jackson* and the *Rockland*. The latter ran daily trips to Albany. Hubbel, Clark & Co. ran the business from 1842 to 1850 and was succeeded by Haviland, Clark & Co.[62]

Jeremiah Bame had the *Columbia* built in 1841. It ran to and from New York City in eight and one-quarter hours. The *Fairfield*, of Hubbel, Clark and Co., was held responsible for the sparks that started the big fire of 1844.

The *Poughkeepsie Telegraph* reported on September 19, 1838: "The Hudson Codfish Company's schooner *General Warren* has just arrived at Hudson from the Banks with a full cargo of fish valued at from $5000 to $6000. She will be immediately dispatched on a mackerel fishing voyage."

Random Recollections of Hudson by Ignatius Jones in 1847 described the city as follows: "There are now no shipping at its docks, and no ships building. There is now no ring of the anvil to be heard,—no sound of the axe or the hammer. There is no bustle of seamen along its wharves, no song of the ropemaker upon its hills, no throng of wagons from the interior, no crowds of men in its streets. The shipyards are overgrown with grass, the wharves have moldered away, the ropewalk is deserted. It is only on the arrival or departure of a steamboat that any decided signs of life are visible: And yet the surrounding scenery is as beautiful as ever. The river has neither diminished in breadth or depth: the tide ebbs and flows as usual."[63]

EPILOGUE

Late-nineteenth-century Warren Street scene including Waldron House hotel.

The City of Hudson did not disappear from the maps as the naysayers predicted. The times advocated a change from shipping to manufacturing, and with Hudson's new advantages for transport by rail, several new firms were established. The major hurdle, which incensed many of the local political writers of the time, was the reluctance of the city's wealthier citizens to invest in business enterprises. These citizens were scolded in the preface of the *1871 Gazetteer of Columbia County* for being "averse to investing their hoarded wealth in business enterprises which give reasonable promise of success and remuneration for invested capital."[1]

The spectacular losses in earlier years had left a lasting impression on future generations.

One early firm, Clapp and Jones, Inc., established in 1869, constructed fire engines, hose carriers, etc. Clapp and Jones stood on land reclaimed from the South Bay. In 1870 it employed over 100 men; it closed in 1872. The Hudson Iron Company, intent on filling up its ninety acres of the South Bay, and the Columbia Iron Works, begun in 1857 on Water Street near the river, were successful for a brief period of time. A depression in the iron industry spelled the end for both enterprises. Hunt and Miller's Stove Works, founded in 1848 by Charles

McArthur, owed its success to the transition from heating rooms by fireplaces in American homes to the use of "parlor stoves" in every room. A kitchen "range," or iron stove, became the standard for cooking. Located on the site of the old distillery, this firm at one time was producing 2,000 stoves a year. The brewery of Phipps and Evans and the Hudson Foundry and Machine Shop of the Gifford brothers expanded and employed a great many workers.

As with all other cities, Hudson enjoyed years of prosperity and suffered through years of adversity. As demand for products and new processes of manufacturing changed, so did the industries. Those that didn't, failed. The Gifford Brothers manufactured agricultural and architectural iron-work in the beginning, but changed to manufacturing machinery for ice harvesting as that need became apparent.[2]

Two industries that brought considerable change to Hudson were brick making and the process of making cement. The clay banks of the North Bay had several brickwork concerns in operation from the beginning of the nineteenth century through the 1930s. An entire area of northwest Hudson was "dug out" (thus giving that name to a road and section of the city) through 100 years of removing the clay to make bricks. Just over the city line in the Town of Greenport, the Greenport Brick Corporation operated on what was referred to as Second Street Extension. Like the railroad builders in 1850, the brickyard men were given a wide berth by the local citizens. Predominantly of Italian descent, the brick-worker families eventually integrated into the population of Hudson, adding a new and exciting element to the formerly staid community.

The two cement plants, both located in the Town of Greenport, required a large workforce to

J.W. Hoysradt Hose Co. No. 8., 515 Warren St., Hudson. Clapp & Jones engine on left.
Photo by Frank Forshew, c. 1880. Rowles collection.

The Union Mills. Postcard, 1908.

mine the limestone and process the stone in the plants. This demand was filled by an influx of immigrants from Eastern Europe, particularly from Poland. A large percentage of these workers made their homes in Hudson, adding another new dimension to the fascinating stew that is Hudson's demographics.

The manufacture of knit goods became an outstanding industry in Hudson toward the end of the nineteenth century. The Union Knitting Mills, to name one, was organized in 1851, and by 1900 was employing 500 workers with an output of 600 dozen fleece-lined and flat shirts and drawers. Many enormous knitting mills sprang up in Hudson, but as the industry moved south and demand decreased, the factories closed. The run-down structures, mostly too large for practical use, are now being renovated for other uses.

Several wars, two of them worldwide, plus the Great Depression of the 1930s, played havoc with Hudson's economy. The closing of the cement plants led to a severe downturn in the city's financial well-being. All the foreboding prophecies that labeled Hudson a finished city in the mid-1800s were being repeated 100 years later. But again the city has rebounded, rejuvenated by an influx of new people bringing in new ideas and cultures, and a respect and admiration for the city and its history.

Today's communities are vulnerable to worldwide events over which they have no control, just as past generations were. Sometime in the future there may be another slump in Hudson's economy, and new prophets of doom will proclaim Hudson as a finished city (once again!), but future generations will have the ideas and improvements now being implemented by today's diverse population to build upon, just as today's generation builds on the foundations set by those able and energetic entrepreneurs known as the Hudson Proprietors.

APPENDIX A

The Quakers and the Hudson Meeting

Rachel Hicks, wearing a typical example of Quaker women's dress.
(Courtesy of Friends Historical Library of Swarthmore College,
Pennsylvania.)

In Miller's *Sketches of Hudson*, he mentions, "it is said that at one time, fully two-thirds of the families of the city were Quakers, and of the remaining third, the greater part were 'half Quaker.'"[1]

A great proportion of the Hudson Proprietors belonged to the Society of Friends, so it is not surprising that they were the first to request, and obtain, a lot of ground to be used for a meetinghouse and school. They chose a lot on the south side of Union Street near the corner of Third Street. A small frame building was constructed, where they held their meeting for ten years.[2] In

1794, with the need for more space, they purchased a lot on the northeast side of Union and Third streets. There the Quakers built a brick building fifty-feet-by-thirty-eight-feet, which was two stories high and held 600 people. Unpainted for years and devoid of any interior or exterior ornament, this building was used by the Friends until 1854.

Paraphrased from Burnham N. Dell's *Quakerism of Nantucket*, published by the Nantucket Historical Association in 1955, the following is a brief explanation of Quaker beliefs.

153

Elias Hicks. (Courtesy of Friends Historical Library of Swarthmore College, Pennsylvania.)

The Quakers followed a doctrine of "the Inner Light," meaning, in part, that an individual could have divine contact with God—a oneness with God, in other words—without the intervention of the sacrament or a priest. The Quakers were reviled by other Christians, even their fellow Protestants, because they rejected the liturgy of the church, the sacraments, and the need for a trained clergy. The Quakers refused to recognize any temporal authority or law because their direct communication with the Divine Will superceded all human authority.

To the Quakers there were no social distinctions; all men and women were created equal. The Quakers used "thou" and "thee," believing that the word "you" had honorific connotations based on differing social levels. Simplicity and humility held the highest virtues; pride and vanity were to be avoided and should be condemned.[3] Quaker dress reflected this rule. Men wore flat hats, somber brown or gray clothes, and square-toed shoes. Women wore plain, somber colors (usually a soft, dove gray), kerchiefs or shawls, and no jewelry. "In their world, there were Friends on one hand, and the world's people on the other."[4] The Quakers sought converts, but protected their societies by insisting that marriages could take place only among members.

Quakers were peace loving; they declared war to be unchristian. They opposed slavery, believing all men were equal as children of God. The Quakers advocated aid to the poor, but usually this aid was reserved for their Quaker brethren. Music, art, and recreational activities such as dancing and card games were frowned upon. (Condemning these activities as "vanity" was what eventually drove many younger members from Quakerism.)

A "Select Committee," whose function was to regulate member behavior, was chosen from among the older and more revered members within the meeting. The final decision was left to the entire meeting.[5] Punishment for all offenses was disownment from the Quaker meeting. A member could be disowned for wearing buckles, refusing to say "thou" and "thee," or for attending a marriage performed by a minister (not of the Quaker faith) where there was music and dancing. A common cause of disownment was the marriage of a member of the society with one of the "world's people." Youthful Quakers could be condemned for such trivial "sins" as wearing ribbons or playing a musical instrument.

Quakers were expected to abstain from taking part in governmental activities, for they would not obey a law if it did not agree with their conscience. They were known to be the most law-abiding members of the community, however. Perhaps paradoxically, many were in demand to hold office in Hudson. Their honesty, sobriety, and peacefulness gained them great respect and influence among the population.

An event occurred in 1828 that divided the members and nearly destroyed the Quaker meeting. Elias Hicks, an active Quaker, became concerned that the Quakers were moving away from the fundamental beliefs of Quakerism as stated by its founder, George Fox. Hicks' influence was so great that by 1828 a split had divided nearly all meetings in America. Hicks' followers were called Hicksite Friends, and those rejecting his ideas were labeled Orthodox Friends. The Hicksites made up three-quarters of the Quakers in Hudson and continued to meet in the large building, while the Orthodox Friends had to find another meeting place.[6] The London Yearly Meeting furnished them with funds for a new meetinghouse, which they used to build a small structure on Union Street near the courthouse park.

According to an article by Florence Mossman, a former Columbia County Historian and an active Quaker, "In 1853, the Hicksites made an agreement to sell the front portion of their property (100 feet along South Street) to the Methodists 'including the meeting house site.'" What we do not know is whether the Methodists demolished the Quaker meetinghouse or remodeled it to

Friends Meeting House, Union Street, Hudson. Photo by Robert Ragaini.

meet their needs. The Hicksites, however, retained the rear portion of the lot—fifty feet facing Union Street. According to one account, the Friends "received in part payment the old Methodist Church building on Diamond (Columbia Street), in which they held their meetings until about 1858, when they sold it to Charles Meyers to be used as a dye-house." Perhaps as early as 1856 they began construction of a new meetinghouse on the Union Street property, which they continued to use until the meetings ended in 1871 when the remaining Friends traveled to Ghent for worship services.[7]

From 1871 to 1951, there were no active meetings of Quakers in Hudson, but a group of Friends began meeting in homes around the county in 1951. After publicity appeared that the Quakers were again active, Isobel Webber, the owner of the old Macy building, offered the Friends the opportunity to purchase this former Orthodox meetinghouse. The deed stipulated that the building would revert back to the original owners if the building ceased to be used for Quaker meetings.

The new group took the name Taghkanic-Hudson Monthly Meeting and acquired the building that had been used as a storehouse. The meetinghouse was cleaned and refurbished. Eighteenth-century benches from the Cornwall-on-Hudson Meeting were donated, and now a weekly meeting is held in the old building.[8]

Most of the old restrictions have disappeared, but Quakers still believe in human brotherhood and essential equality. Their beliefs find expression in simplicity of lifestyle, integrity in personal relations, and at times controversial stands on public issues. Membership has dwindled in the United States since the nineteenth century through attrition and disownment, and the Quaker emphasis on individual divine guidance, plus the lack of a defining authoritative leadership, allowed schisms to develop that are just now being healed.

"One of the Most Gifted of Her Day"

Hannah Barnard was "one of the most gifted of her day, and probably the most intelligent female Friend in the country," wrote Stephen Miller in *Sketches of Hudson*.[9] She was born Hannah Jenkins, in Nantucket, and became a Friend in 1772. "Eight years later she married Peter Barnard, a widower with three children.[10] Soon after, the Barnards came to Hudson, where Peter built a frame house on Main (Warren) Street and set up a carting business." Peter was one of the "kindest-hearted, best tempered men that ever lived."[11]

Hannah became known as an eloquent speaker. She traveled extensively, even to Europe where she talked with the learned men of the day. Aunt Hannah, as she was familiarly called locally, was an extensive reader. She was inquisitive and perplexed her Quaker friends with Latin words and quotations from "heathen" writers. While in Ireland she appalled some Irish Friends, and when she traveled to London in 1800, Hannah was censored after a trial of fourteen months and advised to cease speaking and "quietly return to her own habitation."[12] Back in Hudson, Hannah had conferences with the elders of the Hudson Meeting. The elders believed that her actions were not in keeping with those becoming a woman belonging to the Society of Friends. They reported that they "had no hope of her recovery from the dark and bewildered state of mind into which she had fallen and she had so far become clouded in her mind as to be led away by the spirit of delusion."[13] In 1802 Hannah was told that she was silenced as a minister and was to refrain from speaking in meeting. Finally, they disowned her as a member of the Society of Friends. In her last remarks before the society, she predicted that the "Meeting of Hudson would come to naught."[14]

Quaker Meeting House, Ghent, New York, c. 1880.

Appendix B

Blood for Oil: The Whaling Industry, Illustrated

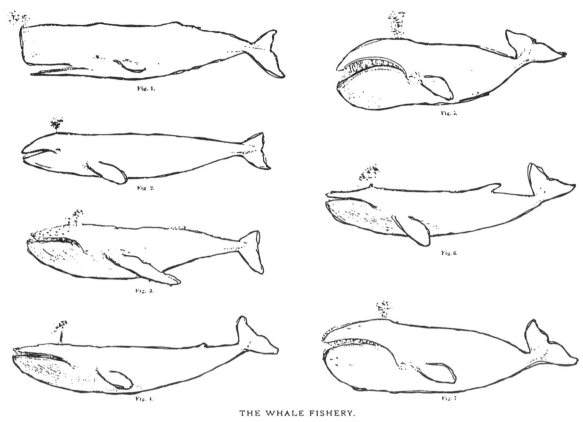

THE WHALE FISHERY.

Fig. 1. The Sperm Whale (*Physeter macrocephalus*).
Fig. 2. The California Gray Whale (*Rhachianectes glaucus*).
Fig. 3. The North Pacific Humpback (*Megaptera versabilis*).
Fig. 4. The Sulphur-bottom (*Sibbaldius sulfureus*)
Fig. 5. The Bowhead (*Balæna mysticetus*).
Fig. 6. The Fin-back or Oregon Finner (*Balænoptera velifera*).
Fig. 7. The Pacific Right Whale (*Balæna japonica*).

Outlines from Scammon's Marine Mammalia.

Drawings are from Charles M. Scammon, *The Marine Mammals of the Northwest Coast of North America, Together with an Account of the American Whale Fishery*, 1874, Plate 184.

Whales

The swimming animals known as whales and dolphins are cetaceans, from the Greek and Latin words for "whales." The two main groups are the baleen whales, known as Mysticeti (mustached), and the Odontoceti, or toothed whales. The "mustache" of the Mysticeti refers to the baleen strips.[1]

Whales are descended from four-legged animals that lived on the shores of ancient seas millions of years ago, and they still retain vestiges of those limbs. A small pair of bones embedded in the trunk muscles is all that is left of the hipbones. The former front limbs remain, but have been modified into flippers, some of which contain bones aligned as finger bones.[2]

These warm-blooded, air-breathing mammals are covered with a layer of blubber up to two feet thick, which serves as a better insulation in water than would a covering of fur. The blubber is firm, fatty tissue, resembling salt pork. It is filled with oil cells and connected by fibrous tissues. Whale oil (which is oil made from the baleen whales), is a fatty acid made almost entirely of glycerides. It is necessary to remove the blubber from the dead whale as soon as possible, for it decomposes rapidly.[3]

Whales must breathe air, so they surface to expel used air and replace it with fresh air using the blowhole on the top of their heads. When the blowhole opens, a vapor of condensation and foam is expelled into the air with a rushing sound. Whales are usually spotted by their spouting, which can be seen from long distances. Baleen whales have a double blowhole; the toothed whales have a single blowhole.[4]

It is thought that whales find their way on their long migrations by using the earth's magnetic field. One theory for the mass beachings of some species of whales puts the blame on something interfering with the magnetic field.[5]

There are seventy-five species of whales and dolphins. Listed are those of interest to the early whalers.

THE BALEEN WHALES (*Mysticeti*)

These whales have no teeth. They have a series of two hundred to over six hundred flat plates hanging crossways from the edge of the upper jaw. The plates are tough and flexible, and made of keratin, the same substance in human hair and fingernails.[6] The edges of the plates are frayed into bristles that act as a strainer for separating food from the water. Because of their feeding habits, the baleen whales are compared with grazing animals. They spend their days feeding on planktonic animals of the ocean. Though minute, these organisms are so numerous that they are found in thick masses like clouds in the sea. The whalemen called this plankton "krill" or "brit," and knew that where these concentrations appeared there were likely to be whales. The baleen whale plows through the water with its great mouth open. When it has a mouthful of krill-filled water it shuts its mouth, presses its tongue against the baleen and filters out the water, leaving the stranded mass of food behind. Some baleen whales also feed on small fish such as herring that in turn feed on the plankton.[7]

Baleen was called "whalebone" by the whalers, leading to confusion. By that name it was assumed by the uninitiated that the bones of the whale were brought back for the many uses attributed to whalebone.[8] Baleen comes in shades from black to white and in sizes that range up to ten feet in length. The uses for baleen were many. In an age before plastics and thin steel, baleen was the only product that had the flexibility for whips, parasols, umbrellas, dresses, corsets, supporters of all kinds, caps,

Whaleman tying up whalebone, *Harper's Weekly*, June, 1860. (Courtesy of General Research Division, New York Public Library, Astor, Lenox & Tilden Foundations.)

hats, divining rods, bows, buskins, canes, rosettes, cushions for billiard tables, fishing rods, tongue scrapers, penholders, paper folders and cutters, and mattress and furniture stuffing.[9]

Why the whales died—women in corsets and hoopskirts, c. 1890.

The oil from the baleen whales was used mostly for illumination. It was called "black" oil, after the black right whale, and also "train oil," causing confusion. The word "train," in this case, came from the early Dutch whaler's word *traan*, meaning "tear" or "drop." As animal fat was used in making soap, soon blubber was used extensively for that purpose. Another use was for lubrication in processing of wool, leather, and ropes.[10] Later, in the industrial age, "black" oil was used for lubricating the moving parts of engines and machinery. In modern times, during the war years, whale oil was used with vegetable oil for making margarine, lard, and shortening. Cosmetics and crayons were later uses, as well as varnishes, linoleum, and printing ink. Glycerin has been another product made from whale oil.[11]

BOWHEAD WHALE
(also called the polar whale, the Greenland whale, etc.)

The bowhead whale (*Balaena mysticetus*) has a large mouth and a great deal of baleen. Its large mouth fills a third of its body and is arched like a bow. It has the largest baleen plates of any whale, up to 600 plates that could be 14 feet long. It plowed the Pacific Arctic seas. In the second half of the nineteenth century, after petroleum had replaced whale oil, the bowhead were decimated for their baleen, which was in high demand for hoopskirts and corsets. There are very few bowheads left today.[12]

THE RIGHT WHALE
(*Balaena glacialis*)

The earliest whalers pursued the right whale. Easy to kill, with great quantities of blubber and an enormous mouth filled with baleen, plus the added convenience of not sinking when killed, made this genus of the family of Balaenidae "right" with the whalers, to the degree that there were few right whales left in the northern Atlantic by 1800. The southern Atlantic, particularly the Brazil Grounds, had right whales with an inferior, dark oil.[13]

HUMPBACK WHALE
(*Megaptera novaeangliae*)

Megaptera means "big wing," referring to this whale's extraordinarily long flippers, and *novaeangliae* means "New England." Though the humpback has throat grooves, it is not included with the rorqual whales (see below). The humpback does not have a humped back, but dives with an arched back. It is noted for "breaching" well out of the water, "lobtailing"—smacking the water with its flukes (divisions of the tail)—and its songs.[14]

Two northern right whales. © Jane A. Sasonow-White.

The Grampus-Grampus was the early name for the killer whale (*Orcinus Orca*),
illustrated above, but the name is now reserved for Risso's Dolphin.

THE RORQUAL WHALES

These baleen whales have numerous ventral pleats that run under their mouths to the center of their bodies. A loose lower jaw allows the whale to scoop up a great amount of krill-filled water, and the grooves open like a pouch to hold it all. Of the rorquals, the blue whale is the largest, and is in fact the largest animal on earth. Some blues have a planktonic algae covering their stomachs, giving them the name "sulfur bottoms." They make the loudest sounds made by any living creature, but humans cannot hear it. It is so low in pitch that only special instruments can detect the sound. The blue is very nearly extinct.[15]

The fin whale, another rorqual whale, is unusual in that its coloring is totally asymmetrical. It is black on one side and white on the other. Even its baleen is asymmetrical. The fin is a narrow, streamlined whale, ignored by the early whalers because of its swiftness.[16]

There also are three smaller rorqual whales: the sei, Bryde's, and the minke.

The Beluga whale, also called the white whale and the "sea canary."

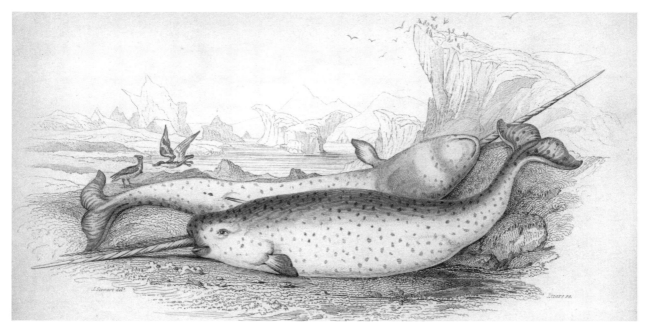

The narwhale. In the male narwhale the canine teeth (or tooth) extends forward into a spiraled tusk up to ten feet long.

THE GRAY WHALE (*Eschrichtius robustus*)

The gray whale has a separate classification among the baleen whales. Grays once were numerous in the Atlantic, but were completely killed off, leaving only the Pacific grays. The gray is the only whale whose upper jaw overhangs the lower. They congregate in the thousands off the coast of lower California, and are the favorites of the whale watchers in the Baja Peninsula.

THE TOOTHED WHALES (*Odontoceti*)

The toothed whales offer the greatest variety. There are six families under the suborder Odontoceti and sixty-seven species, with the sperm whale being the largest. They have five digits in their flippers, and a single blow-hole. Many species have a bulbous forehead, called a melon, filled with oil. The toothed whales have the remarkable ability of "seeing" by echolocation. They

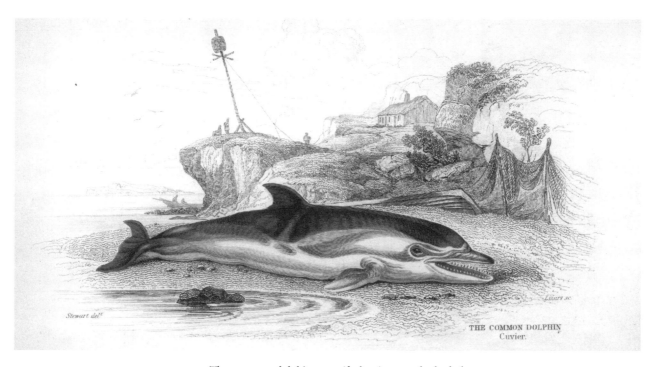

The common dolphin—a swift, leaping, toothed whale.

PLATE 8.

The sperm whale—the largest toothed whale and the mammal that changed whaling.

emit noises (mostly clicks) and hear the echoes that bounce off objects.[17] Like bats, the whales can "picture" their prey or surroundings. Their echolocation is extraordinary, giving the whales the ability to discriminate to the smallest degree.[18]

One of the four families of the toothed whale is the ocean dolphins,[19] which contains the killer whale (the largest of the Delphinidae family).[20] The pilot whale, which the whalers called the blackfish, was taken for its body oil and the valuable oil in its "melon."[21]

The family Monodontidae includes just two whales—the beluga and the narwhal. The beluga is a sixteen-foot whale that is found in the northern Atlantic. It is white and has a "smiling" face. The beluga were called "sea canaries" for their chirping, trilling sounds.[22] The male narwhal has a tusk (really a tooth), one of only two teeth in the upper jaw. This tooth extends eight or nine feet from its jaw. The spiraled and twisted tusk is famous for having been falsely identified as the horn of the mythical unicorn.[23]

The family of beaked whales contains 915 species. The bottlenose dolphin is the most popular species. It is a big attraction at water shows, and displays a remarkable intelligence.[24]

The freshwater dolphins are another family, containing four species.

The most important toothed whale is the sperm whale, *Physeter catodon*. (There are also pygmy sperm and dwarf sperm whales.) The sperm whale is the largest of the toothed whales and is found in all the oceans of the world. It has a unique shape with a large, square head. The sperm's head is asymmetrical, with the upper jaw not aligned with the lower. The S-shaped blowhole is on the left side of the snout, and the spout of the sperm is easily identified. The black skin is only as thick as carbon paper. The unfortunate name for this mysterious whale came from confusion when it was first encountered. The waxy fluid in its head was thought to be sperm.

The principle food of the sperm is squid, all kinds of squid. (There are more squid in the oceans than any other creature.) The sperm is famous for preferring the giant squid, *architeuthis*, an illusive monster that lives in the deep ocean. The scars from its tentacles have been found on sperm whales' bodies.[25] The sperm is known to dive over a mile deep and stay down for over an hour. *Physeter catodon* does not take kindly to being harpooned. His attacks on the whaleboats wreaked havoc, for his tail and jaws were formidable weapons. The discovery of the sperm whale changed whaling. Sperm oil was so superlative to the baleen whale oils that it was given its own, special category. The allegorical *Pequod* in *Moby Dick* was not the only ship sunk by a sperm whale—the *Essex* and the *Ann Alexander* were among actual ships sunk.

Whale Ships and Whaleboats

The bark *North America*, reprinted from Francis Allyn Olmstead, *Incidents of a Whaling Voyage*, 1839-1840, Tuttle Publishing, Boston, Massachusetts.

Whale ships could be barkentines (barks), brigantines (brigs), schooners, ships, or sloops. The difference between these vessels was in the rigging, and many vessels were changed from one to another over the years. A brig has two masts, which are square-rigged. A bark is a three-masted vessel—the foremast and mainmast are square-rigged, and the third (mizzenmast) is fore and aft rigged. A schooner has two or more masts, fore and aft rigged. The three-masted schooner was the one most employed in early whaling. A ship is a full-rigged vessel with three masts.

Depending on the size of the vessel, a whale ship could carry up to thirty men, but only a few were actually required to man the vessel. When the crew and officers were out in the boats after the whales, the ship was manned by the cooper, the blacksmith, or maybe the cook.

Whale ships differed from other types of merchant vessels in that they were not made for speed, but for endurance. They had to be strongly built to withstand the strains of whaling. It was remarked that they "lumbered" along, rather than sailed. Most whale ships averaged between 250 to 400 tons, but were no more than 100 feet

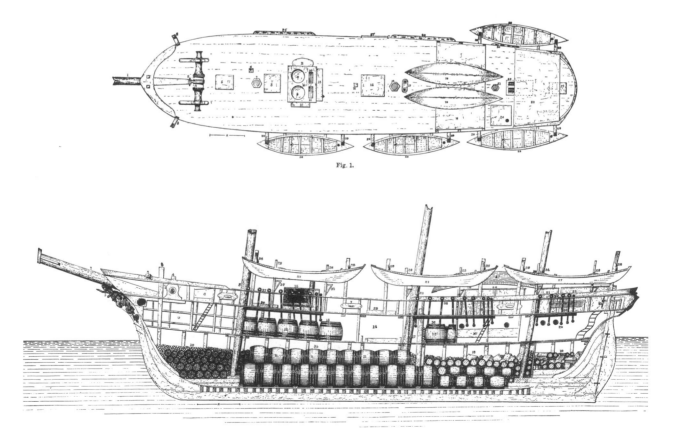

Fig. 1.

Deck plan, side and interior plan of the whaling bark *Alice Knowles* of New Bedford. Plate 189 in *The Fisheries and Fishing Industries of the United States*, G.B. Goode, ed., Government Printing Office, Washington, D.C., 1884-1887.

in length. Below the waterline, room had to be available for the storage of hundreds of barrels of whale oil, food supplies, and whaling gear.[26]

Above the waterline, below the deck in the stern of the ship, the captain had his private stateroom with a dining area adjoining. There, he and the ship's officers would have their meals served by a steward. Forward from there were the private six-by-four-foot bunks for the officers. Mid-ship, in what was called steerage, were bunks for the cooper (barrel maker), blacksmith, carpenter, steward, and cook. Across from them was a stateroom for the harpooners (boatsteerers). These men, by their skills, ranked higher than the rest of the crew.

Forward in the ship was the forecastle, known to seamen as the "fo'c's'le." Jammed between the bows, this wedge-shaped room was the living quarters for as many as twenty men. The sides were lined with double-decker bunks, and there was just room for a seaman's chest in front of the bunk. J. Ross Browne wrote in 1842 his impression of the fo'c's'le: "The forecastle was black and slimy with filth, very small and hot as an oven. It was filled with a compound of foul air, sea-chests, soap-kegs, greasy pans, tainted meat, Portuguese ruffians and seasick Americans."[27] Air and light came through a small opening from the deck above, where the crew entered by means of a ladder.

Trying Out—the greasy, smoky process of boiling the blubber into oil, from "Huntsmen of the Sea," *Harper's New Monthly Magazine*, c. 1870.

There She Blows—watching for a spouting whale, "Huntsmen of the Sea,"
Harper's New Monthly Magazine, c. 1870.

Above the waterline three or four whaleboats hung from cranes on ten-foot wooden davits—three on the larboard side and one on the starboard quarter. The starboard side held only one because that was where the cutting-in platform was located. There, also, the heavy "blanket pieces" of blubber were hauled aboard by tackles lifted by a man-powered windlass. There were usually two extra whaleboats inverted and lashed to the deck.

The tryworks, located on the deck forward of the fore hatch, were two iron pots, each holding 250 gallons, which were bricked in with a firebox underneath. Beneath that, in a wood and brick framework, was the "goose pen" filled with water, which prevented the deck from catching fire when the fires under the trypots were burning. Nearby were the copper cooling tank and the cooper's bench. High above, on the main topmast, was the "crow's nest" of wood or canvas, where a crew member watched the seas for the signs of a whale.[28] Most whale ships had an encircling white border painted on their hulls that indicated they were whale ships.

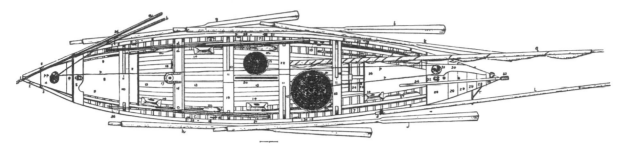

Deck view of a whaleboat ready for the chase. Plate 184 in *The Fisheries and Fishing Industries of the United States*, G.B. Goode, ed., 1884. Note the coiled line running aft and forward to the waiting harpoons.

The Whaleboat

The whale ship was transportation in the search for whales, a factory, and living quarters for up to thirty men. The whaleboat, however, was the killing vessel.

If the whale ship was slow and clumsy, the whaleboat was the direct opposite. The ideal whaleboat was twenty-eight feet long, had a six-foot beam, was sharp at both ends, and had a round bottom. Easily constructed, the boat could move effortlessly with speed over the waves and was easy to maneuver. The gunwale and keel were of heavy timber, and the planking was of one-half-inch cedar. It was clinker-built, meaning the thin boards overlapped one another, strengthening the vessel but keeping it light (1,000 lbs.)

There were six men aboard, five with rowing oars and one, a ship's officer called the boatheader, manning the steering oar, which was up to twenty-eight feet long. This great oar was attached to the sternpost and exerted great power in steering. It could maneuver the boat in circles, if necessary. The five rowing oars, two on the larboard and three on the starboard, were of unequal lengths from fourteen to sixteen feet. There was a reason for this lack of symmetry—the boatsteerer (harpooner) on the starboard bow would put aside his oar and stand, on command, to hurl the harpoon at the whale. That left four

Returning to the ship, without a whale! Pencil on paper by Gordon Grant.

rowers. The men sat on the side opposite the rowlock to add strength to the pull. The thole pins, into which the oars were fastened, were covered with matting to keep noise at a minimum (whales can't see well, but their hearing is excellent).

The whaleboat carried about 900 pounds of equipment, including harpoons, lances, paddles, a sail and mast, emergency rations, hatchet, knives, a waif (a small flag for marking ownership of a dead whale), etc. Two tubs of carefully coiled line (tarred hemp or manila rope) were added just before the boat was lowered. One tub contained 225 fathoms (a fathom equals six feet), the other 75 fathoms.

The boat could carry up to twelve persons if, for example, another boat was smashed by a whale, but was too fragile to be lowered with the men aboard. (Once afloat, the buoyancy of the water added to the whaleboat's strength.) The men had to clamber down the ship's side by ropes (and up again, exhausted, after the chase).

The boatheader stood on a small raised platform aft, where he could watch and steer toward the whale. The other men would not see the whale until they were upon him, for they rowed with their backs to the bow. (This was probably fortunate—some might be inclined to jump overboard when their twenty-eight-foot boat approached a seventy-foot, seventy-ton whale.)[29]

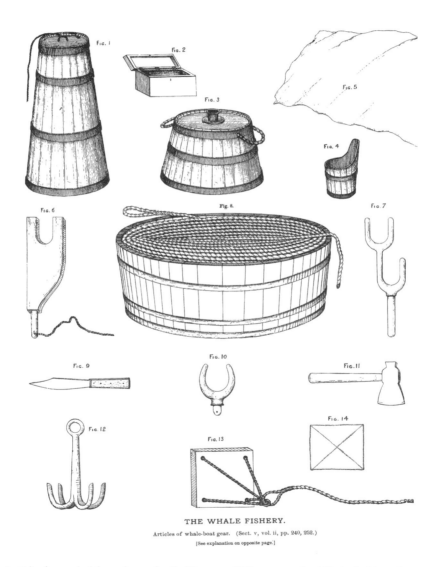

THE WHALE FISHERY.

Articles of whale-boat gear.   (Sect. v, vol. ii, pp. 240, 252.)

[See explanation on opposite page.]

Articles for a whaleboat: kegs of coiled line, a waif (flag to mark a killed whale), and a drogue (at bottom), which was fastened to the line to slow a harpooned whale. From *The Fisheries and Fishing Industries of the United States*, G.B. Goode, ed., Government Printing Office, Washington, D.C., 1884-1887.

From Greenhorn to Whaler

Greenhorn, or "Greenie," was the name given to a young man off on his first whaling voyage. If he was from an established whaling city, he knew the pitfalls, but also was aware that none of the town's young ladies would pay him any attention until he had taken his first whale. It was the boys from the farms and non-whaling communities that suffered the most. After a day or two out, homesickness and seasickness struck with a vengeance, but the officers made sure that the boys' shipboard seamanship education began, despite the fact that the boys were sure they would die if they lifted their heads.[30] (According to the *Tamerlane* journal, seasickness was treated by feeding the victim codfish and peppers.)[31]

Watches were assigned as follows: four hours on duty (headed by a mate), then off for four hours. Two "dog watches" each day, of two hours each, were for free time. The night watches were three hours each. Steering, setting sail, washing decks, and instructions on the use of the ship's instruments were part of the learning experience. Each man was assigned a particular whaleboat and a certain oar, so that there would be no confusion when the boats were lowered. Endless practice lowering the whaleboats, scrambling down the lines into the boat, and learning to row with the long oars was essential. The men practiced again and again under the shouted orders of a ship's officer. Every day, from the rising sun until it set, one or more forecastle men were stationed high up in the mast-heads, watching for whales. Each stayed aloft for two hours.

The forecastle, where the crew slept, was dark, damp, boiling hot in the tropics and freezing in the colder latitudes. Fleas and bedbugs shared the thin straw mattresses, and rats were common visitors.

It certainly wasn't the pay that sent them on these dangerous voyages. Whalers were not paid wages. They received a percentage of the profits of the voyage, called a "lay." The owner or firm owning the ship received the largest percentage, about 60 percent, because of their capital outlay of ship and stores. The captain received one-eighth. The forecastle hand might sign on for 1/175 to 1/150, which averaged out to about $10 a week. Of course, room and board were included … if it could be called that. Then there was the ship's "slop chest." In this chest was found everything a sailor might need during the several years at sea—extra clothes, a new knife, even chewing tobacco. Every item taken from the chest was priced and marked against the sailor's "lay." He might at the end of his journey have little left to show for years of hard labor and much danger.[32]

Nor did they sign on for the food. All the provisions were packed in barrels before the cruise began. "Salt horse" (beef), and "salt junk" (pork), were heavily salted to keep from spoiling, though most of it usually did, becoming rancid and filled with maggots. It had to be boiled, but remained tough and tasteless. "Hardtack," twice-baked crackers that substituted for bread, and molasses (for sweetening) were common rations. The drinking water stored in casks quickly gained a green

A Scramble for Salt Junk, reprinted from J. Ross Browne, *Etchings of a Whaling Cruise, 1846.*
(Courtesy of Belknap Press of Harvard University Press, Cambridge, Massachusetts.)

scum, smelling as bad as it looked. "Longlick," a mixture containing molasses, was what the sailors drank. "Lobscouse" was a common meal, made from salted meat and hard biscuits soaked in the water that had boiled the meat. There were dried fruits, so "plum duff" was a special treat. Plum duff was a form of pudding made from flour, lard, yeast, water, and dried fruits. Beans, rice, and potatoes (before they rotted) were also part of the usual fare. Fish, freshly caught from the ship, added to the menu. If an officer was not looking, the crew would place pieces of hard bread into the boiling whale oil, a treat they thought delicious. So were whale brains, deep-fried in the boiling oil.

The ship's hold was the perfect breeding place for all types of vermin, from rats to fleas to cockroaches. The cockroaches were so numerous that the men grew accustomed to sharing their meals with them or finding them in their food.[33]

The tropical islands were welcomed for their fresh fruits, particularly as every seaman had a fear of scurvy.

Scurvy

> The crew are longing for fresh provisions but do not expect to get them sometime to come and are fearful of the scurvy.
>
> Journal of James L. Harris aboard the whale ship *Tamerlane* out of New Bedford, 1850[34]

Scurvy was called "the plague of the sea." Whalers were particularly susceptible because, unlike merchant ships that sailed from port to port, whale ships spent weeks prowling the oceans searching for whales. A continuous diet of salted meats and hard biscuits aggravated the problem.

Scurvy is caused by a lack of vitamin C, which is found in fresh fruit, particularly citrus fruits, some vegetables, milk, liver, kidney, and fish. The body can store vitamin C for about three months. After that time the connective tissues (collagen) weaken. Hemorrhages occur

The Whale of Captain Debois, Harper's New Monthly Magazine, 1856.
(Courtesy of General Research Division, New York Public Library, Astor, Lenox & Tilden Foundations.)

on the skin, resembling bruises. Blood flows into the joints, causing great pain and eventually immobility. The gums bleed, turning spongy, and the teeth loosen.[35] This led to an inability to eat any of the tough, hard food that was routine on a whale ship. Eventually, death would occur. It was not unknown for all aboard a whale ship to come down with scurvy, leaving the ship foundering in the ocean with none aboard well enough to sail it.

In 1753 a Scottish physician suggested that scurvy could be prevented by "ingesting citrus juice, particularly oranges, lemons and limes." This led to the British practice of requiring its sailors to drink a daily ration of lime juice, thus their nickname, "limeys."[36]

For unknown reasons, American whaling captains never accepted this solution and continued to find novel reasons for scurvy, and even more unique methods to prevent it. A dirty ship was believed to harbor the potential for scurvy. Lieutenant Charles Wilkes was sent by the United States government to explore and survey the "southern ocean." Early on in his voyage, in 1838, he encountered the *America* of Hudson, "homebound and leaky 35 days out of New Zealand. The Master, Topham, had 3800 Bbls. After 18 months out." Wilkes commented: "I have seldom seen at sea a more uncombed and dirty set than his crew. How they preserve any tolerable state of health I know not, and it is not at all surprising that the ravages of scurvy should be felt on board some vessels belonging to the whaling fleet, if this is the state in which they are kept."[37]

Many captains insisted on having their ships totally scrubbed down during or after a voyage. A harpooner aboard the *Rebecca* in 1791 recorded, "cleaned ship foreward and aft betwixt decks, made several fires to dry, smoke and clean ship to prevent scurvy." If any of the men also were required to scrub themselves, it is not mentioned.[38]

Another novel "cure" was championed by some captains. The victim was buried for a day in sand or soil with only his head protruding. The result was not noted.[39]

One captain reported that he had found a sure cure. When the vessel docked in the Sandwich (Hawaiian) Islands, he allowed native women aboard. Undoubtedly the crew was enthusiastic about this form of treatment, but the addition of fresh fruit to their diet, abundant on these islands, was the real reason for their recovery.[40]

In Olmstead's voyage in 1840, he mentions the captain buying barrels of lime juice in Tahiti. Lime trees were "numerous and prolific" on the island. "The natives would ferment the juice with chalk to remove impurities, allowing the juice to keep for years." Some care had to be taken, however, for the natives learned to half-fill the barrel with water, rather than provide a full barrel of lime juice. Thus, by 1840, when the ships stopped where antiscorbutic fruits were available, the captains knew of the benefits.[41]

Busch's *Whaling Will Never Do for Me: The American Whaleman in the Nineteenth Century* mentions that Hudson's Captain Rogers was arrested for leaving two men ashore on Rotuma, one of the remote Fiji Islands. This abandonment created an outcry in the local newspapers. The following appeared in the *Poughkeepsie Telegraph* on April 29, 1840: "The Troy Budget publicly charges against Captain Wm. Rogers of the whaleship *Beaver* of the Hudson Whaling Company on his first cruise out 16 months (in 1837). Many of the crew got scurvy, and asked to get ashore, etc. One man, called Gordon, a ship steerer, complained, etc.—put ashore by Capt. on a cannibal island where he was eaten."[42]

There was no doctor aboard. All injuries and ailments were under the care of the captain. He had, perhaps, a book of remedies, a chest of medicines, and the tools for amputations. Every conceivable injury could occur on a whale ship or in the whaleboat. Strange ports brought exotic diseases, and it was more a matter of luck than skill if a seaman recovered. A book was written by Lot Tripp, a druggist in Hudson, and published in Hudson in 1784: *Directions for Mariners on Voyages, Both in Hot and Cold Climates*. In it were lists of the proper medicines and treatments to be used by the ship captains, who also served as the doctors on board their vessels.[43]

In 1790 a law ordered that "every vessel belonging to a citizen of the United States of the burden of 150 tons or upwards navigated by ten or more persons and bound on a foreign voyage must be provided with a chest of medicine put up by some apothecary of known reputation and accompanied by directions for administering same." Later the law was amended to include 75-ton vessels with a crew of six or more calling on any port in the West Indies. One or two dollars was deducted from the whaleman's "lay" to cover the expense, but whalemen felt some security in the knowledge that help was at hand.[44]

Many men lost their lives while whaling. There were falls from the rigging and disease, but most deaths came from the battle with the whale. The bodies of the deceased were consigned to the sea, and the death noted in the logbook. Relatives would learn of their loss when the ship returned to home port.

After two or three years on a whale ship, a young man would be experienced in navigation and ship basics. He also would have lived through times of deadly terror

Struck on a Breach, "Huntsmen of the Sea," *Harper's New Monthly Magazine*, c. 1870.

and sheer boredom. There was the possibility that if he shipped again, he might be qualified as a third or second mate. There was always the dream, if he could tolerate the hardship, that someday he might be captain. Others just signed on for adventure. Some planned to desert at a tropical island. After 1848 many signed on as whalers just to get to San Francisco and the gold fields. Most boys made one voyage, then swore off whaling forever. Others qualified to join the merchant service, which did not have the risks that whaling did.

"A Dead Whale or a Stove Boat"

When the shout sounds from high above—"Thar she blows!"—excitement reigns. The captain orders the boats lowered, and the men rush to place the line tubs aboard. Then they lower the boats and follow by sliding down to take their assigned places. It was a race to see which boat would reach the whale first. The rowers faced aft with their backs to the whale. They depended on the boat-header, an officer, to guide the boat. All the while he was cajoling the men with: "Pull boys, pull! Set me on the black back! Pull, and I'll sign over my house, my wife, my children! Pull, boys, pull!" Moving quietly so as not

to "gally" (frighten) the whale, they watched it "sound" (dive below) and then endured the long wait until it reappeared. Finally, the officer would shout to the boatsteerer (harpooner) to "Let him have it!" The harpooner would put aside his oar and lift the iron harpoon from the crotch where it (and several others) were held.

Harpoons were clumsy and heavy—eleven feet long, with an eight-foot hickory shaft and a three-foot iron shank with a sharp "flue," or barb. A line ran down the shaft and was attached to the line in the boat. The tubs of line, carefully coiled, did not run directly out to the harpoon. From the tub the line was extended aft around a protruding piece of wood called the "logger head," then forward again, over the oars to the bow box, where part of it was coiled before leaving the boat through a channel called the "bow chuck."

The harpooner rested his thigh against the "clumsy cleat" and darted the harpoon at the whale. When the whale felt the pain of the harpoon, it would do one of several things. Often it would "sound" and the crew would have to wait, hoping it would not emerge under the boat. The whale might decide to attack the boat. If it was a baleen whale, it would use its tail to crush the boat. If it was a sperm whale, the boat would be attacked by the crushing jaws of the whale. Sometimes the whale would take off at high speed across the surface of the waves, dragging the boat behind in a "Nantucket sleigh ride."[45]

The minute the whale was "fast," a time-honored but dangerous tradition took place. With the boat bouncing and rocking over the waves, the line whipping forward, and legs and oars in the way, the boatheader and the boatsteerer changed places. The boatsteerer moved aft to steer the boat and the officer, the boathead-er, moved to the bow to kill the whale. The term "foul line" meant a rope that had not been coiled correctly and had a kink in it. In this change of places, such a line could easily encircle a man's leg and pull him overboard in a second. (From the reports, this is what happened to Captain Clasby aboard the *Meteor*.) When the line was pulled in to bring the boat closer to the whale so that it could be "lanced," the line was carefully but loosely gathered in the bottom of the boat. A sudden accelera-tion by the whale could send the line whipping through

the boat, and anyone caught in its coils was sure to be pulled overboard.

When the whale had tired, the boat moved forward and the officer stood to place the lance in the "life" of the whale. He did not throw the lance, but plunged the "killing iron" time and again into the whale. This was called "reaching for its life." Eventually the whale would bleed to death, going in circles, then into a final "flurry" before turning on its back, dead.[46]

Blubber to Oil

There has been a popular myth in Hudson that the dead whales were towed home behind the whale ship. Did no one consider the impossibility of dragging sixty

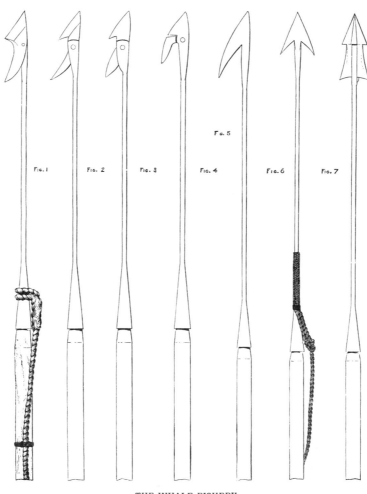

THE WHALE FISHERY.

Harpoons. (Sect. v, vol. ii, p. 250.)

FIG. 1. Improved harpoon or toggle-iron now in general use.
FIGS. 2, 3. First forms of toggle-irons made by Lewis Temple.
FIG. 4. "One-flued" harpoon with hinged toggle.
FIG. 5. "One-flued" harpoon.
FIG. 6. "Two-flued" harpoon.
FIG. 7. Provincetown toggle-iron; not now in use.

From *The Fisheries and Fishing Industries of the United States*, G.B. Goode, ed.

Capturing a sperm whale. *Whaleship* Superior, 1835 aquatint engraving by William Page
from an original painting by Cornelius Hulsart. © Mystic Seaport, Mystic, CT.

tons of rapidly rotting animal carcass, of which only a small part was needed, behind a sailing ship in a rising sea? And what would be left when the sharks got through with it?

The blubber was processed into oil immediately, while the ship was in the open sea. A dead whale decomposes quickly, and sharks attacked the carcass even when it was attached to the ship for cutting-in, presenting a danger

Cutting-in a right whale, hoisting the baleen (upper jaw) aboard.
From *The Fisheries and Fishing Industries of the United States*, G.B. Goode, ed.

to the men engaged in the process. Turning a whale into oil was long and dirty work and began with the whale being towed to the ship by the six exhausted men in their whale-boat. The whale was secured to the ship by chains at the head and flukes (tail). The cutting-in stage was lowered, and strong blocks and tackle with huge grappling hooks at the ends of their chains were set at the ready. Two men, usually officers, stood on the platform with cutting spades (long-handled instruments with sharp, broad blades).

The first piece of blubber was sliced, and a grappling hook was attached to a hole in the blubber. As the hook rose and the cutting continued, the whale was rotated and the blubber unwound like peelings from an orange. These

"blanket pieces" of blubber, weighing about a ton, were hoisted and then lowered to the deck or through a hatch into the blubber room below by the men operating the windlass forward of the foremast.[47] As the ship moved slowly through the sea (one cannot stop a ship in mid-ocean), more and more blanket pieces were hauled on board until all the blubber had been removed.

If the whale was a sperm, the head also was carefully removed. A sperm whale's head is one-third of its body and weighs about thirty tons. If small enough, the whole head was hoisted aboard. If too large, the lower part, called the "junk" (five or six tons), was cut off and brought aboard. The "case," free of bone, contains about

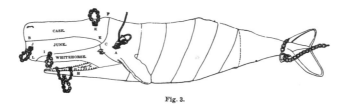

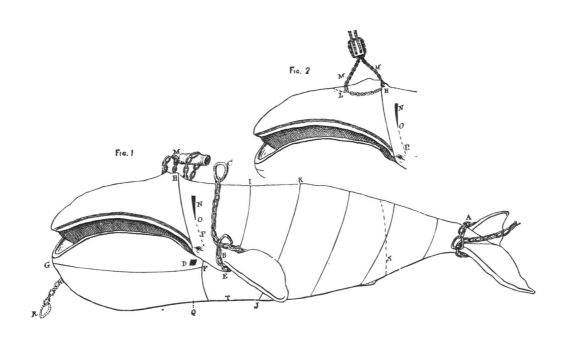

Diagrams showing how the blubber was cut from the bowhead and sperm whale.
From *The Fisheries and Fishing Industries of the United States*, G.B. Goode, ed.

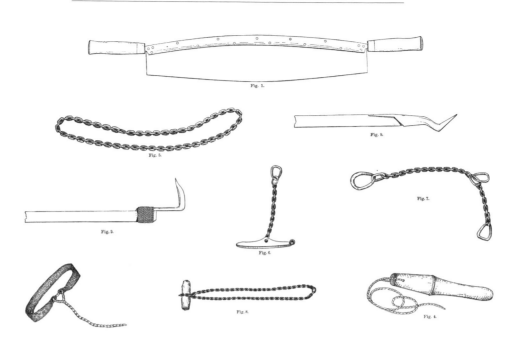

Whaling gear—some of the equipment needed for securing the whale alongside the ship and cutting-in.
The top figure is a blubber-mincing knife. Plate 203 from *The Fisheries and Fishing Industries of the United States*, G.B. Goode, ed.

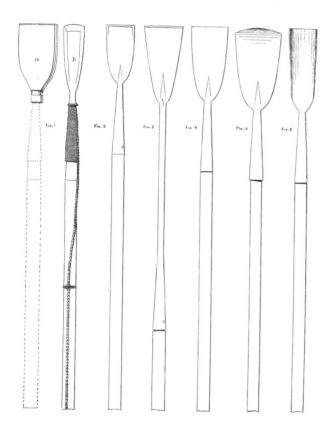

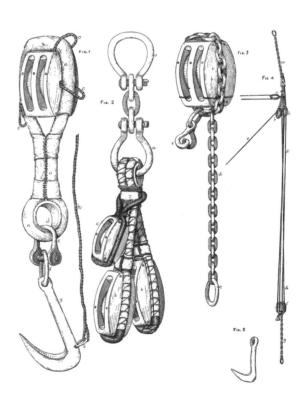

Boat spade and cutting-in spades. The long-handled cutting spades were used from the platform, making cuts into the blubber. Plate 205 from *The Fisheries and Fishing Industries of the United States*, G.B. Goode, ed.

Examples of the tackle used to raise the "blanket" pieces aboard the ship. Plate 206 from *The Fisheries and Fishing Industries of the United States*, G.B. Goode, ed.

fifteen barrels of a clear, fluid wax that congeals like petroleum jelly when exposed to air. This is the valuable spermaceti; it was carefully bailed out.[48]

If the sperm whale was thin or appeared sick, the men on the platform probed the intestines searching for valuable ambergris. Ambergris forms in the sperm whale's intestine around the undigested horny beaks and rings of the squid it eats. Used originally as a medicine, the value of ambergris came from its use as a fixative for perfumes. It once brought $400 an ounce.[49]

The lower jaw of the sperm whale was hauled aboard, the only piece of bone saved from a whale. The peg-like teeth, thirty to fifty in number, occur only in the lower jaw. These teeth were prized by the crew, to be used for scrimshaw. The bone of the lower jaw also was used in scrimshawing and made into canes and tools, etc.

If the whale was a baleen, the whole upper jaw was hoisted aboard. The strips of baleen were cut from the gum, cleaned and scraped, and stored in bundles in the hold.

While all this was going on, men were busy cutting the blanket pieces into smaller pieces, called "horse pieces." These were then cut into book-sized pieces with the blubber sliced to the skin, resembling pages in a book. These were called "Bible leaves," and they were placed in the trypots. Wood fires had been started under the pots, but as the blubber slowly boiled into oil the "cracklings" (undissolved pieces of whale skin) were used to fuel the fire, the whale actually cooking itself. The blubber had to be carefully boiled to extract all of the liquids found in it, or it would spoil. The boiling temperature of oil is higher than that of water, and the oil became so hot it would melt tin, so only iron utensils were used. Care was taken to prevent water from getting into the boiling mixture. That would cause the oil to steam, crackle, and erupt from the pot. There was a man assigned to make sure the water in the "goose pen" did not evaporate away. A fire on the deck of an oil-soaked ship would cause it to burn to cinders in a brief time.[50]

As each pot of oil was boiled, it was put into the cooler—a rectangular container holding six to ten barrels

Cutting-In, "Huntsmen of the Sea," *Harper's New Monthly Magazine*, c. 1870.

Bailing the case—removing the spermaceti oil from the head of a sperm whale.
Plate 208 from *The Fisheries and Fishing Industries of the United States*, G.B. Goode, ed.

of oil. The oil was cooled again in a deck pot, then siphoned into the casks in the hold.

The spermaceti oil (actually, it was a wax) was boiled to remove imperfections, and was stored as "head matter."

When all was taken from the whale that the whalers required, the stripped carcass was set free on the sea to be consumed by sharks and seabirds.

The trying-out process went on night and day. Sometimes several whales were tied alongside waiting to be processed. It was described as a scene from hell, with the stench and soot permeating everything. The men were divided into two watches, one watch working while the other slept. As the ship lurched through the waves, the men slipped and skidded on the oil and blood-covered decks. Terrible injuries occurred when men fell against the sharp cutting instruments or slid overboard into the waiting sharks. Afterward the ship was cleaned using lye made from the ashes of the trypot. The process continued until the hold was filled with casks of oil and the ship began the return trip home.[51]

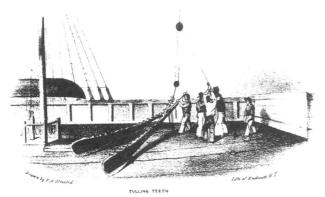

Pulling Teeth—removing the teeth from the lower jawbone of a sperm whale to be used for scrimshaw. Reprinted from Francis Allyn Olmstead, *Incidents of a Whaling Voyage*, 1839-1840, Tuttle Publishing, Boston, Massachusetts.

Spermaceti Candles

Spermaceti candles were the brightest-burning of all candles. They were also smokeless and odor-free. Even today, the term "candlepower" is based on the measure of light given off by one pure spermaceti candle.

Candleworks were started in Hudson as early as 1785. They were small compared to the later oil and candleworks run by Barnard, Curtiss & Co., which began when the whaling industry revived in Hudson in 1830 and continued until the middle of the 1840s. The business report of 1840 lists 60,000 sperm and whale candles manufactured in Hudson.[52]

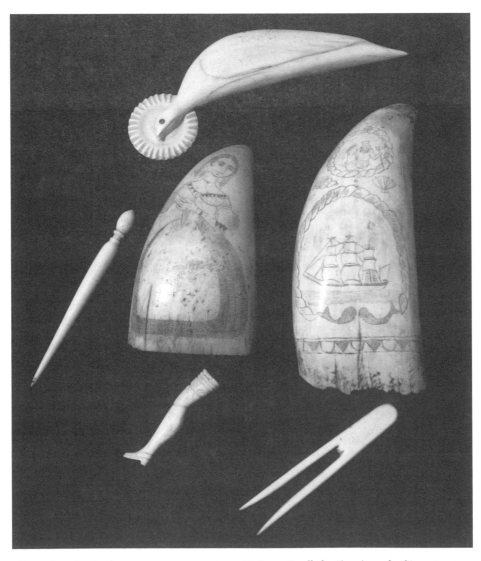

Examples of scrimshaw: *top*, a pastry cutter or "crimper," called a "jagging wheel"; *center*, two scrimshawed sperm whale teeth; *center left*, a pick-wick, used for cleaning wicks or pulling up a too-short wick; *bottom left*, a pipe tobacco tamper in the precisely rendered shape of a lady's leg; *bottom right*, a clothes pin. Photo by Robert Ragaini.

Whalemen chopping blubber into "Bible pieces," the last process before the blubber is boiled.
From J. Ross Browne, *Etchings of a Whaling Cruise, 1846*,
Belknap Press of Harvard University Press, Cambridge, Massachusetts.

THE PROCESS

The sperm oil was placed in large kettles and heated to 180°-200°, evaporating any water that might have mixed with the oil. In late fall when the weather had turned cold, the oil was boiled again to produce granulation. Then it was placed in tubs and open casks to rest until the cold turned it into a semi-solid mass called "blackcake."

In the main part of the factory, one or more spermaceti presses were a permanent part of the building, swung from the ceiling and anchored and counterbalanced by large beams in the cellar. The top beams had one end held between upright posts that were constructed in such a way that the beams could be secured at any height from the floor. Between the posts was the "press box." Bags of the "blackcake," separated by heavy wooden leaves, were placed under a beam. The beam over the press box was weighted, causing a clear oil to gush from the bags. This first pressing was called winter-strained sperm oil, because it would not congeal in a lamp or machinery in the coldest weather. This first pressing, the finest oil, was

Carcass Adrift, "Huntsmen of the Sea," *Harper's New Monthly Magazine,* c. 1870. The remains of the whale were left to be devoured by sharks and birds.

Whale ships at New Bedford with casks of whale oil on the wharf. The ship on the back left is "hove down" for repairs to the hull. Plate 210 from *The Fisheries and Fishing Industries of the United States*, G.B. Goode, ed.

also used as a lubricant in fine watches and chronometers, in addition to fuel for domestic lamps and street lights.

"Spring oil" was made after the first pressing. The oil was again heated in boilers, replaced in casks, and allowed to cool. This time it hardened more than before. In April when the temperature reached 50°, the oil became soft. It was put in bags and pressed again. This oil could be used in all but the coldest months. More boiling and pressing produced an oil that was usable only in the summer months.

What was left in the bags after the final pressing was called "spermaceti," and it was from this that the finest candles were made. To make the candles, the wax was put into boilers and heated to 210°. It was refined and cleared of all foreign ingredients by the addition of potash (lye). The pure, clear wax remaining was molded into spermaceti candles.[53]

Sealing

The Hudson sealers did all their sealing in the far southern hemisphere, including the Falkland Islands and the islands off the coast of western South America.

Seals are carnivorous mammals of the suborder Pinnepedia, meaning "feather foot." Two families exist: the eared seal and the "true" seal (no ears). Eared seals can move forward on their flippers and turn their heads with their long necks. The true seals (or as they are sometimes called, the hair seals) have a tiny, wrinkled ear opening. Their hind limbs are permanently set backward, so they can only slide and wriggle over the ground.[54]

Seals congregate by the thousands in rookeries along the shores in colder climates. They travel with grace and

PLATE 18.

The common seal (true seal) has very small ears and is unable to move on land except by sliding its rear half over the ground.

speed through the water, but are clumsy on land, where they give birth to their young.

The adult sea lion (of the eared seals) grows up to nine feet long. Sea lions were valuable for their hides. Fur seals, which can reach six feet, also were slaughtered for their rich, silky undercoat of fur. The pelts were valued in China, where great quantities were shipped in exchange for cargoes of tea.

"True" seal hides made the finest leather. Their bodies were covered with blubber. Many varieties lived in rookeries on or near the Antarctic shores. The elephant seal is an enormous creature. Adult males are up to 22 feet

A rookery of sea lions. Sea lions are eared seals that can move on their flippers (see pup at left).

long and weigh up to 8,000 pounds. The male has a long proboscis that swells when he is annoyed, accounting for the designation "elephant" seal. The term "elephant oil," used in cargo listings, caused considerable curiosity. Fat was stripped from the elephant seal and tried out as whale oil. The oil was used for lighting and lubrication, and also in tanning leather, making it especially valuable for the Hudson tanneries. Elephant seal oil made leather supple and waterproof.

A sealing voyage required advance preparation. Vessels stopped at the Cape Verde islands for the salt used in preserving the hides. Spare time during the rest of the voyage was spent making thousands of wooden pegs to be used to hold down the pelts while they were drying. One voyage mentions 6,092 pegs completed. Sharpening knives was another essential task.

When the ship reached the island holding the rookeries, men were sent to the rocky shore in whaleboats. Their stay on the beaches would be from several months up to a year. Supplies were left for them, and their shelters usually were overturned whaleboats insulated from the cold with sealskins. During the day the men would move among the herds of seals, slaughtering as many as possible. The seals were hit on the head with clubs or stabbed with lances, then skinned. The skins were pegged down on the ground to dry, then salted and packed in layers. The skins would stay preserved for years if kept dry. The elephant seal oil was sometimes "tried out" on shore; otherwise the blubber was preserved in the snow until the ship returned. It would then be hauled aboard for "trying out" in the ship's trypots.

While the shore crews were at work, the ship was off in other waters, possibly whaling. There was always the worry that the ship might meet with a disaster and be unable to return for the men. Starvation and freezing were a few of the hazards the men faced.

Most crews amassed up to 20,000 hides during a season. Three and a half million sealskins were gathered between 1793 and 1807. By 1820 most of the seal herds had been destroyed.[55]

Clubbing Seals, Harper's Weekly, May 1874. (Courtesy of General Research Division, New York Public Library, Astor, Lenox & Tilden Foundations.)

NOTES

Works frequently cited are identified by the following abbreviations:

AH   "Annals of Hudson," unpublished compilation, Vedder Memorial Research Library, Bronck Museum, Coxsackie, New York. "Annals of Hudson" includes: excerpts from the *Hudson Weekly Gazette*, 1785-1797; Shipping News as recorded in the *Hudson Weekly Gazette*, 1785-1797; memoirs of Laban Paddock, December 8, 1853; memoirs of Deacon H.P. Skinner, April 8, 1854; and memoirs of Captain A. Jordan.

CCC   *Columbia County at the End of the Century* Vol. I & II (Hudson, N.Y.: Record Printing and Publishing, 1900).

ELLIS   Captain Franklin Ellis, *History of Columbia County* (1878: reprint, Old Chatham, N.Y.: Sachem Press, 1974).

HCH   Anna R. Bradbury, *History of the City of Hudson* (Hudson, N.Y.: Record Printing and Publishing, 1908).

LUND   Judith Navis Lund, *Whaling Masters and Whaling Voyages Sailing from American Ports. A Compilation of Sources*: New Bedford, New Bedford Whaling Museum; Sharon, Mass.; and Gloucester, Mass., The Ten Pound Book Co., 2001.

MILL   Stephen B. Miller, *Historical Sketches of Hudson, Embracing the Settlement of the City, City Government, Business Enterprises, Churches, Press, Schools, Libraries, Etc.* (1862: reprint, Hudson, N.Y., Hendrick Hudson Chapter D.A.R., 1985).

MW   Richard Ellis, *Men & Whales* (Guilford, Ct.: The Lyons Press, 1991).

SCHR   Margaret B. Schram, various newspaper articles written for the (Hudson, New York) *Register-Star*, the (Hillsdale, New York) *Independent*, and the (Hudson, New York) *Columbia Request*. These articles, nearly two hundred in all, were written twenty years ago and include quotations from some sources that were not available at the time this book went to press.

STAR   A. Starbuck, *A History of the American Whale Fishery from Its Earliest Inception to the Year 1876*, Report to the Commissioner of Fish and Fisheries, Washington, D.C., Vols. I & II (1878: reprint, New York: Argosy-Antiquarian Ltd., 1964.

TSH   Edouard A. Stackpole, *The Sea Hunters: The New England Whalemen during Two Centuries, 1635-1836* (New York: J.B. Lippincott Company, 1953).

WD   Edouard A. Stackpole, *Whales and Destiny: The Rivalry between America, France, and Britain for Control of the Southern Whale Fishery, 1785-1825* (Amherst, Mass.: University of Massachusetts Press, 1972).

Prologue: A Miracle City

1.   Karl Rodman, "Whalers on the Hudson River," *Hudson Valley Magazine*, October 1980. Rodman wrote his article from a study made at Mystic Seaport Historical Association.

2.   Edouard A. Stackpole to Margaret Schram, April 30, 1985.

3.   John Lambert, as quoted in *CCC*, 326.

4.   Julian Ursyn Niemcewicz, *Under the Vine and Fig Tree: Travels through America in 1797, 1799, 1805*, as quoted in Ruth Piwonka, "Hudson," *Hudson Valley Regional Review* Vol. II, No. 1 (March 1985), 18.

5.   Deacon H.P. Skinner, *AH*.

6.   Laban Paddock, *AH*.

7.   *HCC*, 207.

The River that Flows Two Ways

1.   Wallace Bruce, *The Hudson* (New York: Brant Union Company, 1913), 9.

2.   Carl Carmer, *The Hudson* (New York: Grosset and Dunlap, 1968), 3-7.

3.   Wallace Bruce, op. cit., 18.

4.   Arthur G. Adams, *The Hudson* (Albany, N.Y.: State University of New York Press, 1981), 164-65. At this point the river is 165 feet deep and 3/8 mile wide.

5.   Seventy-fifth Anniversary Publication, *Hudson Daily Star*, December 1923.

6.   ELLIS, 11.

7.   Wallace Bruce, op. cit., 179.

A Little Different: Claverack Landing, 1661-1783

1.   A.J.F. Van Laer, ed. and trans., *Minutes of the Court of Albany, Rensselaerwyck and Schenectady, 1675-1680* Vol. II. (Albany, N.Y.: University of the State of New York, 1928), 358.

2.   Helen Reynolds, *Dutch Houses of the Hudson Valley before 1776* (New York: Dover Publ. Inc., 1965), 11. See also Bruce Wallace, op. cit., 39.

3.   See illustration of the Van Hoesen deed on page 11.

4.   "A map of the Several Farms and

Unappropriated lands in the Town of Claverack and Corporation of the City of Hudson; Belonging to Daniel Penfield, Esqr. Surveyed by Will. Cockburn, Fred. Hauser, & Wm. Cockburn, Jr. 1799." Columbia County Historical Society, Kinderhook, New York.

5.   *HCH*, 3.

6.   For information on the patron system in the Hudson Valley, refer to S.G. Nissenson, *The Patroon's Domain* (New York: Columbia University Press, 1937) or Sung Bok Kim, *Landlord and Tenant in Colonial New York: Manorial Society* (Chapel Hill, N.C.: University of North Carolina Press, 1978).

7.   Van Laer, op. cit., 384.

8.   Ibid., 389-90, 413-14

9.   *CCC*, 294.

10. The Penfield map, Columbia County Historical Society, op. cit.

11. *HCH*, 8. The early name for Athens has been spelled Lunenberg and Loonenberg. This author chose the latter because it is the spelling used in the Athens Bicentennial Committee publication, *Athens, Its People and Industry, 1776-1976*. (Athens, N.Y.: Athens Bicentennial Committee, 1976).

12. Wilhelm Christoph Berkenmeyer, *The Albany Protocol: Wilhelm Christoph Berkenmeyer's Chronicle of Lutheran Affairs in the New York Colony, 1721-1750*, trans. Simon Hart and Sibrandina Geertruid Hart-Runeman, ed. John F. Dern. (Ann Arbor, Mich.: 1971), 480-81.

13. Ruth Piwonka, op. cit., 12.

Between the Devil and the Deep Blue Sea

1.   For more understanding of the problems faced by the Quaker whalemen on Nantucket, see *WD*, 1-13.

2.   *TSH*, 92.

3.   STAR, n. 77.

4.   *WD*, 13.

5.   Ibid., 4.

Five Quakers, Six Opinions

1.   This "memorial" stated that "the whale fishery cannot be preserved in this place, nor any part of the business carried on ... without great loss ... and the only remedy is in placing the island and its inhabitants in a state of neutrality." (*WD*, 27)

2.   Ibid., 26.

3.   Mrs. Paul Szasz, interviewed by author.

4.   Washington County Historical Society, "Some Chapters in the History of the Town of Easton, N.Y." in *History of Washington County, New York* (The Washington County Historical Society, 1959). See also Jane Betsey Welling, *They Were Here Too*, Greenwich, N.Y.: The Washington County Historical Society, 1963).

5.   *WD*, 32-33.

6.   "This afternoon the schooner *Lark*, Cap't. Cottle of Nantucket, with fish, whale-oil, rum, etc. came up the Hudson to Newburgh! This was the first American vessel which had come up the river since the British took possession of New York in 1776." (*TSH*, 99)

7.   MILL, 8.

Those Yankee Heathen

1.   *CCC* Vol. I, 297.

2.   *WD*, 30.

3.   Mill, 8.

4.   Ibid., 9.

5.   Ibid., 11. See also ELLIS, 157.

6.   Ruth Piwonka, op. cit., 13.

7.   MILL, 32-33.

8.   "... with ravines on either side, so near that when graded in after years, the sidewalks in some places required the support of plank and timbers." (MILL, 33)

9.   Ruth Piwonka, op. cit., 13.

10. ELLIS, 167.

11. Ibid., 133. See also Robert M. Terry, *The Hudsonian: Old Times and New* (Hudson, N.Y.: Edwin Rowley Printer, 1895), 140-41.

From the Jaws of a Whale

1.   ELLIS, 155.

2.   MILL, 6.

3.   Ibid., 6.

4.   *HCH*, 34.

5.   *WD*, 5-6.

6.   MILL, 16.

7.   *HCH*, 36.

8.   Ibid., 36.

9.   Ibid., 27.

10. *WD*, 29. See also *HCH*, 37. For more on Coffin, see ELLIS, 162, and *WD*, 15, 29, 30, 41, 268, 271.

11. MILL, 17.

12. Ibid., 17.

13. STAR, 56.

Seals, Whales, and Too Many Sleighs

1.   *HCH*, 22.

2.   MILL, 11.

3.   Ibid., 10.

4.   Ibid., 29.

5.   *Hudson Weekly Gazette*, November 23, 1786. (*AH*)

6.   Ibid., March 28, 1787.

7.   MILL, 30. The Shipping News, *Hudson Weekly Gazette*, April 12, 1807 (*AH*), records the arrival of the "Sloop *Hudson* from Dublin," and "Maritime History of the Port of Hudson,

1784-1810," unpublished manuscript, Hendrick Hudson Chapter, D.A.R. Library, Hudson, N.Y., lists the "Hudson sloop *Hudson*, tonnage 72." Captain A. Jordan in his memoirs in "Annals of Hudson" states, "Titus Morgan, from Boston, ship builder, built the 1st. ship in Hudson, called *Hudson*."

8. Deacon H.P. Skinner, April 8, 1854 (*AH*)
9. *HCH*, 29.
10. MILL, 31.
11. *HCH*, 28.
12. ELLIS, 159.
13. Ibid., 162.
14. MILL, 34.
15. *Hudson Weekly Gazette*, February 1790. (*AH*)
16. Ibid., May 21, 1795.
17. "Maritime History of the Port of Hudson, 1784-1810," op. cit.
18. *Hudson Weekly Gazette*, August 18, 1785. (*AH*) See also *WD*, 32-33.
19. Shipping News, *Hudson Weekly Gazette*. (*AH*) Over thirty listings appear in the Shipping News with various masters listed, such as Latham Bunker, Barker, Cartwright, Rawson, Swain, Sears, and Coffin. Most were packet sloops, meaning they followed a set schedule (as much as possible), But a brig and a schooner also are listed.

The Quasi-War with France

1. George Rogers Taylor, "The Transportation Revolution, 1815-1860," in *The Economic History of the United States* Vol. III (New York: Rinehart & Co., 1951), 137.
2. For American reaction to the French Revolution, see: Fawn Brodie, *Thomas Jefferson: An Intimate History*, 240-41; David McCullough, *John Adams*, 473-559; Alexander Laing, *American Sail: A Pictorial History*, 112-121.
3. *Hudson Weekly Gazette*, July 11, 1793. (*AH*)
4. Among other things the treaty established reciprocal commercial relations between Britain and the U.S. Unfortunately, U.S. trading with the British West Indies was "opened under conditions so harsh and exacting that the article was struck out." No agreement was reached on impressments, and British ships could seize enemy goods as contraband of war. (Harold Underwood Faulkner, *American Political and Social History*, Vol. I [Reprinted for the United States Armed Forces Institute: F.C. Crofts & Co., Inc., 1944], 140-41)
5. David McCullough, *John Adams* (New York: Simon and Schuster, 2001), 484-99. See also Richard C. Malley, *The Early Republic and the Sea* (Washington: Brassey's, Inc., 2001), Chapter

Five "Daniel Caulkin's Voyage: An Incident of the Quasi-War"; and *WD*, 285-313. For more on the X.Y.Z. affair, which changed American sentiment, see Faulkner, op. cit., 142-43.

6. Alexander Laing, *American Sail: A Pictorial History* (New York: Bonanza Books, 1961), 114-19.
7. "In a petition filed at the Court of Claims in January, 1887, the New York Insurance Company requested from the United States Government twenty-five hundred dollars against the loss of the cargo as a result of its illegal seizure by the French." (French Spoilation Claims of the Bureau of Census, Record Group #36, National Archives, Washington D.C. Cited in "Maritime History of the Port of Hudson, 1784-1810," op. cit.)
8. *Hudson Weekly Gazette*, July 9, 1795. (*AH*)
9. *200 Years: A Bicentennial Illustrated History of the United States* Vol. I (New York: U.S. News and World Report, 1973), 171. John Adams considered this his greatest achievement.
10. Faulkner, op. cit., 143.

The First Whaling Voyages

Data on all vessels listed as "arrived" or "sailed" are from the Shipping News of the *Hudson Weekly Gazette* in "Annals of Hudson," Vedder Memorial Research Library, Bronck Museum, Coxsackie, New York.

1. MILL, 30.
2. *Marooned, Being a Narrative of the Sufferings and Adventures of Captain Charles H. Barnard Embracing an Account of the Seizure of his Vessel at the Falkland Islands, Etc., 1812-1816*, ed. Bertha S. Dodge (Middletown, Conn.: Wesleyan University Press, 1979), 16.
3. Ibid., 15.
4. STAR Vol. I, 182-83.
5. Ibid., 184-85.
6. LUND, 612.
7. "Maritime History of the Port of Hudson, 1784-1810," op. cit.
8. STAR, 194-95.
9. ELLIS, 164.
10. STAR, 194-95.
11. *WD*, 378.
12. *HCH*, 46.
13. Shipping News, *Hudson Weekly Gazette*. (*AH*)
14. For more on the use of the word "grounds," see *TSH* index category "whaling grounds."
15. *WD*, 386.
16. *TSH*, 388.
17. For more information on right and sperm whales, see "Whales" in Appendix B.
18. *WD*, 126-28.
19. MILL, 36.

20.   Ibid., 36.
21.   Ibid., 36. See also ELLIS, 165.
22.   *TSH*, 208.
23.   Ibid., 269-70. For another of Coffin's letters—this one from Nantucket alerting Samuel Adams to William Rotch's plan to establish a whale fishery at Bermuda—see STAR, 79.

Rum, Arsenic, and Plumes

1.   Terry, op. cit., 40.
2.   *CCC*, 306.
3.   MILL, 27.
4.   ELLIS, 61.
5.   Ibid., 158.
6.   *HCH*, 39.
7.   *Hudson Weekly Gazette*, August 9, 1787. (*AH*)
8.   ELLIS, 159. Miller mentions that the gaol was reached from Main Street by a footpath through the field. (MILL, 13)
9.   ELLIS, 159.
10.   *Hudson Weekly Gazette*, February 6, 1794. (*AH*)
11.   Terry, op. cit., 63-64.
12.   *CCC*, 84.
13.   Terry, op. cit., 46. See also MILL, 14, and *CCC*, 311.
14.   *HCH*, 63.
15.   Terry, op. cit., 63.
16.   Ibid., 61. In 1796 the American Philosophical Society published Benjamin Franklin's "nautical budget," a map of the Gulf Stream that he charted to aid mariners. A cartouche in the corner of the map pictures a Neptune similar to that on Hudson's first seal. Franklin's Neptune is equally as unclothed as Hudson's, but not quite as muscular. Rather than riding a whale, he sports a mermaid's tail. The map was drawn by James Poupard, "Sculp." It would be interesting to know if Hudson's Neptune originated from this drawing.
17.   In 1791 Secretary of State Thomas Jefferson and Congressman James Madison set out on a journey up the Hudson River Valley to Lake George and Lake Champlain, then over to Bennington, Vermont,, down the Connecticut River to Long Island, and then back to Philadelphia. Jefferson's main inquiries concerned the "Hessian fly," an insect that was ravaging the wheat crops in the valleys. He kept copious notes on wildlife and flora. He also rated the inns where he stayed. (Claverack and Hudson rated "good," Kinderhook "bad.") While in Hudson, Jefferson visited the Jenkins distillery and the textile mill that made sailcloth. He also sent Jenkins his report on the whale fisheries. (Willard Sterne Randall, "Mr. Jefferson Takes a Vacation, *American Heritage*, July/August 1996, 75-85, and John Catanzariti, ed., *The*

Papers of Thomas Jefferson, 434-72.)
18.   Ruth Piwonka, op. cit., 20, and ELLIS, 349-352.
19.   The Penfield map, Columbia County Historical Society, op. cit.
20.   ELLIS, 165. The information concerning the foundation ruins and "druid" stones was told to the author by the late county historian Walter Miller.
21.   *Hudson Weekly Gazette*, July 11, 1793. (*AH*)
22.   Andrew D. Peloubet, "Town of Athens," in J. Van Vechten Vedder, *History of Greene County* Vol. I, 21. Peloubet wrote: "In those days, there was no vegetation—when the tide was at flood tide—the Flat was invisible. ... I have been told the late Dr. A.H. Gelly's father imported—and sowed [the seeds] on the flats and bays. It has multiplied."
23.   *Hudson Weekly Gazette*, April 28, 1890. (*AH*)
24.   MILL, 20.
25.   Ibid., 25.
26.   J.B. Beers, *The History of Greene County*, (J.B. Beers & Co., 1884), 164-65. See also Andrew D. Peloubet, op. cit., 26.

From the Dung Heap: Plagues and Epidemics

1.   Nantucket Historical Society, gift of the Buffalo and Erie Historical Society. Susanna Bunker (1761-1836) was the second wife of Latham Bunker (1755-1827). They married in 1788 and had three daughters. (computer database of the Eliza Starbuck Barney Genealogical Record, Nantucket Historical Association Research Library) Latham Bunker is listed in the *Hudson Weekly Gazette* Shipping News as the master of sloops running to Nantucket. (*AH*)
2.   Terry, op. cit., 82-83.
3.   *Home Medical Encyclopedia* Vol. II, medical ed. Charles B. Clayman, M.D. (New York: Random House, 1989), 1086.
4.   Ibid., 918.
5.   Tina Rosenberg, "When Smallpox Struck during the Revolution," *The New York Times*, December 22, 2001, Editorial Observer.
6.   *Home Medical Encyclopedia* Vol. II, op. cit., 1039.
7.   Terry, op. cit., 69.
8.   Ibid., 72.
9.   *Home Medical Encyclopedia* Vol. I, op. cit., 274.
10.   *CCC*, 94-95.
11.   Terry, op. cit., 181-82.
12.   *Home Medical Encyclopedia* Vol. II, op. cit., 880.
13.   Joel A. Tarr, "Urban Pollution, Many Long Years Ago," *American Heritage* Vol. XXII, No. 6, October 1971, 65-69.
14.   *Home Medical Encyclopedia* Vol. I, op. cit., 362.
15.   Ibid. Vol. II, 883.
16.   Ibid., 1013-14.

17. Ibid., 835-36.
18. *HCH*, 117.
19. Tarr, op. cit.
20. "Proceedings of the Common Council of Hudson, N.Y., 1785-1930." Microfilm. City Hall, Hudson, N.Y.
21. Ibid.
22. *Home Medical Encyclopedia* Vol. II, op. cit., 630.
23. *Hudson Weekly Gazette*, April 2, 1795. (*AH*)
24. Max Berger, *The British Traveler in America, 1836-1860* (New York: Columbia University Press, 1943), 177.
25. Ibid., 178.
26. Jane Louise Mesick, *The English Traveler in America, 1785-1835*, (New York: Columbia University Press, 1922), 91.
27. Elizabeth McClellan, *A History of American Costume, 1607-1870* (New York: Tudor Publishing Co., 1937), 276.
28. Dr. Thomas Brodhead, "Dissertation before the Medical Society of Columbia County," *Hudson Balance*, July 14, 1807.

Traitorous and Lawless Action

1. SCHR, "Scandalize, Traduce and Vilify," *The* (Hillsdale, N.Y.) *Independent*, September 1987.
2. ELLIS, 67.
3. *200 Years: A Bicentennial Illustrated History of the United States* Vol. I, op. cit., 174.
4. Milton Lomask, *Aaron Burr: The Conspiracy and Years of Exile, 1805-1836* (New York: Farrar, Straus, Giroux, 1982), 49-297.
5. McCullough, op. cit., 507.
6. Ibid., 504-05.
7. Ibid., 505-06.
8. *Hudson Weekly Gazette*, April 24, 1787. (*AH*)
9. CCC, 108.
10. ELLIS, 119-20. See also SCHR, "Scandalize, Traduce and Vilify," op. cit.
11. MILL, 69.
12. Lomask, op. cit., 28-29.

Turnpike Fever

1. Herman Melville, *Moby Dick, or, The White Whale* (New York: Harper and Brothers, 1851), chapter 16.
2. ELLIS, 127. See also *CCC*, 49.
3. *Hudson Weekly Gazette*, December 10, 1795. (*AH*)
4. ELLIS, 69-70.
5. *HCH*, 75.
6. ELLIS, 69.
7. Ibid., 157-58.
8. *HCH*, 66-67.
9. Ibid., 67.

10. MILL, 36.
11. ELLIS, 159.
12. *Hudson Weekly Gazette*, June 22, 1786. (*AH*)
13. Ibid., July 5, 1792.
14. Ibid., May 12, 1785.

The Teakettle that Changed the River

1. Cynthia Owen Philip, *Robert Fulton: A Biography* (New York: Franklin Watts, 1985), 204.
2. Ibid., 212.
3. Ibid., 206.
4. ELLIS, 129.
5. Ibid., 129.
6. CCC, 231.
7. Carmer, op. cit., 160-61.

Corsairs and Privateers

1. Ignatius Jones [A. Gorham Worth], *Random Recollections of Albany from 1800-1808*. Second edition. (Albany, N.Y.: Charles Van Benthuysen, 1850), 53.
2. "Maritime History of the Port of Hudson, 1784-1810," op. cit.
3. *200 Years: A Bicentennial Illustrated History of the United States* Vol. I, op. cit., 179-96.
4. Faulkner, Vol. I, op. cit., 151.
5. Laing, op. cit., 102-06. See also Faulkner, Vol. I, op. cit., 150.
6. Judah Paddock, *A Narrative of the Shipwreck of the Ship* Oswego, *on the Coast of South Barbary, and the Sufferings of the Master and Crew while in Bondage among the Arabs, interspersed with numerous remarks upon the Country and its inhabitants, and concerning the peculiar perils of that coast* (New York: Collins & Co., 1818).
7. *HCH*, 52. See also Carmer, op. cit., 132-36.
8. James Riley, *An Authentic Narrative of the Loss of the American Brig* America, *etc.* (New York: James Riley, 1818).
9. Laing, op. cit., 133.
10. LUND, 682.
11. Ibid., 683. See also STAR, 202-03.
12. LUND, 544. See also Star, 202-03.
13. *TSH*, 192.
14. LUND, 704. See also STAR, 202-03.
15. LUND, 673. See also STAR, 202-03.
16. *Hudson Balance*, November 24, 1807.
17. ELLIS, 163. See also CCC, 226; Terry, op. cit., 136-39.

Winds of Change

1. Denis Tilden Lynch, *An Epoch and a Man: Martin Van Buren and His Times* (New York:

Horace Liveright, 1929), 120.

Winds of War

1. Minutes of the Common Council, 1808, in "Proceedings of the Common Council of Hudson, N.Y., 1785-1930," op. cit.
2. Milbert, *Picturesque Itinerary of the Hudson River (and the Peripheral Parts of North America)* (Ridgewood, N.J.: The Gregg Press, 1968), 37. Milbert carefully listed every mineral and all the flora and fauna along the way; however, he never included dates of observation!
3. Joshua M. Smith, "Patterns of Northern New England Smuggling, 1789-1820," in *The Early Republic and the Sea: Essays on the Naval and Maritime History of the Early United States*, eds. William S. Dudley and Michael Crawford. (Dulles, Va.: Brassey's Inc., 2001).
4. *200 Years: A Bicentennial Illustrated History of the United States* Vol. I, op. cit., 180-84.
5. Faulkner, op. cit., 168-69.
6. *200 Years: A Bicentennial Illustrated History of the United States* Vol. I, op. cit., 187.
7. Ibid., 186-96.
8. Ibid., 196.
9. Ibid., 184-85.
10. ELLIS, 143-44.
11. MILL, 36-37.

Commerce, Licit and Illicit

1. MILL, 17.
2. ELLIS, 166.
3. James Thomas Flexner, *That Wilder Image* (New York: Bonanza Books, 1962), 281-84.
4. Bruce Edward Hall, *Diamond Street: The Story of the Little Town with the Big Red Light District* (Hensonville, N.Y.: Black Dome Press Corp., 1994). See also, Thesis. The Graduate School of Public Administration, New York University, June 1962.
5. Minutes of the city recorder, July 25, 1843, in Mary R. Wend, "The Administrative Affects of the Breakdown of Law Enforcement in Hudson, New York," op. cit., 57.
6. Ibid., 61.
7. Hall, op. cit.
8. Milbert, op. cit., 38.
9. CCC, 347; ELLIS, 168.
10. ELLIS, 178.
11. Captain Laban Paddock, memoirs. (*AH*)

The General Disappoints

1. Minutes of the Common Council, August 30, 1824, in "Proceedings of the Common Council of Hudson, N.Y., 1785-1930," op. cit. "That the following Preamble and resolution relative to the reception of General La Fayette be accepted. Whereas the arrival of the intrepid patriot and veteran soldier of the American Revolution General La Fayette upon our shore has been announced to the American people. Whereas the citizens of Hudson, sensible of the important service [provided] by him in our struggle for independence, are desirous of testifying in person their gratitude and respect by suitable demonstrations. ... That Elisha Williams, Alexander Coffin and others be appointed a committee of the Corporation to make suitable arrangements for receiving Gen. La Fayette in a manner suitable to the _____ in which he is held, whatever his _____ determination to comply with our request shall be made known to his honor the mayor."
2. SCHR, "The Man Who Didn't Come to Dinner," (Hudson, New York) *Columbia Request*, bicentenary issue, 1986.
3. MILL, 49.
4. SCHR, "The Man Who Didn't Come to Dinner," op. cit.
5. MILL, 49-50.
6. Octavia Roberts, *With Lafayette in America* (Boston: Houghton & Mifflin, 1919), 16-163.

Bypassed by Progress

1. Taylor, op. cit., 34.
2. Edward F. Locke, "A City in Transition," (Hudson, New York) Register-Star, July 3, 1976.
3. Taylor, op. cit., 38-39, 157.
4. CCC, 351.

Native Sons and Daughters

1. B.F. Jenkins, "The Female Executions," letter to the editor, *Hudson Evening Register*, March 1, 1887.
2. MILL, 51-53.
3. ELLIS, 53-54.

War and Whales

1. *Marooned, Being a Narrative of the Sufferings and Adventures of Captain Charles H. Barnard Embracing an Account of the Seizure of his Vessel at the Falkland Islands, Etc., 1812-1816*, ed. Bertha S. Dodge, (Middletown, Conn.: Wesleyan University Press, 1979), 233.
2. "Expects soon the American brig *Triton* from Hudson, near New York with a cargo of wheat which will be sold readily at our market with (I hope) a handsome profit." Letter from André Limozin to Thomas Jefferson, January 20, 1789, ed. Julian Boyd, *The Papers of Thomas Jefferson* Vol. I-XX (Princeton, N.J.: Princeton University Press, 1951).

3. *200 Years: A Bicentennial Illustrated History of the United States* Vol. I, op. cit., 188.
4. Ibid., 190.
5. Faulkner, op. cit., 171.
6. "Maritime History of the Port of Hudson, 1784-1810," op. cit.
7. MILL, 40.
8. ELLIS, 169.
9. Ibid., 169-70.
10. *Marooned ...*, op. cit.
11. STAR, 218-19. See also LUND, 699.
12. STAR, 218-19. See also LUND, 698.
13. STAR, 224-25. See also LUND, 450.
14. STAR, 224-25. See also LUND, 459.
15. STAR, 229. See also LUND, 504.
16. Nathaniel Philbrick, *In the Heart of the Sea: The Tragedy of the Whaleship* Essex (New York, Viking Penguin, Putnam, 2000), 102.
17. Owen Chase, *Narrative of the Most Extraordinary and Distressing Shipwreck of the Whaleship* Essex, 1821 (reprint, New York: The Lyons Press, 1999), 74-75.
18. Philbrick, op. cit., 213.

Trials, Tribulations, and Catastrophes

1. *CCC*, 339. See also *HCH*, 58.
2. MILL, 105.
3. *CCC*, 87-88.
4. Ibid., 334.
5. Ibid., 93-94. Regarding the almshouse in Ghent, the following disconcerting report was issued in 1844: "The paupers in this institution seem cleanly and appear to be well clothed and under good subjection, and from what your committee can discover, they appear to be controlled without a resort to severe corporal restraint, and without the infliction of any severe punishment." (*CCC*, 96)
6. Ibid., 92.
7. Ibid., 318-20. See also ELLIS, 171-73.
8. ELLIS, 173.
9. Ibid., 174.
10. Ibid., 174.
11. *CCC*, 367.
12. *HCH*, 174.
13. *CCC*, 653.
14. ELLIS, 363.
15. Ibid., 175.
16. Ibid., 54.
17. Locke, op. cit.
18. MILL, 42.
19. Ibid., 40-41.
20. ELLIS, 166.
21. Ibid., 167.
22. Ibid., 167.
23. Locke, op. cit. See also Terry, op. cit., 188.
24. *HCH*, 188.

Railroad Frenzy

1. Taylor, op. cit., 80-83.
2. Ibid., 81.
3. Ibid., 81-82.
4. Ibid., 82.
5. Mesick, op. cit., 73.
6. Berger, op. cit., 35, 64-65. "But the visitor forgot the conductor as he noticed the continuous streams of saliva that every male was expectorating on the floor, on the stove, into corners, or at any likely spot. ... In the winter the stove became the main spittoon, each male endeavoring to hit that target with a louder report than the other." Berger was quoting Alfred Bunn in *Old England and New England* (New York: Columbia University Press, 1943).
7. ELLIS, 130.
8. Ibid., 131.
9. Ibid., n. 132.
10. There is no documentation for this theory, but the directors of the Hudson section certainly profited by having the line run near their business establishments.
11. From an interview at the A.D.M. plant in Greenport, New York.
12. *HCH*, 188. Bradbury wrote that "it was denuded of its fine old forest trees, and paved with cobblestones. ... The Boston and Albany railroad atones in a measure for its presence, by generously furnishing sufficient gravel to fill in the whole surface of the park."
13. ELLIS, 241.
14. Ibid., 131.
15. Taylor, op. cit., 81.
16. ELLIS, 132.
17. Ibid., 132. See also CCC, 339: "the loaning by the city of $50,000 in aid of the Hudson and Berkshire Railroad on bond and mortgage, through the instrumentality of Ambrose Jordan, Robert A. Barnard and James Mellon."
18. *CCC*, 78.
19. Ibid., 79.
20. ELLIS, 134.
21. Ibid., 134.
22. Locke, op. cit.

Labor Unrest

October 1988 the author wrote a three-part article for *The Independent* titled "The Shoemakers' Trial." The trial was not mentioned in any of the local histories, so extensive research was required. In a sidebar to the articles, I listed my sources: *The Daily Albany Argus*, July 8, 1836 (microfilm, New York State Library, Albany, N.Y.); W. Hunt, "The Trial of Journeymen Shoemakers of the City of Hudson," report for the Cordwainers Society, July, 1830 (New York City Public Library); Carl Carmer,

"How Eight Poor Shoemakers of Hudson Won Union's First Victory 105 Years Ago," *PM's Weekly*, June 1, 1941; and Stephen Mayer, "The Shoemakers' Strike of 1833: People v. Fisher" (New York City Public Library).

1. SCHR, "The Shoemakers' Trial," op. cit.
2. Taylor, op. cit., 250-51.
3. Ibid., 263.
4. Ibid., 256.
5. Carmer, "How Eight Poor Shoemakers of Hudson Won Union's First Victory 105 Years Ago," op. cit.
6. Hunt, "The Trial of Journeymen Shoemakers of the City of Hudson," op. cit., 4.
7. Carmer, "How Eight Poor Shoemakers of Hudson Won Union's First Victory 105 Years Ago," op. cit.

A Feudal System Collapses

1. MILL, 61.
2. For more on the anti-rent crisis in Columbia County and elsewhere in New York State, see Henry Christman, *Tin Horns and Calico* (Saugerties, N.Y.: Hope Farm Press, 1978). Christman takes a strong pro-tenant stance. For the opposite viewpoint, see Stephen B. Miller, *A Group of Great Lawyers of Columbia County* (Privately printed, 1904), 214-64. For a useful summary of the tenant-landlord problems, see ELLIS, 36-45.
3. MILL, 55.
4. ELLIS, 44.
5. Ibid., 44.
6. *HCH*, 146-47.
7. ELLIS, 45.
8. Ibid., 45.
9. Ibid., 93-94.
10. SCHR, "Boughton's Second Anti-Rent Trial," *The* (Hillsdale, N.Y.) *Independent*, December 10, 1987.
11. ELLIS, 55.
12. Henry Christman, *Tin Horns and Calico* (Saugerties, N.Y.: Hope Farm Press, 1978), 318.

From Shore to Shore

1. MILL, 53.
2. For the full story of General Worth and his activities during the war with Mexico, see ELLIS, 99-100.
3. Donald Barr Chidsey, *The War with Mexico* (New York: Crown Publishers, Inc., 1968), 167. This book is an excellent study of the war with Mexico.
4. *200 Years: A Bicentennial Illustrated History of the United States* Vol. I, op. cit., 262.
5. *Ibid.,* 269.

Tragedies at Sea and on the River

1. ELLIS, 94-95.
2. Laurie Robertson-Lorant, *Melville: A Biography* (Amherst, Mass.: University of Massachusetts, 1996), 121.
3. Buckner F. Melton, Jr., *A Hanging Offense: The Strange Affair of the Warship* Somer (New York: Free Press, 2003), 143.
4. Ibid., 255. The hanging of John Canfield Spencer deeply affected two great authors of the nineteenth century. Herman Melville's cousin, Lieutenant Guert Gansevoort, presided at the "trial" aboard the *Somers* that condemned Spencer. Melville agonized over the story and finally exorcised it from his conscience with the novella *Billy Budd*, published posthumously in 1924. James Fenimore Cooper and Alexander Slidell MacKenzie had waged a literary war ever since they disagreed in print over Jesse Elliot's role in the Battle of Lake Erie. Readers who are familiar only with Cooper's Leatherstocking tales may be surprised to learn that he was a maritime man and published many nautical novels. Cooper wrote an eighty-page "elaborate review" of MacKenzie's court-martial, "Proceedings of the Case of Court Martial in the Case of Alexander Slidell MacKenzie" (Delmar, N.Y.: Scholars Facsimiles & Reprints, 1992). See also *The Early Republic and the Sea: Essays on the Naval and Maritime History of the Early United States*, ed. William S Dudley and Michael Crawford (Dulles, Va.: Brassey's Inc., 2001).
5. Melton, op. cit., 258.
6. ELLIS, 130.
7. SCHR, "At Your Own Risk: Early Steamboat Travel," *The* (Hillsdale, N.Y.) *Independent*, May 6, 1987.
8. *HCH*, 189.
9. SCHR, "At Your Own Risk: Early Steamboat Travel," op. cit.
10. Ibid.
11. ELLIS, 130.

Hard Times

1. Joseph G. Rayback, *Martin Van Buren* (New York: Eastern Acorn Press, 1982), 25.
2. Marquis James, *The Life of Andrew Jackson* (New York: Garden City Publishing Co., Inc., 1940), 598-706. See also Faulkner, op. cit., 199-200.
3. Jones, op. cit., 4.
4. MILL, 37.

Off to the South Seas

1. Frederick Debell Bennett, *Whaling Voyage*

round the Globe (1840), quoted in Herman Melville, Moby Dick, or the White Whale (London: J.M. Dent, 1922), 501.

2. ELLIS, 164.

3. Frances Diane Robotti, Whaling and Old Salem: A Chronicle of the Sea (New York: Fountainhead Publishers, 1962), 39-43.

4. MW, 55.

5. Hudson Gazette, September 10, 1833, quoted in Poughkeepsie (New York) Telegraph, September 25, 1833.

6. STAR, 278-79. See also LUND, 378. "… this being the largest amount that has been brought by any vessel in the United States this year … In less than two months she was again ready for the sea, and on the 20th of June, she set sail for the South Atlantic, (her former voyage had been to the Brazilian Whaling ground)." (ELLIS, 164)

7. STAR, 288-89. See also LUND 378.

8. STAR, 294-95. See also LUND 378. "The Alexander Mansfield has returned with 1,600 common and 150 barrels of sperm oil, and 1,200 barrels [sic] of whalebone." (Poughkeepsie Telegraph, May 8, 1833)

9. STAR, 304-05. See also LUND 378.

10. STAR, 320-21. See also LUND 378.

11. STAR, 342-43. See also LUND 378.

12. STAR, 360-61. See also LUND 378.

13. Francis Allyn Olmstead, Incidents of a Whaling Voyage (Boston: Tuttle Publishing, 1936), 275. "… having determined to take aboard the Flora, the oil belonging to the Alexander Mansfield. … We then hauled up alongside the dismantled whaler, within a few rods of the shore, to receive her cargo, consisting of a thousand barrels of oil." (Olmstead, 296)

14. STAR, 278-79. See also LUND, 384.

15. STAR, 304-05. See also LUND, 384.

16. STAR, 342-43. See also LUND, 384.

17. STAR, 360-61. See also LUND, 384.

18. STAR, 288-89. See also LUND, 509. "… in the old John Jacob Astor tea ship Henry Astor." (TSH, 397)

19. STAR, 320-21. See also LUND, 509.

20. Judith Downey, "Consequences of California Mania," Historic Nantucket Vol. 48, No. 1 (Summer 1999). The article includes an illustration of the Henry Astor.

21. STAR, 288-89. See also LUND, 569.

22. STAR, 304-05. See also LUND, 569.

23. STAR, 350-51. See also LUND, 569.

24. STAR, 360-62. See also LUND, 569.

25. STAR, 384-85. See also LUND, 569.

26. STAR, 288-89. See also LUND, 707.

27. No Washington with William Clark as master is listed in either Starbuck or Lund; however, Stackpole, in The Sea Hunters, pages 449-50,

mentions the crew of the Lydia being picked up by the Washington.

28. STAR, 294-95. See also LUND, 520.

29. Philbrick, op. cit., 217.

30. STAR, 332-33. See also LUND, 520.

31. STAR, 350-51. See also LUND, 520.

32. STAR, 278-79. See also LUND, 581.

33. Peter M. LaFrance, Surveyer, Quarterly Publication of the American Bureau of Shipping, November 1976, 32.

34. STAR, 279.

35. LaFrance, op. cit., 32. "The Meteor returned to New York on March 30, 1833."

36. STAR, 304-05. See also LUND, 508.

37. STAR, 342-43. See also LUND, 508.

38. STAR, 360-61. See also LUND, 508.

39. STAR, 304-05. See also LUND, 529.

40. STAR, 312-13. See also LUND, 529.

41. STAR, 312-13. See also LUND, 493. Lund lists the George Clinton as "L" (lost) in 1838.

42. Poughkeepsie Telegraph, January 31, 1838.

43. STAR, 304-05. See also LUND, 403.

44. ELLIS, 164. This was Captain Jared Gardner.

45. STAR, 332-33. See also LUND, 403.

46. STAR, 368-69. See also LUND, 403.

47. STAR, 304-05. See also LUND, 455.

48. The Hudson Republic, January 30, 1833.

49. STAR, 320-21. See also LUND, 455.

50. STAR, 332-33. See also LUND, 455.

51. STAR, 350-51. See also LUND, 455.

52. STAR, 368-69. See also LUND, 456.

53. ELLIS, 164.

54. LUND, 663.

55. ELLIS, 137.

56. Karl Rodman, "Whalers on the Hudson River," Hudson Valley Magazine, October 1980, 15-19. See also "Haacker Report for Museum," Newburgh (New York) News, September 21, 1955.

57. Arthur H. Hayward, Colonial Lighting, third ed. (New York: Dover Publications, Inc., 1962), 38.

58. Jeremy Cherfas, The Hunting of the Whale (New York: Penguin Books, 1988), 77.

59. Ivan T. Sanderson, Follow the Whale (Boston: Little, Brown and Co., 1956), 181. "In 1846 more than seventy thousand men were in the whole fleet. Total value of oil brought in was seventy million dollars."

60. Ibid., 256. "Bowheads were first found in the Sea of Okhotsk (off Japan) and the Bering Sea. The whalers destroyed the bowhead population there. After the whale was killed, the baleen was removed, and the rest of the whale released and left to rot. The expense of such a voyage might be eight thousand dollars, but whale oil brought only thirty cents a gallon. The baleen was worth four dollars a pound. By this time, the ships

were registered on the west coast, and the cargo sent back to the east by cargo ship; later, by the transcontinental railroad."

61. ELLIS, 129.
62. Ibid., 169. Samuel Plumb, Oliver Wiswall, Abner Hammond and Rufus Reed began a tow-boat company with barges built on the South Bay and towed by the steamship *Legislature*. The Hudson Tow Boat Company formed in 1830, with Captain George Powers as agent and manager.
63. Jones, op. cit., 5.

Epilogue

1. Hamilton Child, *Gazetteer and Business Directory of Columbia County, 1871-72*, 184.
2. For information on these latter businesses, see ELLIS, 166-69.

The Quakers and the Hudson Meeting

1. MILL, 87.
2. Ibid., 87.
3. Burnham N. Dell, *Quakerism on Nantucket* (Nantucket, Mass.: Nantucket Historical Association, 1955), 9-15.
4. Ibid., 10.
5. Ibid., 15.
6. Florence Mossman, "Meeting House Last Vista of City's Quaker Heritage," (Hudson) *Register-Star*, February 3, 1991.
7. Ibid.
8. Ibid.
9. MILL, 86.
10. Mossman, op. cit.
11. Jones, op. cit., 43.
12. MILL, 86.
13. Ibid., 87.
14. Ibid., 87.

Blood for Oil: The Whaling Industry

1. Cherfas, op. cit., 15.
2. Carl Zimmer, *At the Water's Edge: Fish with Fingers, Whales with Legs, and How Life Came Ashore but Then Went Back to the Sea*. New York: Simon & Schuster, 1998. This is an excellent study on the evolution of whales.
3. Dr. Leonard Harrison, *The Whale* (New York: Simon and Schuster, 1968), 221.
4. Cherfas, op. cit., 33.
5. Ibid., 45.
6. Harrison, op. cit., 70-74.
7. Ibid., 41, 49.
8. *MW*, 55.
9. Ibid., 55.
10. Ibid., 44.
11. Harrison, op. cit., 221-22.

12. *MW*, 8-9.
13. Ibid., 4-5.
14. Ibid., 11-12.
15. Ibid., 71. "Unlike other floating-krill-eating mysticeti, the Blue is a bottom feeder, scooping up mud with its tongue. The mud contains shrimp-like krill that constitutes its food. However, it strains out the mud through the baleen to retain just the food." (Cherfas, op. cit., 30)
16. Ibid., 21-23.
17. Zimmer, op. cit., 125-31.
18. Shannon Brownlee in "Blast from the Vast," *Discovery Magazine* Vol. 24, No. 12, December 2003, 51-57, describes experiments and studies that prove that the sperm whale uses its "amplified clicks" to stun its prey. The article describes how sperm (and other odontoceti) whales use their heads and cases of oil to focus the clicks. "Some clicks are loud enough to temporarily deafen a person."
19. Not to be confused with porpoises, which are a separate family called Phocaenidae. (Sanderson, op. cit., 362)
20. The genus *Orcinus*, the killer whale, will attack seals and other whales, but generally feeds on fish. (Harrison, op. cit., 86)
21. Harrison, op. cit., 83.
22. Ibid., 74.
23. Ibid., 78.
24. Ibid., 82.
25. *MW*, 30-31.
26. Albert Cook Church, *Whale Ships and Whaling* (New York: Bonanza Books, 1938), 21-22.
27. J. Ross Browne, *Etchings of a Whaling Cruise, 1846* (reprint, Cambridge, Mass.: Belknap Press of Harvard University, 1968), 24.
28. Granville Mawer, *Ahab's Trade: The Saga of South Seas Whaling* (New York: St. Martin's Press, 1999), 64-71.
29. STAR, n. 123-25.
30. Briton Cooper Busch, *Whaling Will Never Do for Me: The American Whaleman in the Nineteenth Century* (Lexington, Ky.: The University Press of Kentucky, 1994), 9.
31. James L. Harris, journal of a voyage on the New Bedford whale ship *Tamerlane*, October 24, 1850–January 12, 1852, Kendall Institute Library, New Bedford Whaling Museum, New Bedford, Mass., 1st page.
32. *MW*, 173.
33. Ibid., 178-79.
34. Harris, op. cit., September 24, 1851.
35. *Home Medical Encyclopedia* Vol. II, op. cit., 888.
36. *MW*, n. 55.
37. Mawer, op. cit., 193.
38. *TSH*, 156.
39. Mawer, op. cit., 173.

40.   *TSH*, 448.
41.   Olmstead, op. cit., 303.
42.   *Poughkeepsie Telegraph*, April 29, 1840.
43.   *TSH*, 411.
44.   Susan Kirp Hochwald, "Whaling Ship Medicine," *Historic Nantucket* Vol. 47, No. 4, Fall 1998, 19.
45.   For a sad story of the results of one such "sleigh ride," see Herman Melville, *Moby Dick*, Chapter CXXII ("The *Pequod* Meets the Rachel").
46.   For a description of a whale kill, see *MW*, 183-85.
47.   *MW*, 197.
48.   Philbrick, op. cit., 55-57.
49.   *MW*, 145.
50.   Mawer, op. cit., 70.
51.   Ibid., 73.
52.   ELLIS, 137.
53.   Mawer, op. cit., 15-16. See also Patty Jo Rice, "Beginning with Candle Making," *Historic Nantucket* Vol. 47, No. 3., Summer 1998, 20-23.
54.   Nigel Bonner, *Seals and Sea Lions of the World* (New York: Facts on File Inc., 1994) 8-112.
55.   For further details on early sealing, see *TSH*, 181-92. For more information on the elephant seal, see *TSH*, 191.

BIBLIOGRAPHY

Books

Adams, Arthur G. *The Hudson*. Albany, N.Y.: State University of New York Press, 1981.

Allen, E.S. *Children of the Light: The Rise and Fall of New Bedford Whaling and the Death of the Arctic Fleet*. Boston: Little, Brown and Company, 1973.

Athens Bicentennial Committee. *Athens, Its People and Industry, 1776-1976*. Athens, N.Y.: Athens Bicentennial Committee, 1976.

Barlow, Ronald. *The Vanishing American Outhouse*. New York: Penguin Books, Viking Studio, 2000.

Beers, J.B. *The History of Greene County, New York*. 1884. Reprint: Saugerties, N.Y.: Hope Farm Press, 1969.

Berger, Max. *The British Traveler in America, 1836-1860*. New York: Columbia University Press, 1943.

Berkenmeyer, Wilhelm Christoph. *The Albany Protocol: Wilhelm Christoph Berkenmeyer's Chronicle of Lutheran Affairs in the New York Colony, 1731-1750*. Translated by Simon Hart and Sibrandina Geertruid Hart-Runeman. Edited by John F. Dern. Ann Arbor, Mich.: 1971.

Bonner, Nigel. *Seals and Sea Lions of the World*. New York: Facts on File Inc., 1994.

Boyd, Julian, ed. *The Papers of Thomas Jefferson*. Vols. I-XX. Princeton, N.J.: Princeton University Press, 1951.

Bradbury, Anna R. *History of the City of Hudson, N.Y.* Hudson, N.Y.: Record Printing and Publishing Company, 1908.

Browne, J. Ross. *Etchings of a Whaling Cruise, 1846*. Cambridge, Mass.: Belknap Press of Harvard University Press, 1968.

Bruce, Wallace. *The Hudson: Three Centuries of History, Romance and Invention*. New York: Bryand Union Co., 1913.

Bullen, F. *The Cruise of the Cachelot: Round the World after the Sperm Whales*. London: Smith, Elder & Co., 1899.

Busch, Briton Cooper. *Whaling Will Never Do for Me: The American Whaleman in the Nineteenth Century*. Lexington, Ky.: The University Press of Kentucky, 1994.

Carmer, Carl. *The Hudson*. New York: Grosset & Dunlap, 1967.

Carpenter, Kenneth J. *The History of Scurvy and Vitamin C*. Cambridge, Mass.: Cambridge University Press, 1986.

Catanzariti, John, ed. *The Papers of Thomas Jefferson*. Vols. XXIV-XXVII. Princeton, N.J.: Princeton University Press, 1950.

Chase, Owen. *Narrative of the Most Extraordinary and Distressing Shipwreck of the Whaleship* Essex. 1821. Reprint: New York: Lyons Press, 1999.

Cherfas, Jeremy. *The Hunting of the Whale*. New York: Penguin Books, 1988.

Chidsey, Donald Barr. *The War with Mexico*. New York: Crown Publishers, Inc., 1998.

Child, Hamilton. *Gazetteer and Business Directory of Columbia County, 1871-72*.

Christman, Henry. *Tin Horns and Calico*. 1945. Reprint: Saugerties, N.Y.: Hope Farm Press, 1978.

Church, A.C. *Whale Ships and Whaling*. New York: Bonanza Books, 1938.

Clark, A. Howard. "History and Present Condition of the ... Whale Fishery." In *The Fisheries and Fishing Industries of the United States*. Vol. 12, section 5. Edited by George Brown Goode. Washington: G.P.O., 1887.

Clayman, Charles B., M.D., medical ed. *Home Medical Encyclopedia*. Vols. I & II. New York: Random House, 1989.

Colby, Barnard. *For Oil and Buggy Whips: Whaling Captains of New London County*. Mystic, Conn.: Mystic Seaport Museum, 1990.

Columbia County at the End of the Century. Vols. I & II. Hudson, N.Y.: The Record Printing and Publishing Co., 1900.

Cooper, James Fenimore. *History of the Navy of the United States of America*. 1840. Abridged, Delmar, N.Y.: Scholars Facsimiles and Reprints, State University of New York Press, 1988.

_____. *Ned Myers, or A Life Before the Mast*. Edited by William S. Dudley. Annapolis, Md.: Naval Institute Press, 1989.

Cullen, Charles, ed. *The Papers of Thomas Jefferson*. Vols. XXI-XXII. Princeton, N.J.: Princeton University Press, 1950.

Dana, Richard Henry, Jr. *Two Years before the Mast*. Boston: Houghton Mifflin Co., 1929.

Davis, W.M. *Nimrod of the Sea, or, the American Whalemen*. North Quincy, Mass.: Christopher Publishing House, 1972.

Dell, Burnham N. *Quakerism on Nantucket*. Nantucket, Mass.: Nantucket Historical Association, 1955.

Directory of the City of Hudson, 1851-52. Hudson: Parmenter & Van Antwerp.

Dodge, Bertha S., ed. *Marooned, Being a Narrative of the Sufferings and Adventures of Captain Charles H. Barnard Embracing an Account of the Seizure of his Vessel at the Falkland Islands, Etc., 1812-1816*. Middletown, Conn.: Wesleyan University Press, 1979.

Dows, George Francis. *Whale Ships and Whaling: A Pictorial History of Whaling during Three Centuries*. New York: Argosy Antiquarian, Ltd., 1967.

Druett, Joan. *In the Wake of Madness: The Murderous Voyage of the Whaleship* Sharon. Chapel Hill, N.C.: Algonquin Books of Chapel Hill, 2003.

Dudley, William S., and Michael Crawford, eds. *The Early Republic and the Sea: Essays on the Naval and Maritime History of the Early United States*. Dulles, Va.: Brassey's Inc., 2001.

Ellis, Captain Franklin. *History of Columbia County*. 1878. Reprint: Old Chatham, N.Y.: Sachem Press, 1974.

Ellis, Richard. *Men & Whales*. Guilford, Ct.: The Lyons Press, 1991.

Faulkner, Harold Underwood. *American Political and Social History*, Vol. I. 1927. Reprinted for the United States Armed Forces Institute: F.S. Crofts & Co., Inc., 1944.

Fish, Hamilton. *Lafayette in America during and after the Revolutionary War*. New York: Vantage Press, 1976.

Flayderman, E.N. *Scrimshaw and Scrimshanders, Whales and Whalemen*. New Milford, Conn.: N. Flayderman and Co., Inc., 1972.

Flexner, James Thomas. *That Wilder Image*. New York: Bonanza Books, 1962.

Ford, Paul, ed. *The Writings of Thomas Jefferson*. Vol. III. New York: Putnam, 1894.

Fronenberg, C.W. *Whale-Ho*. Danbury, Conn.: Business Services, Inc., 1969.

Gibson, Gregory. *Demon of the Waters: The True Story of the Mutiny on the Whaleship* Globe. New York: Little, Brown & Co., 2002.

Hall, Bruce Edward. *Diamond Street: The Story of the Little Town with the Big Red Light District*. Hensonville, N.Y.: Black Dome Press Corp., 1994.

Harrison, Dr. Leonard. *The Whale*. New York: Simon and Schuster, 1968.

Hopkins, Donald R. *Princes and Peasants: Smallpox in History*. Chicago: University of Chicago Press, 1966.

Hudson River Sloop Restoration, Inc. *Hudson River Sloops*. Hastings-on-Hudson, N.Y.: Morgan & Morgan, Inc., 1970.

James, Marquis. *The Life of Andrew Jackson*. New York: Garden City Publishing Co., Inc., 1940.

Jones, Ignatius [A. Gorham Worth]. *Random Recollections of Albany from 1800-1808*. Second edition, Albany, N.Y.: Charles Van Benthuysen, 1850.

Laing, Alexander. *American Sail: A Pictorial History*. New York: Bonanza Books, 1961.

Lomask, Milton. *Aaron Burr: The Conspiracy and Years of Exile, 1805-1836*. New York: Farrar, Straus, Giroux, 1982.

Lund, Judith Navis. *Whaling Masters and Whaling Voyages Sailing from American Ports*. A Compilation of Sources: New Bedford, New Bedford Whaling Museum; Sharon, Mass., The Kendall Institute; and Gloucester, Mass., The Ten Pound Book Co., 2001.

Lynch, Denis Tilden. *An Epoch and a Man: Martin Van Buren and His Times*. New York: Horace Liveright, 1929.

Malley, Richard C. *The Early Republic and the Sea*. Dulles, Va.: Brassey's, Inc., 2001.

Martin, Kenneth R. *Whalemen and Whaleships of Maine*. Brunswick, Maine: Harpswell Press, 1975.

Mawer, Granville. *Ahab's Trade: Ahab's Trade: The Saga of South Seas Whaling*. New York: St. Martin's Press, 1999.

McClellan, Elizabeth. *A History of American Costume, 1607-1870*. New York: Tudor Publishing Co., 1937.

McCullough, David. *John Adams*. New York: Simon and Schuster, 2001.

McNeil, William H. *Plagues and People*. New York: Anchor Press, 1976.

Melton, Buckner F., Jr. *A Hanging Offense: The Strange Affair of the Warship* Somers. New York: Free Press, 2003.

Melville, Herman. *Moby Dick, or The White Whale*. New York: Harper and Brothers, 1851.

Mesick, Jane Louise. *The English Traveler in America, 1785-1835*. New York: Columbia University Press, 1922.

Milbert, J. *Picturesque Itinerary of the Hudson River (and the Peripheral Parts of North America)*. Ridgewood, N.J.: The Gregg Press, 1968.

Miller, Stephen B. *Sketches of Hudson, Embracing the Settlement of the City, City Government, Business Enterprises, Churches, Press, Schools, Libraries, Etc.* 1862. Reprint: Hudson, N.Y.: Hudson D.A.R., 1987.

Morris, Paul C. *Maritime Sketches*. Orleans, Mass.: The Lower Cape Publishing Co., 1985.

New Bedford Whaling Museum. *The Whale*. New York: Simon & Schuster, 1968.

Olmstead, Francis Allyn. *Incidents of a Whaling Voyage*. Boston: Tuttle Publishing, 1936.

Paddock, Judah. *A Narrative of the Shipwreck of the Ship* Oswego, *on the Coast of South Barbary, and the Sufferings of the Master and Crew while in Bondage among the Arabs, interspersed with numerous remarks upon the Country and its inhabitants, and concerning the peculiar perils of that coast*. New York: Collins & Co., 1818.

Philbrick, Nathaniel. *In the Heart of the Sea: The Tragedy of the Whaleship* Essex. New York, Viking Penguin, Putnam, 2000.

Philip, Cynthia Owen. *Robert Fulton: A Biography*. New York: Franklin Watts, 1985.

Piwonka, Ruth. *Mount Merino, View of Mount Merino, South Bay and the City of Hudson*. Kinderhook, N.Y.: Columbia County Historical Society, 1978.

Piwonka, Ruth, and Roderic H. Blackburn. *A Visible Heritage: A History in Art and Architecture, Columbia County, New York*. 1977. Reprint: Hensonville, N.Y.: Black Dome Press Corp., 1996.

Rayback, Joseph G. *Martin Van Buren*. New York: Eastern Acorn Press, 1982.

Reed, John. *The Hudson River*. New York: Bonanza Books, 1960.

Riley, James. *An Authentic Narrative of the Loss of the American Brig* America, *etc.* New York: James Riley, 1818.

Roberts, Octavia. *With Lafayette in America*. Boston: Houghton & Mifflin, 1919.

Robertson-Lorant, Laurie. *Melville: A Biography*. Amherst, Mass.: University of Massachusetts, 1996.

Robertson, R.B. *Of Whales and Men*. New York: Alfred A. Knopf, 1954.

Robotti, Frances Diane. *Chronicles of Old Salem*. New York: Bonanza Books, 1958.

_____. *Whaling and Old Salem: A Chronicle of the Sea*. New York: Fountainhead Publishers, 1962.

Sanderson, Ivan T. *Follow the Whale*. Boston: Little, Brown and Co., 1956.

Sawfell, Clement Cleveland. *The Ship* Ann Alexander *of New Bedford, 1805-1851*. Mystic, Conn.: The Marine Historical Association, 1962.

Scammon, C.M. *The Marine Mammals of the North-Western Coast of North America with an Account of the American Whale Fishery*. San Francisco: John H. Carmany, & G.P. Putnam, 1874.

Schlesinger, Arthur M., Jr. *The Age of Jackson*. Boston: Little, Brown and Co., 1950.

Shapiro, Irwin, and Edouard A. Stackpole. *The Story of Yankee Whaling*. New York: American Heritage Junior Library, Golden Press, 1959.

Simon, James F. *What Kind of Nation: Thomas Jefferson, John Marshall & the Epic Struggle to Create a United States*. New York: Simon & Schuster, 2002.

Sloan, Eric. *America Yesterday*. New York: Wilfred Funk, Inc., 1956.

Stackpole, Edouard A. *The Sea Hunters: The New England Whalemen during Two Centuries, 1635-1836*. New York: J.B. Lippincott Company, 1953.

_____. *Whales and Destiny: The Rivalry between America, France and Britain for Control of the Southern Whale Fishery, 1785-1825*. Amherst, Mass.: University of Massachusetts Press, 1972.

Stanton, Samuel Ward. *The Flyers of the Hudson (Hudson River Steamboats)*. Meriden, Conn.: Meriden Gravure Co., 1965.

Starbuck, A. *History of the American Whale Fishery from Its Earliest Inception to the Year 1876.* Report to the Commissioner of Fish and Fisheries, Washington, D.C., 1878. Vols. I & II. New York: Argosy-Antiquarian Ltd., 1964.

Taylor, George Rogers. "The Transportation Revolution, 1815-1860." In *The Economic History of the United States.* Vol. III. New York: Rinehart & Co., 1951.

Terry, Robert M. *The Hudsonian: Old Times and New.* Hudson, N.Y.: Edwin Rowley Printer, 1895.

Town of Greenport Historical Society. *Greenport: The Forgotten Town.* Hudson, N.Y.: Town of Greenport Historical Society, 1987.

Tucker, Glen. *Dawn Like Thunder: The Barbary Wars and the Birth of the U.S. Navy.* Indianapolis, Ind.: Bobbs-Merrill, 1963.

200 Years: A Bicentennial Illustrated History of the United States. Vol. I. New York: U.S. News and World Report, 1973.

Van Laer, A.J.F., ed. and trans. *Minutes of the Court of Albany, Rensselaerwyck and Schenectady, 1675-1680.* Vol. II. Albany, N.Y.: University of the State of New York, 1928.

Vedder, J. Van Vechten. *History of Greene County, 1651-1800.* Vol. I. 1927. Reprint: Saugerties, N.Y.: Hope Farm Press, 1985.

Wallace, Alfred Russel. *The Wonderful Century: Its Successes and Its Failures.* New York: Dodd, Mead & Co., 1898.

Washington County Historical Society. "Some Chapters in the History of the Town of Easton, N.Y." In *History of Washington County, New York.* Fort Edward, N.Y.: The Washington County Historical Society, 1959.

Welling, Jane Betsey. *They Were Here Too.* Greenwich, N.Y.: The Washington County Historical Society, 1963.

Zimmer, Carl. *At the Water's Edge: Fish with Fingers, Whales with Legs, and How Life Came Ashore but Then Went Back to the Sea.* New York: Simon & Schuster, 1998.

Periodicals

Anderson, William G. "John Adams: The Navy and the Quasi-War with France." *American Neptune* XXX, No.2, April 1970.

Cable, Mary. "Bringing up Baby." *American Heritage* Vol. XXIV, No. 8, December 1972.

Carmer, Carl. "How Eight Poor Shoemakers of Hudson Won Union's First Victory 105 Years Ago." *PM's Weekly,* June 1, 1941.

Downey, Judith. "Consequences of California Mania." *Historic Nantucket* Vol. 48, No. 1.

Hochwald, Susan Kirp. "Whaling Ship Medicine." *Historic Nantucket* Vol. 47, No. 4, Fall 1998.

Hudson Balance, February–June 1802, January–December 1807.

Hudson Bee, November 1819, April 1821.

Hudson Weekly Gazette, April 1785–May 1790, April 1792–November 1797.

Jenkins, B.F. "Recollection of Execution of Margaret Hotaling." *Hudson Daily Register,* March 1, 1887.

"Labor's Right to Strike First Upheld." *Chatham (New York) Courier,* January 29, 1959.

LaFrance, Peter M. *Surveyer* Quarterly Publication of the American Bureau of Shipping, November 1976.

Locke, Edward F. "A City in Transition (Thesis)." *Hudson Register-Star,* July 3, 1976.

Mossman, Florence. "The Society of Friends in Hudson." *Hudson Register-Star,* February 3, 1991.

Northern Whig, May–August 1821.

Piwonka, Ruth. "Dutch Settled Claverack Landing 135 Years Before It Became a City." *Hudson Register-Star,* May 17, 1985.

_____. "Hudson." *The Hudson Valley Regional Review* Vol. 2, No. 1, March 1985.

Poughkeepsie Telegraph, 1833, 1835, 1836, 1837.

Randall, Willard Sterne. "Mr. Jefferson Takes a Vacation." *American Heritage,* July/August 1996.

Rice, Patty Jo. "Beginning with Candle Making." *Historic Nantucket* Vol. 47, No. 3.

Rodman, Karl. "Whalers on the Hudson River." *Hudson Valley Magazine,* October 1980, 15-19.

Rosenberg, Tina. "When Smallpox Struck during the Revolution." *The New York Times,* December 22, 2001.

Rural Repository (Columbia County, New York), January 6–December 13, 1807, 1832, 1833, 1844.

Tarr, Joel A. "Urban Pollution, Many Long Years Ago." *American Heritage* Vol. XXII, No. 6, October 1971.
"The Trial of the Hudson Shoemakers." *Daily Albany Argus*, July 8, 1836.

Unpublished

The Annals of Hudson Vol. I. Vedder Memorial Research Library, Bronck Museum, Coxsackie, New York.
Barker, Marks. "The Narrative of Marks Barker, 1764-1839."
Harris, James L. Journal of a voyage on the New Bedford whale ship *Tamerlane*, October 24, 1850–January 12, 1852. New Bedford Whaling Museum, New Bedford, Mass.
Hunt, W. "The Trial of Journeymen Shoemakers of the City of Hudson." Reported for the Cordwainers Society, July 1836. New York City Public Library.
"Maritime History of the Port of Hudson, 1784-1810." Paper. Hendrick Hudson Chapter, D.A.R. Library, Hudson, N.Y.
"Proceedings of the Common Council of Hudson, N.Y., 1785-1930." Microfilm. City Hall, Hudson, N.Y.
Wend, Mary R. "The Administrative Affects of the Breakdown of Law Enforcement in Hudson, New York." Thesis, the Graduate School of Public Administration, New York University, June 1962.

Index

Margaret B. Schram is a lifelong resident of Columbia County and has researched the history of the City of Hudson and its role in early American whaling for more than fifty years. Mrs. Schram has written hundreds of newspaper articles on Hudson's history, has lectured on whaling at numerous museums and schools, and is featured in the public television documentary *Hudson River Journeys*. She is a member of the New Bedford Whaling Museum, the Nantucket Historical Association, the Columbia County Historical Society, and Historic Hudson.